Phonetic transcription

From first steps to ear transcription

Holger Schmitt

ERICH SCHMIDT VERLAG

Bibliografische Information der Deutschen Nationalbibliothek
Die Deutsche Nationalbibliothek verzeichnet diese Publikation in der Deutschen Nationalbibliografie; detaillierte bibliografische Daten sind im Internet über http://dnb.d-nb.de abrufbar.

Weitere Informationen zu diesem Titel finden Sie im Internet unter
ESV.info/978 3 503 12283 7

Hinweis

Die Lösungen zu den mit @ gekennzeichneten Aufgaben finden Sie unter http://phonetic-transcription-key.esv.info

ISBN 978 3 503 12283 7

www.ESV.info

Dieses Papier erfüllt die Frankfurter Forderungen der Deutschen Bibliothek und der Gesellschaft für das Buch bezüglich der Alterungsbeständigkeit und entspricht sowohl den strengen Bestimmungen der US Norm Ansi/Niso Z 39.48-1992 als auch der ISO-Norm 9706.

Druck: Difo-Druck, Bamberg

For Colin Foskett, who first taught me the principles of phonetic transcription.

And for Achim Hescher, friend and colleague, who inspired me to write this book.

Contents

List of abbreviations and notation conventions 9

List of exercises 11

Foreword 15

Foundations of transcription 19

Does transcription matter? 19
Transcription outside linguistics 20
Spelling vs. sound 23
What is phonetic transcription? 24
The International Phonetic Alphabet 27
Choosing a pronunciation dictionary 28
Speech models 31
Received Pronunciation 31
General American 32

A Basic transcription 35

Background 35
The Standard Lexical Set 35
The choice of symbols 39
Some practical advice 43
Practice 45

B Advanced transcription 79

Background 79
Transcription depth 80
Transcription conventions and transcription tolerance 82
Weak forms 84
The happY and the inflUence vowel 88
Practice 90

C Transcribing actual speech ... 115

Background ... 115

Phonetic knowledge relevant for ear transcription ... 115
Factors that influence auditory perception ... 117
From theory to practice: Analysing unfamiliar sounds ... 121
Analysing unknown languages ... 124
Data interpretation ... 125
The limitations of ear transcription ... 126

Practice ... 128

Key ... 137

Bibliography ... 179

List of abbreviations and notation conventions

CV: cardinal vowel

GA: General American

RP: Received Pronunciation

SF: strong form

WF: weak form

(ə) as in [ˈkʊʃ(ə)n]: optional sound

(æ/ə) as in [t(æ/ə)ˈbuː]: alternative sounds

[rəʊp]/[roʊp]: RP/GA transcription

close$_A$: ‘close’ as an adjective

use$_N$: ‘use’ as a noun

use$_V$: ‘use’ as a verb

ˈ as in [ˈɪŋglənd]: primary stress

ˌ as in [ˌɛntəˈtɛɪn]: secondary stress

< >: denotes words in their orthographical form, i.e. spelling.

☑: Answers for this exercise provided in this book.

@: Answers for this exercise provided online.

For the symbols used in sections A and B for RP and GA, see section A ‘Standard Lexical Sets’.

The International Phonetic Alphabet is reproduced in the back inside cover of this book. Reproduction courtesy of the International Phonetic Association.

List of exercises

Section	Exercise	Key	Title/Task
A			
	A1	☑	Standard Lexical Sets
	A2	☑	Words with [iː]
	A3	☑	Words with [ɪ]
	A4	☑	Words with [ɛ]
	A5	☑	Words with [æ]
	A6	☑	Words with [ʌ]
	A7	☑	Words with [ɑː]
	A8	☑	Words with [ɒ] (RP)
	A9	☑	Words with [ɔː]
	A10	☑	Words with [uː]
	A11	☑	Words with [ʊ]
	A12	☑	Words with [ɜː]/[ɜːr]
	A13	☑	Words with [ə]
	A14	☑	Words with [aɪ]
	A15	☑	Words with [aʊ]
	A16	☑	Words with [ɛɪ]
	A17	☑	Words with [ɔɪ]
	A18	☑	Words with [əʊ]/[oʊ]
	A19	☑	Words with [ɪə]/[ir]
	A20	☑	Words with [ʊə]/[ʊr]
	A21	☑	Words with [ɛə]/[ɛr]
	A22	@	Medley 1
	A23	☑	Words with <o>
	A24	☑	Silent letters
	A25	☑	TRAP vs. DRESS
	A26	☑	Inflectional affixes 1 (-s/'s)

	A27	☑	Inflectional affixes 2 (-ed)
	A28	☑	The dental fricatives: [ð] or [θ]?
	A29	☑	Homophones 1
	A30	☑	Spot the mistake
	A31	@	[ŋ], [ŋg] or neither?
	A32	☑	Medley 2
	A33	☑	[z] or [s]? (1)
	A34	@	Homographs
	A35	☑	Medley 3
	A36	@	Homophones 2
	A37	☑	Medley 4
B			
	B1	☑	Weak form or strong form?
	B2	☑	happY, KIT, inflUence or FOOT?
	B3	☑	Homophones 3
	B4	☑	[t] or [t̬] (GA)?
	B5	☑	Stress 1: Proper nouns and compounds
	B6	☑	Mid and high front vowels
	B7	☑	Academic English 1: Phonetics
	B8	☑	[z] or [s]? (2)
	B9	☑	Base allomorphy
	B10	@	Homophones 4
	B11	☑	Low and mid front vowels
	B12	☑	Text: Through the Looking Glass
	B13	☑	The prefix *re-*
	B14	☑	Medley 5
	B15	☑	Low vowels
	B16	☑	Alternative pronunciations
	B17	☑	Low and mid back vowels
	B18	@	Academic English 2: Dialectology
	B19	☑	Stress 2: Stress shift
	B20	☑	High back vowels

	B21	☑	Medley 6
	B22	☑	Funny you should say this: Homophone jokes 1
	B23	☑/@	Text: Limericks
	B24	☑	Frequently mispronounced words 1
	B25	☑	Text: Jokes
	B26	☑	RP vs. GA
	B27	@	Frequently mispronounced words 2
	B28	☑	Text: Psalm 23
	B29	☑	Text: Interview
	B30	@	Funny you should say this: Homophone jokes 2
	B31	☑	Proper nouns 1
	B32	☑	Text: Pygmalion (RP)
	B33	@	Language terms
	B34	☑	Proper nouns 2
	B35	☑	Medley 7
C			
	C1	☑	Casual speech
	C2	☑	Words with non-canonical speech sounds
	C3	☑	Locating the German 'vocalic r'
	C4		Reading transcribed speech
	C5		Transcribing actual speech data
	C6	☑	Analysing authentic data 1: Vowels
	C7	☑	Analysing authentic data 2: Consonants
	C8	☑	Analysing authentic data 3: Intonation
	C9	☑	Analysing authentic data 4: Lexis and grammar
	C10	☑	Analysing authentic data 5: Idiosyncra-sies
	C11		Analysing authentic data 6: Doing your own research project
	C12		The Speech Accent Archive

Foreword

There are many excellent textbooks on the phonetics and phonology of English. They range from practical pronunciation guides to highly abstract theoretical treatises. This book is not meant to replace but to supplement them and to assist students of English linguistics in an area they tend to find particularly difficult: phonetic transcription. Its aim is to familiarise learners with the principles of transcribing and, by giving many tips and providing numerous exercises, help them become proficient in this skill.

This book, however, is meant to be more than just an exercise book for one class. Its division into the three practical 'sections' A, B and C (rather than chapters) implies that each part is quite self-contained and covers material that may be relevant at different stages of your university course. Thus, the book is meant to be a companion throughout your life as an undergraduate or even graduate student.

Before we turn to the more practical aspects of transcription, however, we start by looking at some of its foundations. These include, among other things, the purpose of transcription (why do we need transcription at all?) and its subject (what is it that we transcribe?), the relationship of spelling and sound, and a short discussion of the reference varieties used (this book covers both British and American English). You will find information on where to look for phonetic fonts for your computer and, since having a pronunciation dictionary is essential for students of English, I have also included a brief survey of the most important works available.

The practical sections A-C are each divided into a 'Background' and a 'Practice' part. The sections follow a general progression from simple to complex, and the prerequisites for each section are quite different. Section A aims at basic transcription competence. The idea is that it can be used by beginners to transcription, for example in introductory courses to linguistics (or even in the advanced classes in secondary schools), if there are more specific phonetic follow-up classes. It only presupposes basic phonetic concepts like place and manner of articulation, lip rounding (for vowels), the difference between voiced and voiceless sounds, and the concepts of the phoneme and the allophone. We start with very frequent and comparatively simple words and disregard phonological processes such as weakening.

Section B is intended for undergraduate classes on English phonetics and phonology. It requires more advanced skills, and it assumes a general understanding of phonological processes. In the 'Background' part, we discuss questions of transcription depth, transcription conventions and transcription tolerance. We introduce weak forms and the two allophones [i] and [u] (which are also used by most modern dictionaries). In the exercises, more difficult constructions and entire texts will be transcribed.

Section C, finally, is different from the two previous parts in that it goes beyond transcribing abstract standard pronunciations. It provides background information for those who want to transcribe actual speech, and it offers several exercises based on audio material that is freely available on the internet. This section presupposes a more thorough understanding of the workings of phonetics and phonology, especially articulatory phonetics. It is intended to supplement classes on World Englishes, Dialectology, Sociolinguistics etc.

This textbook is designed both for self-study and for practical sessions in class. Most of the exercises have a key in the 'Key' section. These exercises are marked with the symbol '✓'. The answer section, however, is more than simply the part where the solutions are given. It contains comments that explain special usages, providing some statistical information and pointing out idiosyncratic cases. Most other exercises (those with the symbol '@') are intended for class work. The key to these exercises can be found on the internet pages of Erich Schmidt publishers (www.esv.info).

'Phonetic Transcription' is primarily aimed at university students in the German-speaking countries. This is reflected in the words chosen for practice and in the design of some of the exercises. For example, many speakers of German find it difficult to distinguish the dental fricatives ('th-sounds') and the alveolar fricatives ([s] vs. [z]) in transcription, and there are special exercises to cater for these problems. Since, however, the transcription result is ultimately the same for everyone, the book can be used by people of any linguistic background. The models we follow in sections A and B are the prestige accent of British English, usually referred to as Received Pronunciation (RP), and General American (GA). Questions that are only relevant for British English are marked 'RP'; those that solely refer to American pronunciation are labelled 'GA'. The emphasis in this book is on segmental phonology, i.e. the identification and transcription of individual phonemes and allophones; to a lesser extent, we look at stress and intonation.

The backbone of the words in the exercises, particularly of those in section B, are words I collected over the years from student presentations and oral exams for the simple reason that the students struggled with these words. I have, however, avoided technical or foreign terms that students of English are not likely to come across. Thus you will neither find *Szechwan*, *haemoglobin* or *ichthyophobia* in this book (which may come as a relief). Nor have I included proper nouns that are not common currency in English departments. But I *have* included both proper nouns (*Thames*, *Edinburgh*, *Greenwich* etc.) and technical terms (*diphthong*, *euphemism* etc.) that students of English encounter and that they find hard to master. Additionally, this book lists a number of words which display unique features of some kind (e.g. words with extraordinary sound-letter correspondences, alternating pronunciations or stress patterns). The texts I have chosen range from informal spoken discourse and jokes to written classical and academic texts, covering a wide variety of material. However, once you have grasped the basic principles of transcribing connected speech (e.g. weak forms, linking), the major problem remains the representation of the difficult words just mentioned, typically words of classical origin, and it is for this reason that these words receive special attention.

Sometimes students find transcription a bit hard to come to terms with. It is my hope that once you have understood the basic ideas and developed some fluency in transcription, you will actually find it quite interesting. I have even known people who started to write postcards or letters to their friends and loved ones in phonetic transcription. In any case, transcription is a useful and indispensable tool for teachers of English and linguists alike.

Foundations of transcription

This section provides you with some background information on transcription. Its aim is to answer questions like “Why do we transcribe speech at all?”, “How are sound and spelling related?” and “What is it that we transcribe?” It also gives you a short overview of the history of the International Phonetic Alphabet and some tips on using IPA symbols on your computer. We will take a brief look at some of the pronunciation dictionaries available and then conclude this part by sketching the varieties that we use as a model (‘Received Pronunciation’ and ‘General American’). The question of which symbols we use for each sound is dealt with at the beginning of section A.

Does transcription matter?

Why, as a student of English linguistics, should you learn to transcribe in the first place? There are many good answers to this question, but the following are probably among the most relevant for you:

- On the most basic level, you have to be able to look up the pronunciation of words in pronunciation dictionaries. You cannot afford to (or at least should not) teach English in a school setting or make a presentation in English using words whose pronunciation you are not sure of. This is true for all kinds of words (if, for example, you see the word *yacht* for the first time and don’t hear it spoken, you will probably come up with various ideas of how it might be pronounced), but this is particularly true for proper nouns, i.e. names of places or people.
- Transcription skills are not the same as pronunciation skills, and yet the two feed into each other. As you struggle to master transcription, you develop an awareness of the pronunciation of English in general and the idiosyncrasies of many of its lexemes and their combination in connected speech in particular. If you take that extra step and apply your newly developed understanding to your own pronunciation, you will no doubt benefit from it. Conversely, the more you know about sound patterns and their representations, the more you will be able to distinguish and describe the subtle differences of real language.
- Many linguistic disciplines rely on transcription as an essential tool. The most obvious ones are, of course, phonetics and phonology, but the importance of

transcription does not end here. When you study varieties of English, you will realise that most of the differences between one form of English and another are due to pronunciation. As Mair (2008: 152) puts it, "In our comparison of British and American standard English we were able to observe that, to put it simply, accent divides and syntax and the lexicon unite. This trend is much in evidence when it comes to the new and emerging standards." The same is true for social variation. It is essential to know, for example, that the pronunciation of the word *singing* as [ˈsɪŋɪn], often written as *singin'*, is not caused, as it is commonly described, by 'dropping one's "g"' but by the replacement of the phoneme [ŋ] by another ([n]). In other words, whenever we analyse variation in English, we have to be able to recognise the differences in pronunciation and to describe them. Other areas of linguistics where the representation of pronunciation plays an important role are morphology, first and second language acquisition, and many fields of applied linguistics like language teaching, speech therapy, lexicography, forensic linguistics and alphabetisation.

- If you are training to be a teacher, you will have to teach transcription in the higher classes of secondary education in some educational systems. If this applies to you, you should have more than a vague idea of how transcription works and how you can pass on this knowledge to others.

As you can see, transcription is not a luxury for linguists, but an essential tool, and it pays to develop one's skills in this field to a high standard. If you want to join those who write postcards or letters in phonetic transcript and if you are on very friendly terms with your addressee, you may even employ the symbol 'ʘ' to finish off your letters to them. This symbol represents a voiceless bilabial click, a sound that is actually used in some languages. To produce it, close your lips (for our purpose it helps to round them, too), creating something like a vacuum behind them and then suddenly release the lips, sucking in air, not into your lungs, but just into your mouth (phoneticians speak of 'velaric ingressive airstream'). What you are forming is ... a kiss.

Transcription outside linguistics

Is transcription something that is only relevant for language students and linguists, or do we encounter words or passages transcribed in everyday life, too? The answer is yes to the latter. We do find it in non-philological contexts, and we find it in two different forms. The first one concerns imitations of dictionary entries like the following:

Fig. 1: Shop window in New England, USA

Such mock dictionary entries typically occur in contexts where local or regional words are printed on merchandise like mugs, t-shirts or beer mats, which are then sold to the public, particularly to tourists. These 'transcriptions' are usually far from accurate. Note, for example, that the transcription of the word *vegetarian* above is enclosed in round brackets, that it has two primary stresses and that it uses the symbol [ɘ]. This symbol *does* exist as part of the International Phonetic Alphabet; it is, however, not the schwa (which it was probably meant to imitate), but its upside down version. The point is, of course, that linguistic accuracy is not aimed at in these cases. All that is needed is the *impression* of a transcription that is created by a combination of vaguely phonetic symbols to keep the reader happy. This function is sometimes referred to as the indexical function of language, in this case of transcription. The same function applies when, for example, people in Asian countries wear t-shirts with English words on them that make little or no sense at all, just to benefit from the image of progressiveness that the English language carries in these countries. Similarly, when you enter a Chinese restaurant outside Asia and find Chinese characters on the wall or on the menu, you don't usually call out for the waitress to translate them for you, enjoying instead the slightly more authentic feel that these characters add to the atmosphere.

Sometimes, however, people do have a serious intention of conveying a particular pronunciation to the public. This is especially true when companies try to enter a foreign market or when they try to sell products whose pronunciation is potentially difficult or ambiguous. Some years ago, a camera manufacturer offered a digital camera called 'µ'. Since not too many people outside Greece know Greek letters beyond alpha, beta, gamma and delta nowadays, the company decided to include the transcription [mjuː] on each camera. Since, apparently, this did not help in countries where English isn't used as a major language, the company abandoned this policy later on.

The photo below shows a poster advertising the *Zentrum Oberwiehre* shopping mall in Freiburg, Germany. Its abbreviation, ZO, can be pronounced both as an acronym (as if the letters constitute a word, like 'NATO') or as an initialism (with a pronunciation of the individual letters, like in 'USA'). It was probably due to the fact that the former would have made the short form of the *Zentrum Oberwiehre* homophonous with the German word *Zoo*, 'zoo', that caused the people who were responsible for the mall to include a 'transcription' to guide readers in their pronunciation.

Fig. 2: Poster in Freiburg, Germany

This transcription is not accurate, either, but at least it aims at giving the reader an idea of how to pronounce 'ZO'. Instead of using phonetic symbols (which would probably confuse more than help; the accurate transcription would be [ˌtsɛt ˈoː]), it utilises German spelling conventions to achieve this goal.

Spelling vs. sound

The first 'transcription' system that most people get to know is the written codification of their own language. Indeed, most spelling systems start out as an attempt to represent the sounds of that particular language. The problem is that pronunciation changes faster than spelling, and as a result most languages display mismatches between the pronunciation of their words and their spelling. English, in particular, is known for its notoriously difficult spelling. 'Difficult' here means, of course, that there are only a few reliable rules that tell you how a word is pronounced (when you start from the written form) or spelt (cf. Collins & Mees 2008: 105–115). George Bernard Shaw even jokingly suggested that the word *fish* should be respelled as 'ghoti': <gh> for [f] as in *tough*, <o> for [ɪ] as in *women* and <ti> for [ʃ] as in *nation*. This lack of correspondence between sound and spelling in English is the reason why British television stations can offer prime-time programmes with spelling competitions, and this is also the reason why there are societies and individuals who aim at a reform of the spelling system (cf. www.spellingsociety.org).

English boasts a large number of homophones (words with identical pronunciation but different spellings and meanings), such as *meat* – *meet*, several homographs (words with the same spelling but different pronunciations, e. g. *read*, pronounced as [riːd] or [rɛd]), a fair number of words with letters that are not pronounced (as in *please*, *hymn* or *write*) and even some words with sounds that are not reflected in the spelling (like the [w] in *one*). On top of this, the same spelling may represent completely different sounds. Take the words *tough*, *though* and *through*. Each of them ends in <ough>, yet the pronunciation changes from [tʌf] to [ðəʊ]/[ðoʊ] to [θruː]. The schwa in particular (the sound at the beginning of the word *about* or the end of the word *letter* in RP, represented by the symbol [ə]) is used in many unstressed syllables, regardless of their spelling. Some examples would be *about*, *cruel*, *objective*, *upon*, and *adoption*. Sometimes it is not even clear which letter or letters a sound relates to, at least not synchronically. Take the word *righteous*, pronounced [ˈraɪtʃəs]. The letters *gh* have no correlation in pronunciation (they are 'silent'), but what about the schwa in the second syllable? Is it represented by all three of the vowels? What about the fricative [ʃ]? It seems as if it has no reflection in the spelling at all.

The reason for this confusion is largely historical. If, for example, you compare the words *crime* and *criminal*, you find that in either case the vowel of the stressed syllable is spelled *i*, yet in *crime*, it is pronounced [aɪ], whereas the pronunciation of the first vowel in *criminal* is [ɪ]. The reason is that during the time of the Great Vowel Shift (roughly from 1400 to 1600), only the long vowels (as in *crime*) changed, while short vowels (as in *criminal*) remained the same. Another reason for the irregular sound-letter correspondences in English is loanwords. If you 'borrow' a word from a foreign language, you usually also adopt its spelling. This spelling, however, was developed on the basis of another linguistic system, which possibly has different sound-letter correspondences and may even include sounds that English does not have at all. Take, for instance, the word *envelope*. In French, the first sound is a short nasalized low back vowel (technically [ɑ̃]). The perception of foreign sounds is largely determined by the intricacies of one's own phonological system (cf. section C). The perceptually closest phoneme that English (RP) provides in this case seems to be the vowel [ɒ], which we find in words like *on*, *lot* etc. If, as a native speaker of English, you try to imitate the stressed vowel of the French original, you arrive at [ˈɒnvələʊp] for *envelope* – which is what a fair number of RP speakers do. This, of course, leads to a new sound-letter correspondence (the letter <e> for the sound [ɒ]) that is unlike those commonly used in English.

What is phonetic transcription?

If spelling is not a reliable guide to pronunciation, what is it that we transcribe? At first sight, the answer to this question seems straightforward: transcription is the graphic representation of speech sounds. However, when we look at this answer more closely, we find that it leaves a decisive aspect unanswered: what exactly in pronunciation do we transcribe? As Kennedy (1998: 82) nicely puts it, "transcription is an imperfect written approximation of a speech event which exists initially as a dance of air molecules."

No two sounds ever produced by humans are actually exactly the same. Even if I pronounce a short word, say, 'hit' twice in a row, there will be minute differences in articulation and, thus, in the actual sounds. There might, for example, be differences in the volume with which I speak, in the pitch of my voice, in the exact time that I take to pronounce these words, maybe also in vowel height etc. If I cannot pronounce the same word in exactly the same way twice, how much more will there be differences in my ways of pronouncing words in more unrelated contexts, e.g. when I lecture or when I talk to a friend, when I am healthy or when I have a cold, and even between different speakers that have a different gender, age or linguistic background?

Furthermore, when we speak, we do not produce individual speech sounds (or even less so: letters) and string them together. Rather, what comes out of our mouth (and nose, for that matter) is a continuous flow of noise, modulated by various speech organs like our vocal folds, our tongue, our teeth and others. Even if you use machines to analyse this flow, it is not always possible to say exactly where one sound ends and the next one begins. However, when we transcribe, we represent speech by individual, non-continuous symbols. In transcription, therefore, "a continuously changing speech signal is reduced to a linear sequence of discrete symbols." (Cucchiarini 1993: 48) This means that, no matter how precise or 'narrow' our transcription is, it will always be an abstraction. And the question is: How do we abstract sound waves into discrete symbols?

Let us look at an individual word, say 'food'. Why is it that we usually transcribe it as [fu:d]? Why do we use three symbols (plus a length mark) and not one, two or fifteen symbols to represent this word? Theoretically at least, we could single out the second half of the sound transcribed here as [f] and the first part of [u:] and invent a symbol for it, say [Ψ] (pronounced [(p)saɪ]). The first problem with this approach, however, would be that the sound [Ψ] would have a very limited range of use in English. It would only occur in a few more words like *fool, tofu* and *kung fu*. This, in itself, would make the idea of setting up the symbol [Ψ] for this particular sound look very inefficient. Secondly, and more importantly, there is no word in the English language where you could replace [Ψ] by another sound and end up with a new word, whereas there are many words where you can replace either [f] or [u:] by another sound, resulting in a totally different meaning (e.g. *fell-bell, fine-shine, soon-seen, loop-lap* etc.). The major principle, therefore, is that we start by transcribing those units of speech that are relevant for a given language, i.e. those sounds that, potentially at least, have the power to distinguish meaning, and we call these sounds the **phonemes** of the language.

It is also only in the context of a known language that the use of length marks for vowels (such as [i:] or [u:]) makes sense. In actual speech, the sound [i:] may even be shorter than the sound [ɪ]. Let us assume, for example, a slow speaker who pronounces the word *bid* and a fast one who says *beat*. If you measure the exact time the two speakers take for their vowels, you are likely to find that the [ɪ] in *bid* takes longer than the [i:] in *beat*. This is not just due to the speed of the two speakers, but also to the phonetic environment the two vowels occur in (vowels are usually shorter before [t] than before [d]). Thus, we will only find a systematic difference in vowel length (and, thus, a justification for using length marks) if the context of the speech act is the same, i.e. if we can assume the same language, the same speed of speaking, the same phonological context.

The concept of a phoneme is not just a useful linguistic tool; it seems to reflect a psychological reality (cf. Sapir 1949 and Liberman et al. 1957 for two classic studies). When we listen to the content of a spoken message, we tend to ignore all those elements of speech that are not relevant for a semantic understanding, e.g. the general pitch level, the volume, the voice quality and even minor deviations from our own accent. All of these features tell us a lot about the speakers themselves (e.g. their sex, their current mood or their attitude to us), but they are not relevant for a semantic understanding of the message and are therefore processed at a different level.

If we assume that there are roughly 5,000 languages in the world and that an average language has, say, 40 different phonemes (actual numbers vary greatly), we would expect, allowing for some overlap, hundreds, if not thousands of different phonemes worldwide. It turns out, however, that at least as far as consonants are concerned, these distinctive sounds are amazingly similar across the languages of the world. (The similarity of vowels is more difficult to assess since vowels are, almost by definition, more continuous in nature.) Many languages would, for example, have a sound that involves closing your lips, building up pressure behind them, and then suddenly releasing this pressure – and all this without making the vocal folds vibrate. What we arrive at is a voiceless bilabial plosive – the sound we conventionally transcribe as [p]. The phonological status of this sound, however, may vary from language to language. In English, [p] may be aspirated (i.e. it may be followed by a little puff of air. You can test this by holding your flat hand in front of your mouth and saying the word *pin*), unaspirated (as in *spin*) or even unreleased (i.e. without the last phase just described, as in the phrase *the top button*). The distribution of these three realisations in English is rule-governed and therefore predictable. In other words, what we have here are **allophones** of one phoneme, which could be represented by the symbols [p^{h}], [p] and [p˺] in transcription. The question of whether or not we employ both [p] and [p^{h}]/[p˺] when we transcribe English depends on how accurate we want to be. In other languages, like Chinese or Korean, the difference between [p] and [p^{h}] is used to distinguish words. For example, /pal/ in Korean means 'sucking', whereas /p^{h}al/ means 'arm'. Thus, the two sounds are phonemic, and no matter how much or how little detail we want to include in our transcription of these languages, the difference between the two 'p'-sounds has to be represented. (We will come back to the issue of transcription depth in section B.)

What we have just described is the basic principle of transcription: we transcribe – even at the broadest level – those sounds that have the power to distinguish meaning in any given accent. This principle is sometimes referred to as the **phonemic principle** of transcription, and we will use this term here, too. When we want to include more detail, we can do this, either by using more accurate symbols in the first place or by including extra symbols (like ˺ ˧ ̥ or ˜). These symbols, which only act as additions to specify another, more general, symbol, are referred to as '**diacritical marks**', '**diacritical signs**' or simply '**diacritics**'. The question which characters are used to represent which sounds depends of course on the phonetic alphabet we choose. Since the International Phonetic Alphabet is the most highly developed and the most widely used transcription system for speech sounds, we will now take a brief look at its history and the question of how you can use the symbols on your word processor.

The International Phonetic Alphabet

As we said earlier, most writing systems start out as a reflection of the pronunciation of their respective language, but since writing is always more conservative than speech, the close connection between the two is often lost in the course of time. Thus, there is a need for a representation that adheres to actual sounds – and not to the conventions of writing. A unified system for transcription, however, is nothing that can be taken for granted. For a long time, various transcription systems stood side by side (for a historical overview see Kemp 2006 and Cucchiarini 1993: 1–3). Today, the **International Phonetic Alphabet** (**IPA** for short – the same abbreviation is also used for the **International Phonetic Association**) is not the only system for the transcription of speech sounds, but it is easily the most developed one.

The International Phonetic Association was founded under the name of *Dhi Fonètik Tîcerz' Asóciécon* in Paris in 1886 by a small group of language teachers, originally to develop a phonetic notation to support foreign language teachers. The Association's reputation soon grew and exceeded that of France, and in 1889, the name was changed to *L'Association Phonétique Internationale* or, in English, the *International Phonetic Association.* In 1888, the association published their first alphabet, based on a number of fixed principles, which, to a large extent, are still valid today. Among other things, these principles stated that each 'distinctive sound' should be represented by an individual symbol (what we referred to as the 'phonemic principle' above), that each symbol may stand for slightly different, but very similar sounds in different languages and that ordinary Roman letters should be used as far as possible.

As time went by, the alphabet gradually changed its status from a mere tool to support foreign language teachers to one that could be used for detailed phonetic work in general. In 1917, the famous British phonetician (and later president of the Association) Daniel Jones set another milestone in the history of the Alphabet when he developed the concept of '**cardinal vowels**', 16 pre-defined vowels which act as reference points for all the vowels in the world (cf. section A under the heading 'DRESS, SQUARE, FACE'). The International Phonetic Alphabet today recognises some additional vowels, but the basic principle of the cardinals is still in operation.

In the course of the last century, the Alphabet was further developed in line with new insights, and it has also undergone some revisions (the last major one as a consequence of the Kiel convention in 1989). Today it enjoys almost universal recognition. One of the countries that has found adopting the IPA more difficult than others is the United States (cf. Sampson 1980: 209), but even here this international norm has gained ground in more recent years. If you want, you can listen to all the IPA sounds at www.paulmeier.com/ipa/charts.html. A chart with all the current IPA symbols is reproduced in the inside back cover of the book.

If you want to use IPA symbols on your computer, you will probably find that your word processing programme provides some of the non-Roman symbols you need in the 'special characters' section, but usually not all of them and in particular not the diacritical marks that can be used together with the main symbols. What you need, therefore, is a complete set of IPA fonts for your computer. Probably the easiest way is to download them as freeware from the internet. One of the most commonly used sets is 'Doulos SIL', which is also employed for this book. It is available from the Summer Institute of Linguistics (www.sil.org). Alternatively, you may download various types of fonts from the linguistics section of University College London (www.phon.ucl.ac.uk/resource/phonetics/). In any case, make sure that you install the fonts in the 'fonts' folder of your operating system, otherwise you may have to reload them every time you start your computer. If you intend to use your phonetic fonts regularly, or if you want to type entire texts in phonetic transcript, there are two options. Either you create your own shortcuts ('hot keys'). You may, for example, choose the combination 'ALT + v' for the vowel [ʌ] or 'ALT + ?' for the glottal stop ([ʔ]). This method is particularly useful if the text you are writing is a combination of ordinary (Roman) text and phonetic transcription because you can write using your standard fonts (e.g. Times New Roman) and simply 'insert' IPA fonts whenever necessary. If, on the other hand, your text consists entirely of phonetic symbols or if you want to or need to include many specialised symbols, you may completely switch to the phonetic font set. In this case you have to familiarise yourself with the new function of the keys of your keyboard.

Choosing a pronunciation dictionary

As a student of English, you cannot really do without a pronunciation dictionary. Not only do these works provide you with the transcriptions for proper nouns like *Leicestershire* or *Sioux* (which ordinary mono- or bilingual dictionaries don't). They also include many technical terms and variants that you will not find elsewhere, and they tell you how inflectional endings are pronounced. In a bilingual dictionary, for example, you will always find the transcription for the word *young* ([jʌŋ]). But what about the word *younger*? Is it pronounced [jʌŋə] or [jʌŋgə] in British English? In all probability, you will find the answer in a pronunciation dictionary, but not in an ordinary one. Finally, today at least, pronunciation dictionaries contain transcriptions for both British and American English.

Three of the major pronunciation dictionaries are the *Cambridge English Pronouncing Dictionary* (EPD; edited by Roach et al.), the *Longman Pronunciation Dictionary* (LPD; Wells) and the *Oxford Dictionary of Pronunciation for Current English* (OPD; Upton et al.). To help you choose the best dictionary for yourself, a brief overview of some of their features and transcription conventions is given here. (The words in small capitals in the first column represent the vowel that is used in all the words that have the same vowel as the key word itself; cf. 'Standard Lexical Sets' in section A.)

	EPD	LPD	ODP
British and American English	√	√	√
Inflectional suffixes	√	√	√
Stress shift indicated	√	√	partly
Info boxes (e.g. on 'assimilation')	√	√	
Graphs indicating preference for controversial pronunciations		√	
Native pronunciations of foreign words		√	
CD available	√	√	
Representation of DRESS	[e]	[e]	[ɛ]
Representation of SQUARE	[eə]	[eə]	[ɛː]
Representation of TRAP	[æ]	[æ]	[a]
Representation of NURSE	[ɜː]	[ɜː]	[əː]
Representation of PRICE	[aɪ]	[aɪ]	[ʌɪ]
Representation of happY	[i]	[i]	[i]
Representation of inflUence	[u]	[u]	[ʊ]

To give you a better idea of how these dictionaries treat more complicated cases, the entries for *chanson* and *nephew* are reproduced here (excluding AmE and inflection):

Cambridge (EPD):

- ˈʃɑ̃ː*n*.sɔ̃ː*ŋ*, -sɒn, -ˈ-
- ˈnef.juː, ˈnev-

Longman (LPD):

- **ˈʃɒ̃ sɒ̃** ˈʃɒn-, -sɒn *–Fr* [ʃɑ̃ sɔ̃]
- **ˈnef juː** ˈnev- *–Preference poll, BrE:* ˈnef- *79%,* ˈnev- *21%. It is evident that the traditional form with* v *has been largely displaced by the spelling pronunciation [...].* (The entry is also accompanied by two charts, one showing the overall distribution and one representing the preferences according to age.)

Oxford (ODP):

- ˈʃɒ̃sɒ̃, ˈʃɒnsɒ̃, ˈʃɒnsɒn
- ˈnɛfjuː, ˈnɛvjuː

When you compare these entries, you will see that

- not even pronunciation dictionaries always agree on the way a word is pronounced.
- no matter which dictionary you go for, you have to acquaint yourself with a peculiar set of transcription conventions. For example, the EPD uses dots to indicate syllable boundaries, whereas the LPD marks syllable divisions by spaces and the ODP does not mark syllables at all (except by stress marks). Both EPD and LPD use italicised symbols to indicate optional sounds (as in the *chanson* example of the EPD), while the OPD places optional sounds in brackets. (For a discussion of the abbreviatory conventions used in these dictionaries, see Wells 2008a.)
- it is often the LPD which gives the most detailed information. This includes empirical data on native speaker preferences of controversial words like *schedule*, *garage* or *data*. The LPD also uses bold type for the main pronunciation recommended for learners of English in order to set it off from other stylistic, regional or social variants.

All of these dictionaries cover both British and American English pronunciation. We finish off this *Foundations* section by taking a closer look at these two reference accents of English.

Speech models

When we want to transcribe words or complete texts that were not produced by an actual speaker (i.e. if we do not transcribe live speech or speech that was recorded) but that only exist in our minds, we need a model. The models chosen for this textbook are the prestige varieties of British and American English, commonly referred to as **Received Pronunciation (RP)** and **General American (GA)**, respectively. Both varieties have much in common in terms of status and function, but there are also some features that distinguish them socially.

Received Pronunciation

When you hear the term *Received Pronunciation* for the first time, you may wonder how an accent can be 'received'. A baby 'acquires' an accent, and later on you may learn or acquire a new one, but 'receive' it? The term *received*, however, is simply used in a formal or older sense here, meaning 'socially accepted'; it is still sometimes used in this sense in the expression 'received wisdom'.

The term *Received Pronunciation* is not without its competitors, though. Outside linguistic circles, it is not even known very well. Most people in the UK would use *BBC English*, *Oxford English* or *the Queen's English* when they talk about similar concepts, but each of these terms has its own problems. First, it is true that you would have needed a very clear RP accent before the Second World War to be employed by the BBC; however, the Corporation changed its policies many years ago so that today you will hear newsreaders, presenters and other public radio and television figures that have slight (and sometimes not so slight) but identifiable regional features in their pronunciation. Second, RP is not the accent that is typical of the city of Oxford (or even Oxfordshire), but at its very best (and presumably mostly in historical respect), it is characteristic of the scholars of the universities of Oxford and Cambridge. Probably the popular term that comes closest to the meaning of RP is *Queen's English.* Being Queen, Elizabeth II is still a model for many of her subjects, even though this number today may not be as large as it used to be. However, Her Royal Highness, too, has changed her accent over the decades (cf. Harrington et al. 2000), and the accent she uses is a rather conservative variety of RP.

Received Pronunciation is originally associated with the south-east of England, particularly, of course, with the universities of Oxford and Cambridge and the Public (i.e. fee-paying) Schools. Nowadays, it is no longer a regional accent. You can meet RP speakers in every part of the UK, and it is the only accent that does not give away anything about where you grew up. Today, RP is very much a social accent. It is closely associated with the higher classes, business executives and other professionals. It is also still widely, but not exclusively, used by radio or television presenters. In matched-guise experiments (i.e. experiments where informants are asked to rate speakers of different accents, not knowing that some of the voices they hear come from the same speakers who only change their accent), it is RP speakers who usually score highest as regards social and professional criteria (cf. Romaine 1980, Dretzke 2008 ch. 8.1.1). In its pure form, it is said to be spoken by only 3–5 per cent of the population. However, many educated people in Britain speak some kind of modified RP, i.e. RP with some regional traces.

In many parts of the world, RP is used as a pronunciation model for foreigners who learn English. It is also one of the most widely understood accents of the word – another feature which is true for both RP and GA and which makes them unique. RP and GA are the two world reference accents of English, i.e. they are often used to compare other varieties to – even though, of course, you could also compare, say, Edinburgh English to Ghanaian English. RP is practically always used with standard grammar (you wouldn't expect to hear a sentence like *He ain't done nothing wrong* in RP), whereas you *will* hear many examples of standard grammar with regional accents.

RP, however, is not a uniform entity, nor is it immune to change. Various scholars have identified different subgroups of RP. The most widely adopted classification seems to be the one by Gimson (1962: 84f.), who distinguishes Conservative RP, used mainly by older speakers with certain social and professional backgrounds (if you want to get an idea of how Conservative RP sounds, listen to track 1 of the CD that accompanies Collins & Mees 2003), Mainstream RP and Advanced RP, spoken by some young professionals.

In more recent years, the term and the concept of Received Pronunciation have been discussed and sometimes rejected (cf. Macaulay 1988). Some linguists tend to avoid the term RP altogether (cf. Roach 2000: vii). Nevertheless, if we allow for language (and pronunciation) to change, there is no problem in applying this term to the current prestige accent of the UK. (Also see Trudgill 2001 and Roach 2008: 393f. For recent changes in RP, see Przedlacka 2008.)

General American

Like its British counterpart, the term *General American* is not uncontroversial. Van Riper (1973) points out that the term has undergone a series of subtle shifts in meaning and challenges it on the ground that speech in America is more diverse than was originally thought when the term *General American* was devised. Kretzschmar rejects the term "because it implies that there is some exemplary state of American English from which other varieties deviate" (2008: 43) and suggests *Standard American English pronunciation* instead. Nevertheless, the term *General American* has been widely accepted both by linguists (cf. Trudgill & Hannah 2002: 42) and laypeople.

There are many similarities, but also some striking differences between the social status of RP and that of GA. Like RP for the United Kingdom, GA is the least regionally determinable accent of the United States. It is widely used in the media (and is therefore also sometimes known as *Network English*), and it is the accent used in teaching English as a foreign language in classes where American English serves as the model. It is said to be spoken as a regional accent in the American Midwest (i.e. southern and central Iowa and neighbouring regions) and, of course, by many educated speakers throughout the United States. It is, however, not so strongly associated with social class as RP in class-conscious Britain, and it is used by a far greater proportion of the population. Kortmann (2005: 260), for example, estimates that two thirds of the US population speak GA. There is, however, generally less linguistic diversity in the US than in the UK. Scholars do not always agree about how to represent the dialectal makeup of the US. Three things seem to be clear, though: 1. the diversity is greatest in the east, 2. the major isoglosses run horizontally from east to west, along with the settlement history of the US, and 3. the dialects tend to merge in the west.

Another difference between RP and GA is that the American variety is less clearly defined and demarcated than its British counterpart. With reference to North American English, Trudgill & Hannah (2002: 35) write that "there is no universally accepted totally regionless standard pronunciation as in EngEng [English English]." This variability of GA refers both to the actual pronunciation of many words and to the symbols that are used for the transcription of the accent. Thus, GA is perhaps best defined negatively as "a number of very similar accents which all have the property of sharing neither the characteristics of the accents of the southern US (Southern) nor of New England (Eastern)." (Kortmann 2005: 260) We will discuss both the question of variability within GA and the question of which symbols we use to represent each sound at the beginning of section A.

A Basic transcription

Background

As we said in the *Foundations* section, the major principle in transcription is the phonemic principle: in any given accent, we use one distinct symbol to represent each phoneme. Theoretically, we could therefore simply introduce the phonemes of English now and say which symbol we use for each one of them to get started. This, however, would eventually lead to a number of problems. First, it is sometimes necessary to refer to phonemes in a simple and reliable way. While this is normally not a problem with consonants ('The last sound in *red* is [d], not [t].'), it becomes more problematic when we pronounce vowels in isolation, since vowels are more continuous in nature. Second, it would be handy to have a simple way of referring to all the words in a given accent that share the same vowel, e.g. if you want to compare one accent with another one that uses a different vowel in this position ('All the words like *luck, fun, hut* etc. have the vowel [ʊ] in Northern England.'). Third, on an even more practical level, it is a good idea to have one word per vowel which can be used to compare any given word that you are trying to transcribe ('Does the first vowel in *worry* sound like the one in *lot*, in *luck* or in *nurse*?'). All of these problems can be avoided if we start by looking at a set of universally acknowledged key words known as the 'Standard Lexical Set', and this is what we will be doing first in this section. We will then discuss which symbols are best used for each phoneme (both for RP and GA). Finally, there will be some practical advice for beginners of transcription before we move on to attempt our first exercises.

The Standard Lexical Set

In 1982, John Wells, famous British dialectologist and phonetician, published his seminal three-volume work *Accents of English*, for many years a standard work on variation and world varieties of English. In it, Wells introduced what he referred to as the 'Standard Lexical Set'. These are words, printed in small capitals, which represent all the words that share the same vowel. Thus, for example, the FLEECE set contains words like *knee, mean, key, people* etc., regardless of their spelling. However, these words can also be used to refer to the vowels used in the words themselves. It is, for instance, easier to talk about 'the TRAP vowel in RP' than to imitate it, describe it phonetically ('the short mid-low to low front vowel') or to describe the shape of the IPA symbol that represents it ('the symbol that looks like, erm, a cross between an x and an 8'). Here are the key words and their corresponding symbols as they are used in this book for Received Pronunciation (for General American see below); we will introduce one set that Wells did not use (the inflUence words).

FLEECE	KIT	DRESS	TRAP	STRUT	NURSE	LOT	BATH
iː	ɪ	ɛ	æ	ʌ	ɜː	ɒ	ɑː

THOUGHT	FOOT	GOOSE	PRICE	MOUTH	FACE	CHOICE	GOAT
ɔː	ʊ	uː	aɪ	aʊ	ɛɪ	ɔɪ	əʊ

NEAR	CURE	SQUARE	happY	inflUence	commA
ɪə	ʊə	ɛə	i	u	ə

The last three of these sounds are not considered to be phonemes of English, and we will introduce the happY and inflUence vowels only in section B. The sound in commA is commonly referred to as **schwa**. The term comes from Hebrew, and the sound is used in many languages of the world, often as a reduced vowel in unstressed syllables.

As for American English, the situation is more complicated. First, as mentioned above, there is more flexibility in GA than there is in RP; or, in other words, GA is not as clearly defined as RP. Second, the lexical sets listed above for RP do not correspond one to one to GA (or with only a potential shift in the quality of the vowel). Instead, we have several splits *within* lexical classes, particularly in the region of the back and low vowels. The following is a slightly simplified account of how RP vowels relate to their GA counterparts (for more detailed discussions, see e.g. Wells 1982 Ch. 2.2, Kretzschmar 2008 and Trudgill & Hannah 2002).

RP	ɒ	
	relates to	
GA	ɑː	ɑː, ɔː
Example	lot	long

Most words that have /ɒ/ in RP can have /ɑː/ in GA. However, many Americans would use the rounded mid-low vowel /ɔː/ when the following consonant is one of the voiceless fricatives /θ/, /f/ or /s/ or the nasal /ŋ/ (sometimes also before the phonemes /n/, /g/ and /r/). Examples of the latter group would be *moth, off, cost, long* and *gone/frog/foreign*. We therefore need another lexical set to describe this group, and the word that is commonly used to denote this class is CLOTH. There is, however, a lot of variability in educated American speech in this field, and the distribution is not always predictable. Trudgill and Hannah (2002: 37) offer some reassuring words for those who try to master this intricacy of American speech: "Foreign learners may find the distribution of /ɑ/ and /ɔ/ in USEng confusing and hard to learn. They can take comfort, however, from the fact that many NAmEng accents in fact do not distinguish between these two vowels at all [...]." In other words, some American speakers would use the same slightly rounded, slightly raised low back vowel in both *lot* and *long*. However, as long as many other North Americans distinguish between these two sets, it makes sense to maintain the distinction between LOT and CLOTH for American English.

RP		ɔː	
		relates to	
GA	ɔː, ɑː		ɔːr
Example	thought		bore

Similarly, RP /ɔː/ relates either to GA /ɔː/ or /ɑː/. This means that for those GA speakers who pronounce both LOT and THOUGHT with the vowel /ɑː/, there is a merger of two RP phonemes into one GA phoneme. Since GA is a rhotic accent, /r/ is not only pronounced before vowels (as in RP), but in all contexts. Before /r/, however, only /ɔː/ is possible in GA. This lexical set is referred to as the NORTH set.

RP		ɑː	
		relates to	
GA	ɑː	ɑːr	æ
Example	father	bar	staff

Some words that have /ɑː/ in RP have /ɑː/ in GA, too; in the context of American English, they are referred to as the PALM words (or START if the vowel is followed by /r/). However, if the consonant that follows is either one of the voiceless fricatives /f/, /θ/ or /s/; or /n/ or /mp/ (as in *example*), Americans use /æ/ instead; these words constitute the BATH set. In other words, there are many more words in GA that are pronounced with the TRAP vowel than there are in RP.

RP		æ	
		relates to	
GA	æ		ɛ
Example	trap		marry

Most words that have /æ/ in RP also have /æ/ in American English. Before /r/, however, many American speakers raise the vowel to /ɛ/, so that *marry* and *merry* are homophones in this accent (cf. Wells 1982: 482). These words form the MARRY group for American English.

RP		ə	
		relates to	
GA	ə		ər
Example	<u>a</u>bout		profess<u>or</u>

Once again, American English rhoticity leads to two different forms where RP only has a schwa. Those without /r/ are referred to as commA words; those with /r/ as lettER.

Below you find a comparison of the RP and the GA vowels. Bear in mind that the lexical distribution of these sets may not be identical, i.e. these sets may not refer to exactly the same words in each dialect.

Lexical set	RP	GA	Lexical set	RP	GA
FLEECE	iː	iː	FOOT	ʊ	ʊ
KIT	ɪ	ɪ	GOOSE	uː	uː
DRESS	ɛ	ɛ	PRICE	aɪ	aɪ
TRAP	æ	æ	MOUTH	aʊ	aʊ
MARRY	æ	ɛ	FACE	ɛɪ	ɛɪ
STRUT	ʌ	ʌ	CHOICE	ɔɪ	ɔɪ
NURSE	ɜː	ɜːr	GOAT	əʊ	oʊ
LOT	ɒ	ɑː	NEAR	ɪə	ir
CLOTH	ɒ	ɑː, ɔː	CURE	ʊə	ʊr
BATH	ɑː	æ	SQUARE	ɛə	ɛr
PALM	ɑː	ɑː	happY	i	i
START	ɑː	ɑːr	inflUence	u	u
THOUGHT	ɔː	ɑː, ɔː	commA	ə	ə
NORTH	ɔː	ɔːr	lettER	ə	ər

Some of these symbols are rather uncontroversial, both for GA and for RP. FLEECE and GOOSE, for example, are nearly always transcribed [iː] and [uː], respectively. (Some transcribers that do not distinguish vowel length would not use the length marks, however.) In other cases, there is no unanimity. We will therefore take a look at the rationale for the choices made here.

The choice of symbols

Strange as it may seem for someone who has never dealt with the question of which symbols are to be used to transcribe a particular sound, transcribers always need some principles to guide them through the process. In this book, we follow three basic principles in sections A and B (cf. IPA 1999: 159f.):

- The major principle is, of course, the phonemic principle. If there are two sounds in an accent that potentially distinguish words, different symbols must be used.
- Second, the symbols we employ are those that correspond closest to the actual realisation of the sound in question. This is one of the reasons why we use the epsilon symbol for the DRESS, SQUARE and FACE sets both for RP and GA (see below) and [ɪr] for NEAR in GA. However, we avoid diacritics. Thus, we neither use symbols like [ɚ] (the 'r-colored schwa' as in GA *winn<u>er</u>*) or [ɝː] (as in *n<u>ur</u>se*) in the transcription of GA nor do we mark consonants as syllabic in syllables that have no vowel (as in [bɒtl̩], *bottle*). An exception to this rule is the length mark [ː], which is employed both for RP and GA.
- Third, established conventions are respected wherever possible. This is reflected by the fact that, in RP, the STRUT vowel is not transcribed as [ɐ] and the FACE, PRICE and MOUTH diphthongs do not feature as [ɛe], [ae] or [ao] either, nor GOOSE as [ʉː] and TRAP as [a], even though these transcriptions would possibly reflect actual present-day pronunciations more accurately than the established ones. Compare, for example, the diphthong in *mail* with the monophthong [eː] in the German word *Mehl*. Unless you pronounce the former very carefully and slowly, you will find that the endpoint of the diphthong in *mail* is only around the same height as the vowel in *Mehl* – possibly even lower. However, there is a firmly established tradition of transcribing FACE and PRICE with [ɪ] and MOUTH with [ʊ] as endpoints, probably due to the fact that speakers *aim* for these vowels but, in actual speech, move on to the next sound before they have actually reached them (a phenomenon referred to as *vowel undershoot*, cf. Reetz & Jongman 2009: 252). Also, in American English, words like *latter* and *ladder* are virtually homophonous. Thus, theoretically, these two words could be transcribed as [ˈlædr], and some transcribers actually follow this pattern. However, many textbook writers employ a different policy; since the [d] would be a phoneme in *ladder* but an allophone in *latter*, they would use [t̬] for (the) *latter*. This convention is widely in use, and we follow it here, too.

DRESS, SQUARE, FACE

When you look up words of the lexical DRESS set (like, for example, *weather*, *plenty* or *said*), you will probably find that the editors of your dictionary used the symbol [e] for these words. Other dictionaries (particularly those published by Oxford University Press) and many linguistic treatises, however, employ the symbol [ɛ] for the same set of words. The International Phonetic Association itself transcribes the word *Phonetic* in its name as [fəˈnɛtɪk], using the epsilon in the stressed syllable of the word. How is it possible that the same vowel is transcribed by two different symbols?

To answer this question, we have to go back about a century. When Daniel Jones devised his transcription system, he defined 16 **cardinal vowels** (**CVs**), two sets of eight vowels which were meant to act as reference points for all the vowels in the world (see graph below). CVs 1, 4, 5 and 8 are defined by their physical qualities: one cannot raise ([i, u]) or lower ([a, ɑ]) these vowels any further without causing some kind of friction. Jones then filled the space between [i] and [a] on the one hand and [u] and [ɑ] on the other with two additional 'equidistant' vowels each ([e, ɛ] and [o, ɔ], respectively). These eight vowels form the first set of cardinals. In this first set, the CVs 1–5 are unrounded, while the last three are rounded. The second set utilises the same positions of the vowels, but reverses the lip rounding (e.g. cardinal vowel 1, [i], is an unrounded high front vowel, whereas cardinal vowel 9, [y], is a rounded high front vowel, similar to the stressed vowel in German *Bühne*). For the first set, Jones used the following symbols:

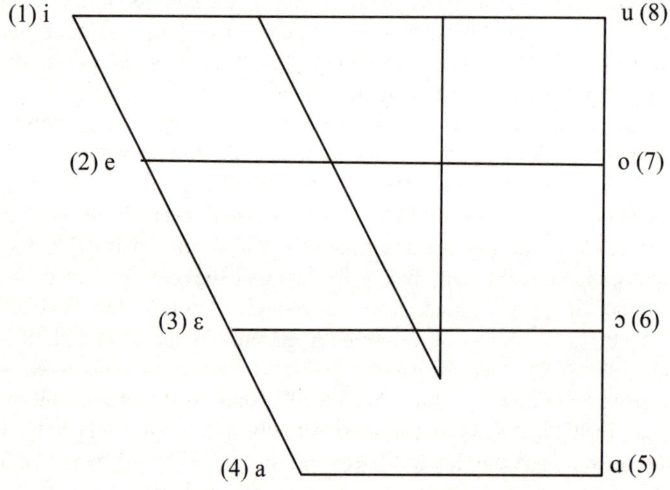

Fortunately, we still have his original recordings, so we can know exactly which sounds he had in mind.[1] The second cardinal vowel, represented by the symbol [e], stands for a mid-high (or 'mid-close') vowel like the one we find in German words like *Seele* or *Besen* or French words like *les* or *été*, while the symbol [ɛ] represents a mid-open vowel as in *Bett* or *ferme* in German or French, respectively. It is quite clear, then, that RP DRESS words are much closer to the latter set than to the former; words like German *Bett* and English *bet* are even as close to being homophones as words from two different languages can be.

The problem arose, however, when Jones published his first *English Pronouncing Dictionary* in 1917. For reasons we cannot be entirely sure about today, he chose the symbol [e] to represent the vowel of the DRESS words, even though, apparently, he was not happy with this decision himself. He remarked (Jones 1917: xxii):

> « e » varies between cardinal « ɛ » and a point little above half-way between cardinal « e » and cardinal « ɛ ». Some authors write the sound with the sign « ɛ », and there is much to be said in favour of this mode of representing it.

We can only assume that he wanted to keep this monophthong symbolically distinct from the starting point of the SQUARE diphthong, for which he used the combination [ɛə]. In the 14th edition of the dictionary (Jones was no longer editor at that point), the symbols for SQUARE were changed from [ɛə] to [eə]. The problem with these decisions is, of course, that they do not represent the facts – and that the *English Pronouncing Dictionary* (from the 11th to the 14th edition renamed *Everyman's English Pronouncing Dictionary*) served as a model for many other dictionary makers. What we have, therefore, is an unfortunate setting of points a hundred years ago whose influence can still be seen in many publications today. Since, on the other hand, many other linguists and publishers decided to use the more appropriate symbols, we have this situation of divided usage as it is today.

When we accept that the appropriate symbol for RP DRESS is the epsilon, we must also accept [ɛə] (or [ɛː]) for SQUARE, since the starting point of this diphthong is even lower than the monophthong in DRESS. The only case that is slightly more problematic is the diphthong in FACE. Most of the treatises that use [ɛ] for DRESS still use [eɪ] for FACE. The reason is that, generally, the starting point of FACE tends to be slightly higher than the monophthong in DRESS. (You can test this claim by comparing the two pronunciations of the word *again*, whose stressed syllable may be either pronounced with a monophthong or a diphthong.) It is, however, not so high that the use of [e] as a starting point would be justified. On the contrary, "[t]he qualitative difference between the starting point of FACE and

---

1 You can download the recording at http://www.let.uu.nl/~audiufon/data/e_cardinal_vowels.html.

DRESS may be lost in RP." (Wells 1982: 141) Phonetically, [e] is even more likely to be the endpoint of FACE than its starting point in ordinary (i.e. unselfconscious) speech, as we have just seen in the *mail*/*Mehl* example. Alternatively, if you pronounce a word like *saying*, you will probably realise that the endpoint of *say* is slightly different from the beginning of *-ing* and that you reach the highest and most fronted position only at the suffix. Since, however, most speakers *aim* at a fairly close position and may actually reach it in careful speech, the most appropriate representation would probably be [ɛɪ], and this is how we transcribe FACE in this book.

Another reason for choosing these symbols is to set the diphthong off from the monophthong that is used for the same set of words in many varieties of English. For example, the word *bay* in Scottish English sounds pretty much like <B> in German when referred to as a letter of the alphabet, and the transcription for both would be [beː]. You will notice that the vowel used here is not like the starting point for FACE in RP.

It is for these reasons that we use the epsilon symbol in all three lexical sets and in both RP and GA, representing DRESS as [ɛ], SQUARE as [ɛə]/[ɛr] and FACE as [ɛɪ]. For a more detailed discussion of the issues raised here, see Schmitt 2007.

The representation of /r/

The symbol used in sections A and B of this textbook for any English 'r'-sound is simply [r]. Strictly speaking, this IPA symbol represents an alveolar trill, such as occurs in Spanish words like *barrio*; the appropriate symbol for the post-alveolar approximant found in RP would be [ɹ]. As for the American version of /r/, it is sometimes said that it is retroflex, so the right symbol here would be [ɻ]. Since most transcribers do not care about these distinctions (unless they specifically pay attention to the way the 'r' is pronounced) and since even pronunciation dictionaries use the Roman symbol, we will do the same here.

The question remains how we treat NEAR, CURE and SQUARE (words that have centring diphthongs in RP) and the lettER words in GA. Since /r/ does not occur before a vowel here, many Americans do not pronounce it clearly, but finish the word 'early'. The result is a mid-central vowel that has some 'r-colouring'. Many transcribers use the symbol [ɚ], a schwa with a hook, to account for this situation. 'Square', for example, would then be transcribed as [skwɛɚ]. A similar case can be made for NURSE, which some transcribe with the symbol [ɝː]. However, for the sake of simplicity and since the exact pronunciation of the postvocalic /r/ is quite flexible in American English (cf. Kretzschmar 2008: 46), we use the symbol [r] here, too. Notice, though, that NEAR usually has a higher, more decentralised starting point in GA than in RP and that, therefore, we transcribe it as [ir] (rather than [ɪr]).

Some practical advice

Students often struggle with similar problems when they start transcribing. The following tips are meant to help you get started and avoid some of the commonest mistakes.

- If you've got the choice between GA and RP, choose one variety and stick with it. It is important that you have a reference accent with which you can compare other accents or actual speech later on. Remember that GA is less fixed than RP, which may make transcription slightly more complicated.
- Initially, you will probably use spelling as a guideline. In some cases (particularly in the question of TRAP vs. DRESS in RP) this can be a help. Generally, however, the English spelling is notoriously unreliable or even misleading. As you practise transcription, set your mind on losing your orientation towards spelling and get used to 'listening' to your 'inner ear'.
- You will probably find that transcribing most consonants is not a big problem. The sound [m], for example, is usually represented either by <m> or <mm> in many Indo-European languages, and the International Phonetic Alphabet reflects this fact by using this letter as a symbol for this sound. However, many students find it somewhat difficult to distinguish the dental fricatives [ð] and [θ] and, perhaps, the alveolar fricatives [z] and [s]. These consonants will receive special attention in sections A and B.
- Many students, however, struggle when they try to identify vowels. For example, is the vowel in the second syllable of *captain* a schwa, or is it the same as the one in DRESS, FACE or KIT? And what about the stressed syllable of *because*? Is this vowel like the one in LOT or in THOUGHT? Or could it even be either? For this reason, and because every word has at least one vowel, it might be a good idea to memorise a word for each vowel phoneme with which you can compare the word that you are trying to transcribe. A useful set of words is the one provided in the 'Standard Lexical Sets' section above, since these words have come to be used internationally to compare different accents. In other words, if you attend classes on variation later on in your studies (e.g. sociolinguistics, varieties of English), you are likely to come across these terms again anyway. In the *Practice* section below, the vowels will be briefly characterised, followed by examples of typical graphemic representations. You will then find a few words with rather unusual spellings for this vowel. These examples are by no means exhaustive; they only list a few words which are still fairly common in English but whose spelling is a bit off the beaten track. (As was mentioned above, spell-

ing-sound correspondences multiply if you include foreign (esp. French) loan-words and alternative pronunciations.)

- Do not confuse the symbol used for the BATH or PALM monophthong and the first symbol of the PRICE and MOUTH diphthongs. The former is [ɑː] (a 'round a' with length mark), the latter is [a], as it is typically used in printing. We use two distinct symbols here because the place of articulation of [ɑ] and [a] is different (cf. the graphs for BATH and PRICE/MOUTH below).
- Do not confuse the symbols for the DRESS and NURSE vowels. DRESS has the epsilon [ɛ], NURSE the 'reverse epsilon' [ɜ] with a length mark.
- Note that the FLEECE vowel has a dot on top while KIT hasn't, thus [iː] and [ɪ].
- If you use a word-processor for your transcription (i.e. if you don't transcribe by hand), the symbol for the 'g-sound' (as in *great, bag* etc.) should strictly speaking look like this: ɡ, not like this: g. However, since the International Phonetic Alphabet does not distinguish between the two, inappropriate use of the symbol is not likely to cause misunderstanding.
- Even more strictly speaking, the correct symbol that indicates length is two triangle-like figures that point at each other, thus: 'ː', and this is how length is indicated in this book. However, even many linguists use simple colons for ease of use, and you may be forgiven if you do the same.
- If you struggle with the transcription of a longer word, look out for the syllable that receives the main stress first. Mark it with the symbol ˈ at the beginning (as in [əˈraɪv] for *arrive*). Since this syllable cannot be weak (i.e. reduced to schwa), try to identify the vowel or diphthong here. Then ask yourself if there is another full vowel in the word which receives secondary stress. In most words (with the exception of compounds), this will precede the syllable with the primary stress.
- Last but not least, one piece of advice is particularly true for transcription: practice makes perfect. If you have learned to spell English words, transcription should not be such a challenge since you have a rough idea of the pronunciation of a word anyway. As a guideline, you need approximately 20–30 hours of practice to be reasonably proficient in broad phonetic transcription; ear transcription (section C), of course, takes a lot longer.

Practice

Exercise A1. Standard Lexical Sets (☑)

The following poem illustrates that words with a similar spelling can be pronounced quite differently. Do not transcribe the words underlined; instead, use the Standard Lexical Sets to indicate which (stressed) vowel is used in each of them.

A moth is not a moth in mother, ____________________________
Nor both in bother, broth in brother. ____________________________
And here is not a match for there ____________________________
Nor dear and fear for bear and pear. ____________________________
And then there's dose and rose and lose – ____________________________
Just look them up – and goose and choose, ____________________________
And cord and word and card and ward, ____________________________
And font and front and word and sword, ____________________________
And do and go and thwart and cart – ____________________________
Come, come, I've hardly made a start!
A dreadful language? Man alive!
I'd mastered it when I was five!

[iː]: FLEECE (RP & GA)

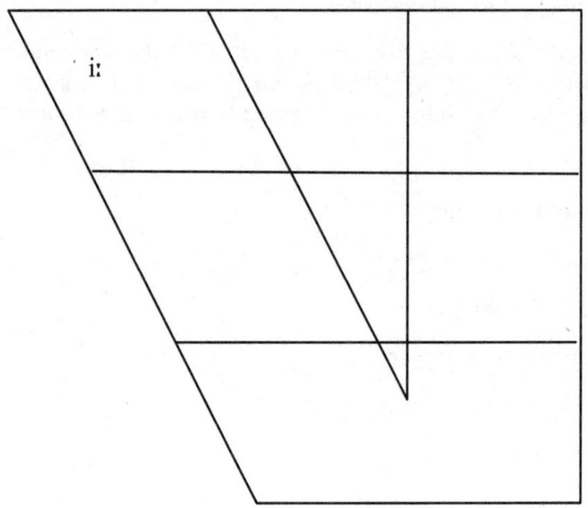

- Characterisation: long high front vowel.
- Typical graphemic representations: s<u>ee</u>, s<u>ea</u>
- Less common spellings include: p<u>eo</u>ple, k<u>ey</u>, d<u>e</u>mon, rec<u>ei</u>pt, un<u>i</u>que, n<u>ie</u>ce, qu<u>ay</u>.

Exercise A2. Words with [iː] (☑)

In each of the exercises A2–A21, you will find a number of words which all share the vowel phoneme under discussion. Please transcribe the words listed.

deep	________________	receipt	________________
people	________________	Eve	________________
eagle	________________	equal	________________
mean	________________	agree	________________
knee	________________	idea (GA)	________________
believe	________________	Z (GA)	________________

[ɪ]: KIT (RP & GA)

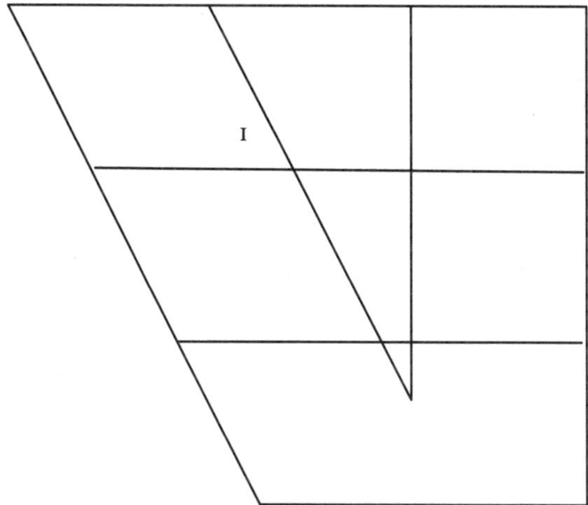

- Characterisation: short centralised high front vowel.
- Typical graphemic representation: pin, symbol, catches (RP).
- Less common spellings include: women, busy, build and village. Note that in English, the letter <y> is never pronounced like in German *Psyche* or *Rhythmus* (i.e. as [yː] or [ʏ]). Thus, the first syllable of the word *syntax* actually sounds like the word *sin* and the middle part of *Olympic* like *limp*.

Exercise A3. Words with [ɪ] (☑)

hit	________	women	________
build	________	biscuit	________
wind	________	bushes (RP)	________
miss	________	Miller	________
ring	________	singer	________
riddle	________	business	________

[ɛ]: DRESS (RP & GA), MARRY (GA)

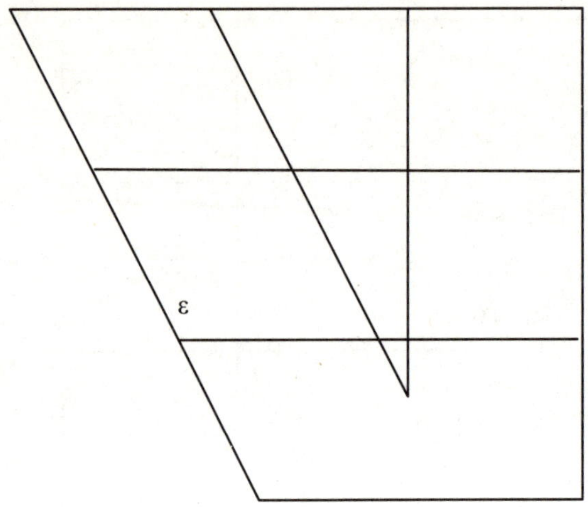

- Characterisation: short mid-low front vowel.
- Typical graphemic representations: bell, deaf
- Less common spellings: leopard, friend, lieutenant (RP), bury. There are very few words where the DRESS vowel is represented by the letter <a> (or a combination starting with <a>). These exceptions include: *any* (and compounds like *anywhere* etc.), *many*, *says*, *said*, *again* (also [ɛɪ]), and the more historical pronunciation of *ate* (the modern one is [ɛɪt]). Also note that the river *Thames* is pronounced with [ɛ].
- In GA, words that have an [æ] in RP are typically raised to [ɛ] before /r/, so that words like *carry, Marilyn* or *narrow* tend to have a higher vowel in GA than in RP.

Exercise A4. Words with [ɛ] (☑)

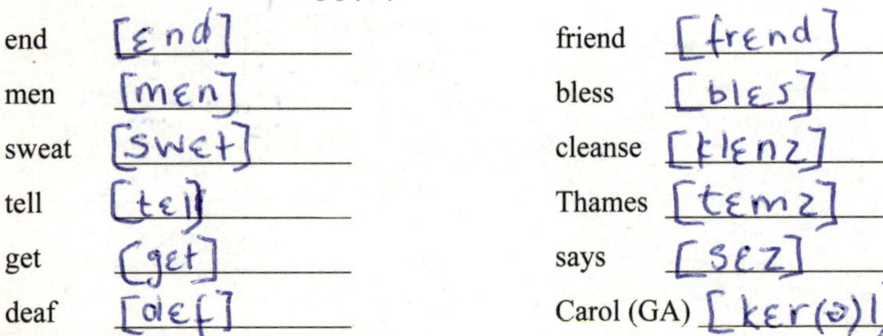

end [ɛnd]
men [mɛn]
sweat [swɛt]
tell [tɛl]
get [gɛt]
deaf [dɛf]
friend [frɛnd]
bless [blɛs]
cleanse [klɛnz]
Thames [tɛmz]
says [sɛz]
Carol (GA) [kɛr(ə)l]

[æ]: TRAP (RP & GA), BATH (GA)

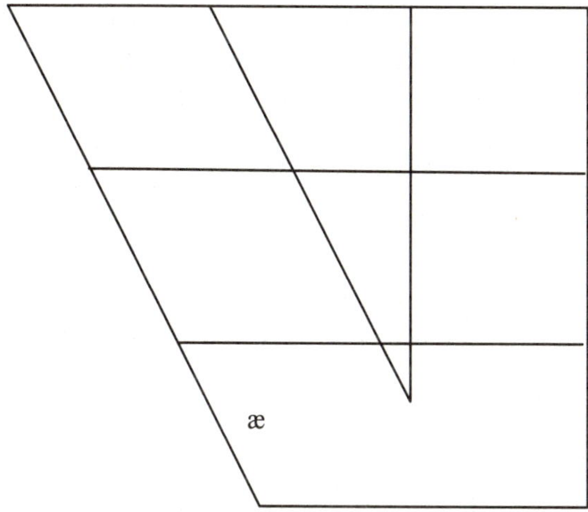

- Characterisation: short mid-low to low front vowel.
- Typical graphemic representations: g<u>a</u>s. In the case of TRAP, spelling *is* actually a rather reliable guideline, but note the exceptions mentioned under DRESS.
- Less common spellings: In GA, the spelling might be <au> (as in *laugh*).

Exercise A5. Words with [æ] (☑)

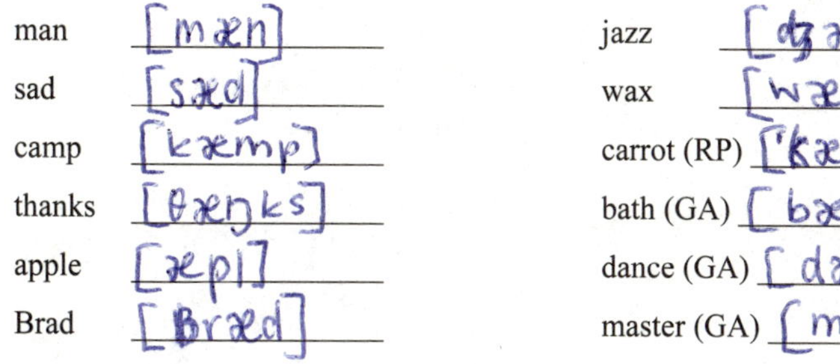

man	________	jazz	________
sad	________	wax	________
camp	________	carrot (RP)	________
thanks	________	bath (GA)	________
apple	________	dance (GA)	________
Brad	________	master (GA)	________

[ʌ]: STRUT (RP & GA)

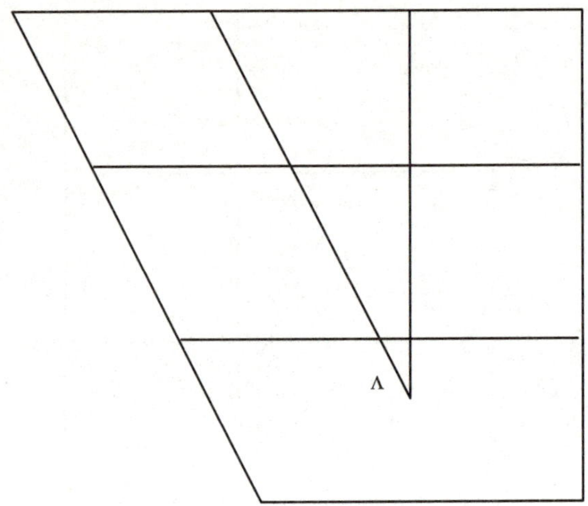

- Characterisation: short mid-low to low central vowel.
- Typical graphemic representations: luck, one.
- Less common spellings include: blood, courage (RP), curry (RP). The problem with this vowel is that the letter <o> may represent either STRUT or LOT (or other sounds), cf. exercise A23.

Exercise A6. Words with [ʌ] (☑)

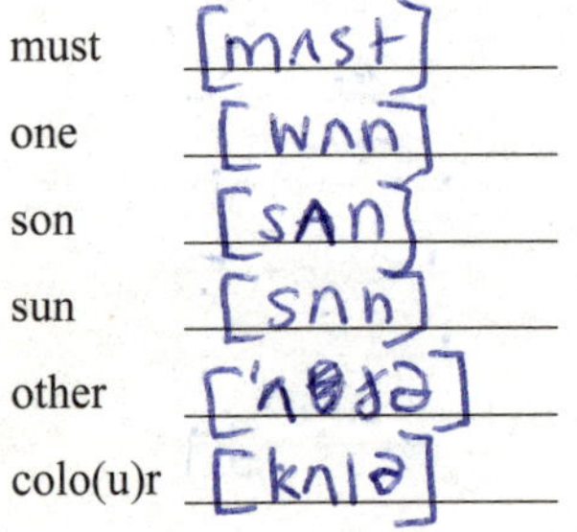

must ____
one ____
son ____
sun ____
other ____
colo(u)r ____

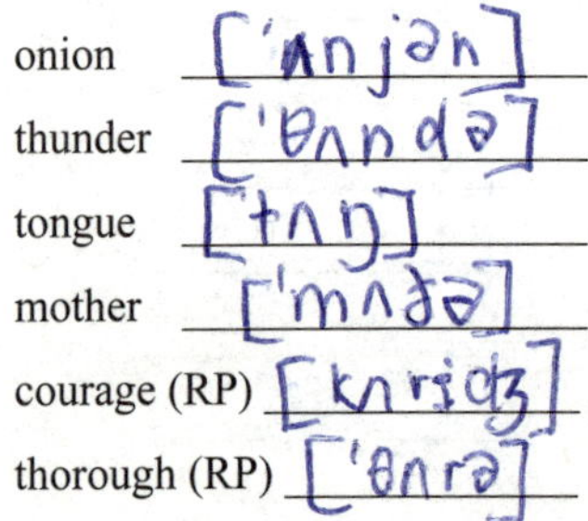

onion ____
thunder ____
tongue ____
mother ____
courage (RP) ____
thorough (RP) ____

[ɑː]: BATH (RP), PALM (RP & GA), LOT (GA), CLOTH (GA: option), THOUGHT (GA: option)

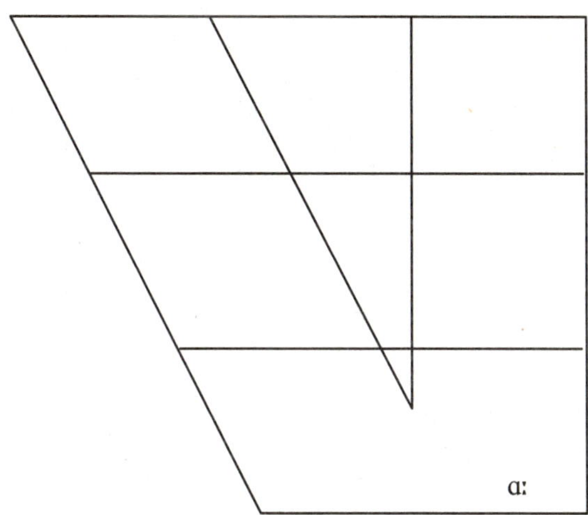

- Characterisation: long low back vowel.
- Typical graphemic representations: father, car (RP), shot (GA).
- Less common spellings include: clerk, bizarre (RP), laugh (RP).

Exercise A7. Words with [ɑː] (☑)

palm	______	dance (RP)	______
schwa	______	branch (RP)	______
star	______	stop (GA)	______
card	______	solve (GA)	______
bath (RP)	______	Tom (GA)	______
laugh (RP)	______	watch (GA)	______

[ɒ]: LOT (RP)

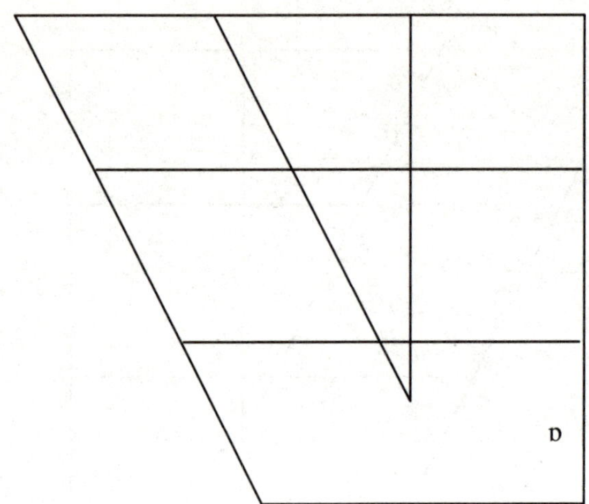

- Characterisation: short low back vowel, rounded.
- Typical graphemic representation: l<u>o</u>ck.
- Less common spellings include: y<u>a</u>cht, c<u>ou</u>gh, <u>e</u>nvelope (option). Some words with initial <a> (*alter*) or <au> (*auction*) can be pronounced either with THOUGHT or LOT.

Exercise A8. Words with [ɒ] (☑)

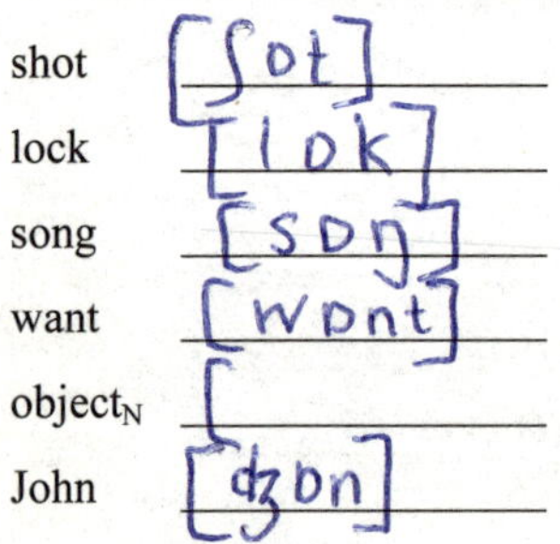

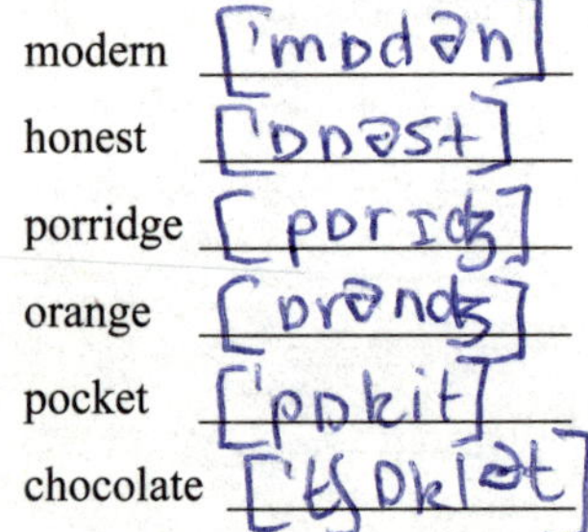

[ɔː]: THOUGHT (RP, GA option), CLOTH (GA option), NORTH (GA)

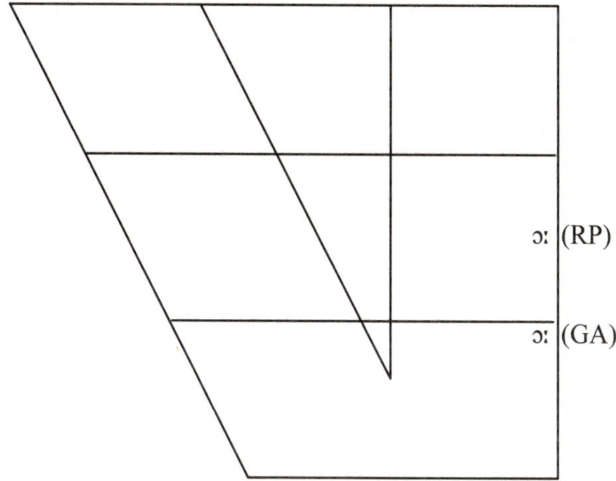

- Characterisation: The actual realisation of this vowel is decidedly different between RP and GA. Whereas it is a long rounded back vowel between cardinal vowel 6 and 7 in RP, it tends to be slightly lower than CV 6 in GA.
- Typical graphemic representations: b<u>ough</u>t, s<u>aw</u>, t<u>au</u>ght, sh<u>o</u>re, b<u>oa</u>r, d<u>oo</u>r
- Less common spellings: Note that some RP speakers pronounce CURE words with [ɔː]. Thus, you may add the patterns you find under that entry here, too.

Exercise A9. Words with [ɔː] (☑)

Note that the first four words have [ɔː] both in RP and GA; *brought, caution, clause* and *Chaucer* have [ɔː] in RP and, optionally, in GA, and for the last four, [ɔː] is an option only in GA (in addition to [ɑː]).

door	[dɔː]	clause	[klɔːz]
shore	[ʃɔː]	Chaucer	[
north	[nɔːθ]	long (GA)	[lɔːŋ]
boring	[bɔːrɪŋ]	boss (GA)	[bɔːs]
brought	[brɔːt]	offer (GA)	[ɔːfər]
caution	[kɔːʃən]	across (GA)	[əkrɔːs]

[uː]: GOOSE (RP & GA)

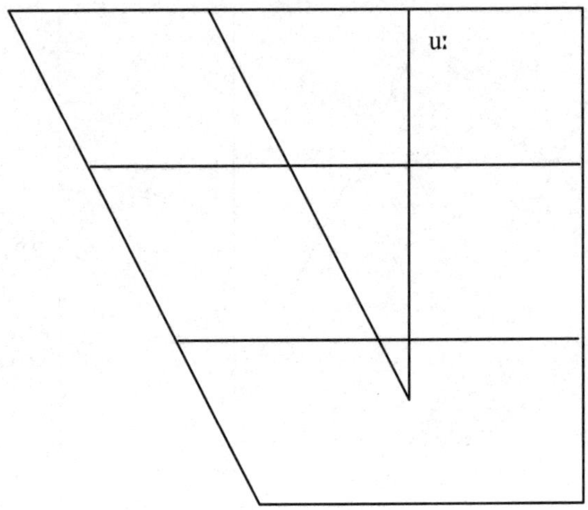

- Characterisation: long high back vowel, rounded.
- Typical graphemic representations: boot, route.
- Less common spellings include: new, tomb, juice, queue, view, shoe, due.

Exercise A10. Words with [uː] (☑)

new	________________	Ruth	________________
fruit	________________	taboo	________________
soon	________________	union	________________
glue	________________	queue	________________
juice	________________	UK	________________
lose	________________	smooth	________________

[ʊ]: FOOT (RP & GA)

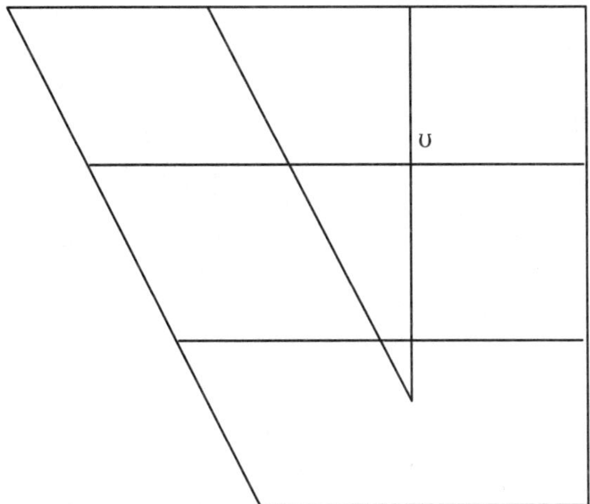

- Characterisation: short centralised high back vowel, rounded.
- Typical graphemic representation: p<u>u</u>t, f<u>oo</u>t.
- Less common spellings include: w<u>o</u>man, sh<u>ou</u>ld.

Exercise A11. Words with [ʊ] (☑)

cook	____________	wool	____________
wood	____________	cushion	____________
push	____________	wolf	____________
full	____________	sugar	____________
should (SF)	____________	woman	____________

[ɜː] (RP), [ɜːr] (GA): NURSE

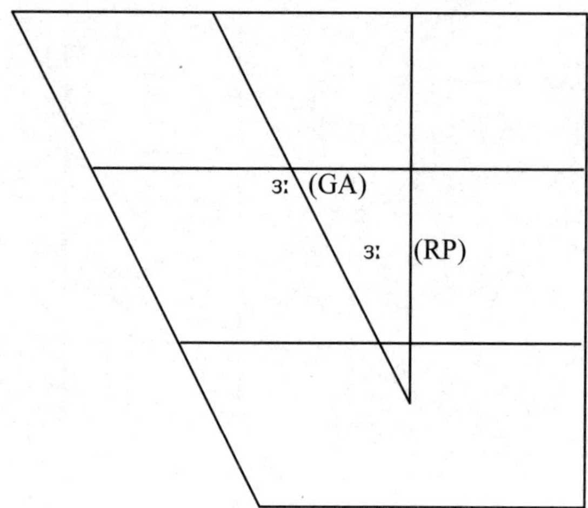

- Characterisation: long mid central vowel. It is slightly more fronted and raised in GA than in RP.
- Typical graphemic representations: bird, word, fur, were, earn.
- Less common spellings include: journalist, milieu, myrrh

Exercise A12. Words with [ɜː]/[ɜːr] (☑)

turn	____________	nerve	____________
verb	____________	murder	____________
heard	____________	urge	____________
worth	____________	person	____________
worse	____________	Wordsworth	____________

[ə] (RP & GA): commA and lettER

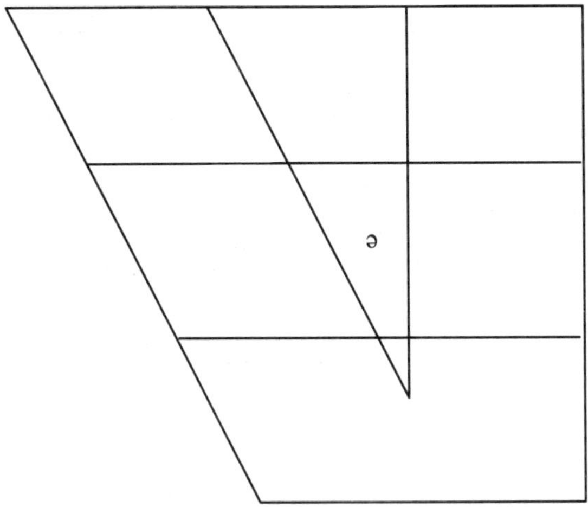

- Characterisation: short mid central vowel, unstressed. As far as place of articulation is concerned, the schwa may be identical to the nurse vowel. Compare, for example, the two vowels in the word *German*: they differ in length but not in quality. (This is the reason why some transcribers prefer [əː] for NURSE.) However, the schwa only occurs in unstressed syllables (i.e. it is a reduced vowel), and it is also more flexible in terms of allophonic variation.
- Typical graphemic representations: Note that in English, all kinds of vowels and diphthongs (not only those which are typically represented by <e>) can be reduced to schwa. Compare, for example, about, operate, computer, succeed, nation etc. Thus, it is difficult to determine typical graphemic representations of this vowel. Note further that because the schwa (as a single vowel) only occurs in unstressed syllables, it is often elided in connected speech (especially if it stands between a plosive and /l/ or /n/ as in *bottle* or *button*). Furthermore, the schwa can sometimes be used interchangeably with [ɪ], as in *beginning* or *accident*, or with [ʊ], as in the suffix *-ful*. In cases where there is a choice between [ə] and [ɪ], the former seems to be more common in GA and the latter in RP.

Exercise A13. Words with [ə] (☑)

sofa	________	diet	________
about	________	nation	________
dealer	________	pleasure	________
comma	________	palace	________
teacher	________	professor	________

[aɪ]: price (RP & GA)

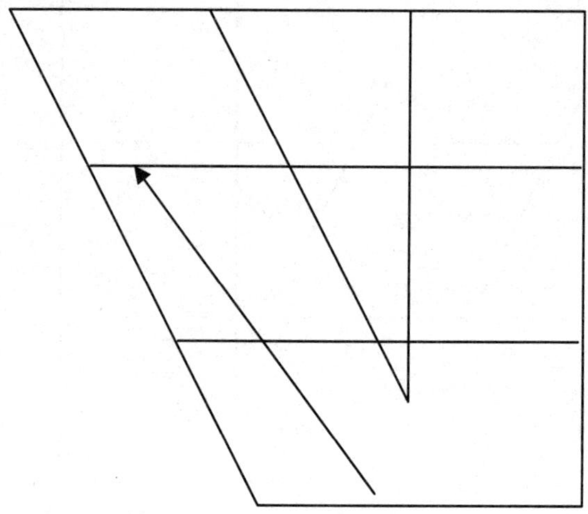

- Characterisation: diphthong, starting in low central position and ending in the area of cardinal vowel 2.
- Typical graphemic representations: shy, idol, night.
- Less common spellings include: either (most common RP pronunciation), eye, buy, die, dye.

Exercise A14. Words with [aɪ] (☑)

fight	________________	choir	________________
knife	________________	tiger	________________
sigh	________________	decide	________________
write	________________	science	________________
fire	________________	island	________________

[aʊ]: MOUTH (RP & GA)

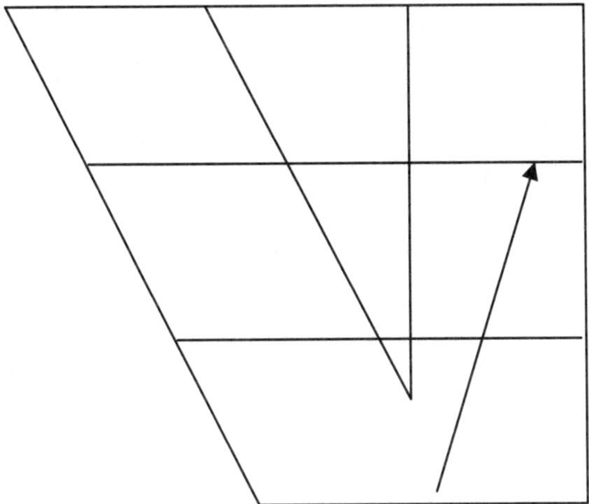

- Characterisation: diphthong, starting in low central position and ending in the area of cardinal vowel 7.
- Typical graphemic representations: loud, cow.
- Less common spellings include: ciao, plough.

Exercise A15. Words with [aʊ] (☑)

shout	________________	house	________________
browse	________________	flower	________________
south	________________	trousers	________________
crowd	________________	mountain	________________
power	________________	however	________________

[ɛɪ]: FACE (RP & GA)

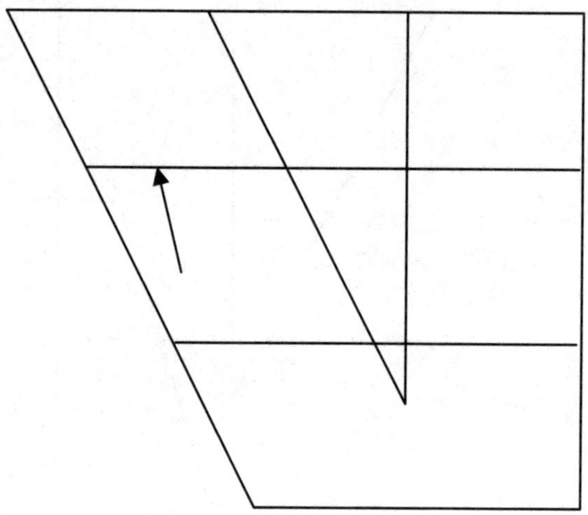

- Characterisation: diphthong, starting between front mid-low and front mid position and ending in the area of cardinal vowel 2 (or, when very carefully pronounced, around [ɪ]).
- Typical graphemic representations: <u>a</u>ble, <u>ai</u>m.
- Less common spellings include: <u>eig</u>ht, gr<u>ea</u>t, w<u>ay</u>.

Exercise A16. Words with [ɛɪ] (☑)

name	________	bacon	________
steak	________	nature	________
came	________	obey	________
wave	________	station	________
jail	________	arrange	________

[ɔɪ]: CHOICE (RP & GA)

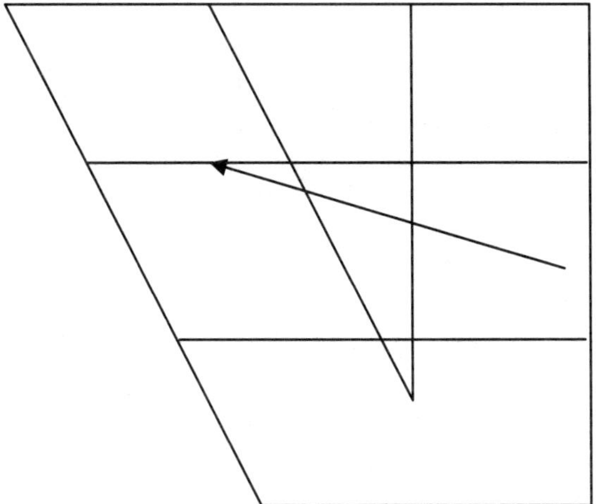

- Characterisation: diphthong, starting in mid back position and ending in the area between cardinal vowel 2 and KIT.
- Typical graphemic representations: boy, noise.
- Less common spellings include: buoy (RP).

Exercise A17. Words with [ɔɪ] (☑)

voice	________________	annoy	________________
coin	________________	oyster	________________
boy	________________	employ	________________
noise	________________	rejoice	________________
moist	________________	soya	________________

[əʊ] (RP), [oʊ] (GA): GOAT

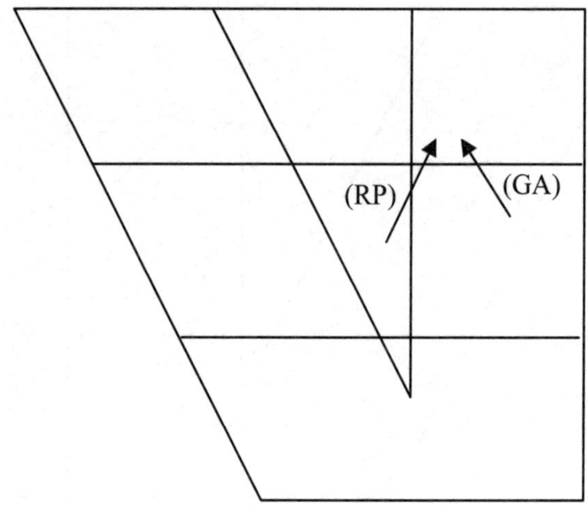

- Characterisation: diphthong, starting in mid central position (RP) or in a somewhat centralised and more open position than CV 7 (GA), and ending in the area of FOOT.
- Typical graphemic representations: <u>o</u>ver, sh<u>ow</u>, b<u>oa</u>t.
- Less common spellings include: <u>au</u>bergine, s<u>ew</u>, ob<u>oe</u>, d<u>ough</u>.

Exercise A18. Words with [əʊ]/[oʊ] (☑)

hole	____________	joke	____________
don't	____________	ocean	____________
rose	____________	okay	____________
comb	____________	clothe	____________
though	____________	control	____________

[ɪə] (RP), [ir] (GA): NEAR

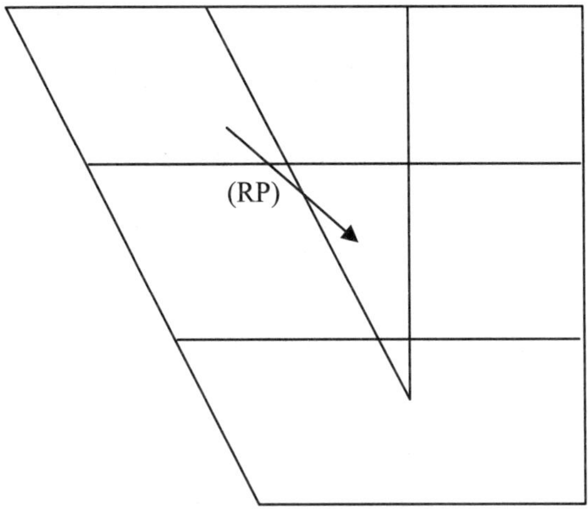

- Characterisation: In RP, a diphthong starting in KIT position and ending in a (broadly defined) mid central position. In GA, a combination of high front vowel + /r/. This vowel tends to be considerably more decentralised than in RP, hence the representation of it as [ir] (not [ɪr] as in other textbooks). If, for example, you compare the two vowels in *sincere* with an American accent, you will realise that the one in the stressed second syllable sounds decidedly different from the one in the first.
- Typical graphemic representations: cl<u>ear</u>, b<u>eer</u>, h<u>ere</u>.
- Less common spellings include: cash<u>ier</u>, <u>e</u>ra.

Exercise A19. Words with [ɪə]/[ir] (☑)

ear	________________	weird	________________
era	________________	sincere	________________
sheer	________________	career	________________
cheer	________________	appear	________________
beard	________________	persevere	________________

[ʊə] (RP), [ʊr] (GA): CURE

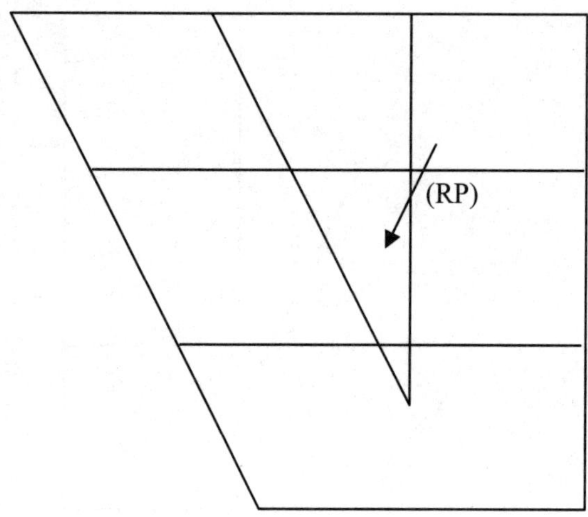

- Characterisation: In RP, a diphthong starting in FOOT position and ending in a (broadly defined) mid central position.
- Typical graphemic representations: ass<u>ure</u>.
- Less common spellings include: y<u>our</u>, pl<u>u</u>ral, <u>eu</u>ro, liqu<u>eur</u>, p<u>oor</u>. Note that some RP speakers pronounce CURE words with [ɔː].

Exercise A20. Words with [ʊə]/[ʊr] (☑)

sure	________________	ensure	________________
tour	________________	Europe	________________
poor	________________	secure	________________
cure	________________	tourism	________________
mature	________________	plural	________________

[ɛə] (RP), [ɛr] (GA): SQUARE

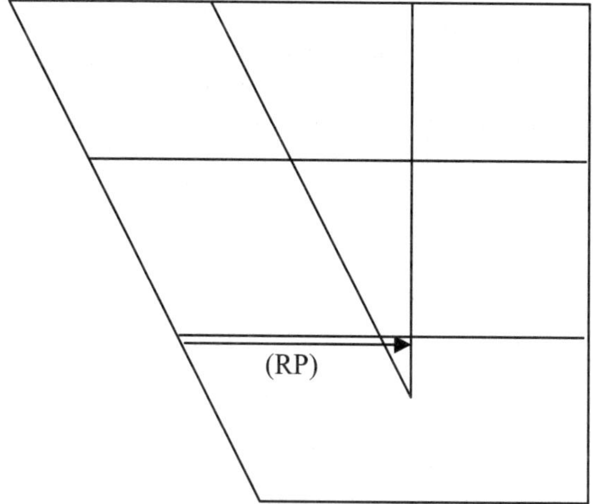

- Characterisation: In RP, a diphthong starting in CV3 position and ending in a (broadly defined) mid central position.
- Typical graphemic representations: d<u>are</u>, f<u>air</u>.
- Less common spellings include: h<u>eir</u>, wh<u>ere</u>, b<u>ear</u>.

Exercise A21. Words with [ɛə]/[ɛr] (☑)

their	______________	prayer	______________
heir	______________	scarce	______________
air	______________	upstairs	______________
swear	______________	unfair	______________
where	______________	mayor (RP)	______________

Exercise A22. Medley 1 (@)

The words in the medley exercises have been specifically selected because, for some reason or other, students tend to struggle with them. Like the exercises in sections A and B in general, they are roughly graded, starting with easier words and progressing to more challenging ones. When you have finished one medley, see whether your results display any systematic errors before you proceed to the next one.

1. such
2. three
3. back
4. work
5. long
6. old
7. world
8. life
9. last
10. might
11. great
12. house
13. told
14. white
15. mean
16. name
17. brought
18. wife
19. young
20. next
21. year

Exercise A23. Words with <o> (☑)

There are some words with an <o> in the spelling that tend to confuse students, partly because <o> is commonly realised as LOT but sometimes also as STRUT (plus a number of other pronunciations), and partly because sometimes the American pronunciation differs from the British in a non-systematic way. See if you can find the right transcription for your variety.

worry	____________	lorry	____________
stomach	____________	once	____________
doctor	____________	comfort	____________
onion	____________	oven	____________
sponge	____________	font	____________
front	____________	wonder	____________

Exercise A24. Silent letters (☑)

All of the following words have at least one letter that is 'silent', i.e. that is not pronounced. Spot the silent letter and transcribe the word.

1. should
2. hymn
3. sword
4. hour
5. psalm
6. write
7. listen
8. debt
9. gnaw
10. heir
11. folk
12. climb
13. build
14. height

Exercise A25. TRAP vs. DRESS (☑)

Minimal pairs are words that differ only in one phoneme, e.g. *bin/pin*, *ban/bang* or *should/shed* (note that the spelling is irrelevant here). These minimal pairs can be powerful tools when we need to understand (and later on, perhaps, teach) differences in the phoneme inventory that we tend to miss due to our own phonological system. German, for example, does not have the vowel [æ]; speakers of this language therefore commonly replace the TRAP vowel in English by the DRESS vowel [ɛ], pronouncing *Pat* as if it were *pet* and *pan* like *pen*. Find three other minimal pairs for these two phonemes.

Exercise A26. Inflectional affixes 1 (-s/'s) (☑)

When nouns and verbs are inflected regularly, they follow a straightforward pattern in English. The plural *–s*, the possessive *'s* (for nouns) and the third person singular *-s* (for verbs) are realised as [z] when the base ends in a vowel or a voiced consonant. If it ends in a voiceless consonant, the suffix is [s]. The only exception are words that end in a sibilant, i.e. any of the phonemes [z, s, ʒ, ʃ, dʒ, tʃ]. In these cases the affix tends to be realised as [ɪz] in RP and [əz] in GA. Generally, these rules also hold for the contracted form *'s* when it stands for *is* or *has* (*He's just turned 40.*). Note that it is the pronunciation of the word which is relevant, not the spelling. Thus, the plural of the word *rope* is [rəʊps]/[roʊps], even though the last letter is an <e>. Also note that there are some nouns that end in a voiceless consonant in the singular, but change to a voiced consonant plus [z] when they form the plural (*wife – wives*). And, of course, there are several irregular forms, which we

 HA week 1

do not consider here. Transcribe the following inflected forms, allocating them to the correct column.

	[z]	[s]	[ɪz]/[əz]
Bob's	* bɔbz		
churches	' ~~tʃɜːtʃ~~		*'tʃɜːtʃɪz
hits		* hɪts	
Sarah's	*'seərəz		
buses			*'bʌsɪz
misses			*'mɪsɪz
plays		* ~~pleɪ~~	pleɪz
breaks		* breɪks	
smashes			*'smæʃɪz
Sue's	* sjuːz		
knives	* naɪvz		
lifts		* lɪfts	
marks		* maːks	
stairs	* steəz		
promises			*'prɔmɪsɪz
presses			*'presɪz
sings	* sɪŋz		
helps		* helps	
climbs	* klaɪmz		
shows	* ʃəuz		
Smith's		* smɪθs	
Jones's			*'dʒəunzɪz

HA week 1

Exercise A27. Inflectional affixes 2 (-ed) (☑)

As for the past tense affix *-ed*, we find similarly conditioned allomorphs. If the base ends in a voiceless consonant, the affix is realised as [t]. If it ends in a vowel or a voiced consonant, it will be [d]. Only if the base has a final [d] or [t] itself will the suffix be [ɪd]/[əd] (with the former preferred in RP and the latter in GA). Again, irregular forms will be disregarded here. Transcribe the following past-tense verbs and allocate them to the correct column.

	[d]	[t]	[ɪd]/[əd]
selected	sɪˈlektɪd		
needed			ˈniːdɪd
transcribed	trænsˈkraɪbd		
missed		mɪst	
showed	ʃəʊd		
wanted			ˈwɔntɪd
promised	~~ˈprɔmɪst~~	ˈprɔmɪst	
arranged	əˈreɪndʒd		
laughed		lɑːft	
licked		lɪkt	
subdued	səbˈdjuːd		
decided			dɪˈsaɪdɪd
smoked		sməʊkt	

Exercise A28. The dental fricatives: [ð] or [θ]? (☑)

In terms of all the languages of the world, dental fricatives are an exception rather than the rule, and some students find it hard to decide which one of the two (voiced vs. voiceless) they should use in a particular word. However, there are some fairly reliable rules (cf. Wells 2008: 804). The easiest way is to start by looking at the position of the fricative in the word.

- If it is at the beginning, ask yourself whether the word is a function word (like an article, pronoun or conjunction) or a content word (like a verb, noun or adjective). The former always begin with a voiced fricative (like *the, these, they, them* etc.), the latter with a voiceless one (as in *three thin thumbs*). Adverbs like *then* and *there* have a pronominal character and are also pronounced with [ð]. Note that the word *then* can also be an adjective (as in *the then president of the United States*); this, however, does not alter its pronunciation.
- If the fricative occurs in the middle, the decision of [ð] vs. [θ] mostly depends on the etymology of the word. Generally, words from Greek have voiceless fricatives (*method, ethnology, mathematics*), whereas words of Germanic origin tend to use [ð] (*father, heathen, leather*). There are some exceptions like *rhythm*.
- At the end of a word, the *th* is usually voiceless. Exceptions are *smooth*, *mouth*$_V$ and *with* (the latter in RP) as well as some other rare words. If, however, the fricative is followed by a silent <e> in the spelling (as in *breathe, clothe*), it is voiced.

All of the above statements refer to morphologically simple words. Thus the *th* in *births* (plural of *birth*) is of course voiceless even though it is a word of Germanic origin and the fricative is not at the end of the word. If the *-th* is a suffix itself (as in *width* or *twelfth*), it is voiceless. In some cases, affixation can cause a final [θ] to become [ð], as in *mouth-mouths*. Sometimes this change is an option (e.g. *oaths, truths, youths, paths*).

Transcribe the following words.

1. month ____________________
2. method ____________________
3. thread ____________________
4. breath ____________________
5. breathe ____________________
6. smooth ____________________
7. with ____________________
8. either ____________________
9. both ____________________
10. thirteenth ____________________
11. oath ____________________
12. oaths ____________________
13. bath ____________________
14. baths ____________________
15. width ____________________
16. there ____________________
17. weather ____________________
18. north ____________________

Exercise A29. Homophones 1 (☑)

There are literally hundreds of homophones (words with the same pronunciation but a different spelling and a different meaning) in English. Below you will find a selection of fairly easy ones. See if you can find out which words are represented by each transcription.

1. [æd]	a) ______________	b) ______________
2. [baɪ]	a) ______________	b) ______________
	c) ______________	
3. [hɪə]/[hir]	a) ______________	b) ______________
4. [haɪ]	a) ______________	b) ______________
5. [njuː]/[nuː]	a) ______________	b) ______________
6. [nəʊ]/[noʊ]	a) ______________	b) ______________
7. [rɛɪn]	a) ______________	b) ______________
8. [sʌn]	a) ______________	b) ______________
9. [stiːl]	a) ______________	b) ______________
10. [ðɛə]/[ðɛər]	a) ______________	b) ______________
11. [miːt]	a) ______________	b) ______________
12. [piːs]	a) ______________	b) ______________
13. [wiːk]	a) ______________	b) ______________
14. [siː]	a) ______________	b) ______________

Exercise A30. Spot the mistake (☑)

All of the following transcriptions contain a mistake. Spot it and correct it.

1. write [wraɪt] ______________________
2. finger [ˈfɪŋə]/[ˈfɪŋər] ______________________
3. father [ˈfaːðə]/[ˈfaːðər] ______________________
4. honest [ˈhɒn(ɪ/ə)st]/[ˈhɑːnəst] ______________________
5. kids [kɪds] ______________________
6. biggest [ˈbɪgg(ɪ/ə)st] ______________________
7. symbol [ˈsimbl] ______________________
8. know [knəʊ]/[knoʊ] ______________________
9. word [wɛːd]/[wɛːrd] ______________________
10. professor [prəʊˈfɛsə]/[proʊˈfɛs(ə)r] ______________________
11. just [jʌst] ______________________
12. ring [rɪŋg] ______________________
13. weather [ˈwɜðə]/[ˈwɜð(ə)r] ______________________
14. highlights ______________________

Fig. 3: Shop sign in Bonn, Germany

Exercise A31. [ŋ], [ŋg] or neither? (@)

Transcribe the following words. All of them have an <ng> in the spelling. Which are realised as [ŋ] or [ŋg], and which have a different pronunciation altogether?

1. finger ____________________
2. strange ____________________
3. angel ____________________
4. angle ____________________
5. anger ____________________
6. Aer Lingus (Irish Airline) ____________________
7. long ____________________
8. longer ____________________
9. longed ____________________
10. English ____________________
11. strangle ____________________
12. language ____________________
13. linguistics ____________________
14. Engels (proper noun) ____________________

Exercise A32. Medley 2 (☑)

1. build ____________
2. pure ____________
3. slow ____________
4. teach ____________
5. these ____________
6. third ____________
7. throat ____________
8. trouble ____________
9. warm ____________
10. thunder ____________
11. size ____________
12. rather ____________
13. wealth ____________
14. suppose ____________

Exercise A33. [z] or [s]? (1) (☑)

One of the problems in transcription is the question of [z] vs. [s]. Try to work out which one is used in each case.

1. use_V ______________________________
2. use_N ______________________________
3. please ______________________________
4. result ______________________________
5. false ______________________________
6. difference ______________________________
7. house ______________________________
8. houses ______________________________
9. of course ______________________________
10. cause ______________________________
11. his ______________________________
12. example ______________________________
13. Miss ______________________________
14. Ms ______________________________
15. $excuse_N$ ______________________________
16. $excuse_V$ ______________________________
17. $close_A$ ______________________________
18. $close_V$ ______________________________
19. loose ______________________________
20. lose ______________________________
21. this ______________________________

Exercise A34. Homographs (@)

Homographs are words that have the same spelling but that can be pronounced differently depending on their meaning or function. There are not nearly as many homographs in English as there are homophones, but here you will find a selection. Determine the pronunciation for each meaning.

1.	read	____________________ (a) present tense	____________________ (b) past tense
2.	rebel	____________________ (a) to oppose authority	____________________ (b) someone who rebels
3.	lead	____________________ (a) to go in front	____________________ (b) a heavy metal
4.	refuse	____________________ (a) to say no	____________________ (b) waste
5.	row	____________________ (a) a line of things	____________________ (b) a quarrel
6.	bow	____________________ (a) to bend your body	____________________ (b) instrument for shooting arrows
7.	tear	____________________ (a) liquid from your eye	____________________ (b) to rip something
8.	sow	____________________ (a) to scatter seeds	____________________ (b) a female pig

Exercise A35. Medley 3 (☑)

Several of these words have more than one possible form. Transcribe one that you find most likely.

1. worm ______________________
2. suit ______________________
3. suggest ______________________
4. tradition ______________________
5. process ______________________
6. business ______________________
7. tension ______________________
8. view ______________________
9. theatre ______________________
10. often ______________________
11. debt ______________________
12. pressure ______________________
13. pleasant ______________________
14. tomorrow ______________________

Exercise A36. Homophones 2 (@)

1. [raɪt] a) ________________ b) ________________

   c) ________________

2. [bɛə]/[bɛr] a) ________________ b) ________________

3. [siːn] a) ________________ b) ________________

4. [bluː] a) ________________ b) ________________

5. [nəʊz]/[noʊz] a) ________________ b) ________________

6. [ˈwɛðə]/[ˈwɛð(ə)r] a) ________________ b) ________________

7. [rɛd] a) ________________ b) ________________

8. [pækt] a) ________________ b) ________________

9. [hɪm] a) ________________ b) ________________

10. [həʊl]/[hoʊl] a) ________________ b) ________________

11. [wɛə]/[wɛr] a) ________________ b) ________________

12. [hiːl] a) ________________ b) ________________

13. [dɪə]/[dir] a) ________________ b) ________________

14. [naɪt] a) ________________ b) ________________

Exercise A37. Medley 4 (☑)

1. primitive ________________________________
2. ruin ________________________________
3. axis ________________________________
4. Switzerland ________________________________
5. strength ________________________________
6. examine ________________________________
7. equal ________________________________
8. superficial ________________________________
9. courage ________________________________
10. transcribe ________________________________
11. elegance ________________________________
12. universal ________________________________
13. closure ________________________________
14. criticism ________________________________

B Advanced Transcription

Background

In this section, we go beyond what we have dealt with so far, and we do this in three respects:

- We will be transcribing not just words, but also sentences or texts. This implies two things: First, we will be using weak forms, i.e. those reduced forms of (mostly) function words that are typical of connected speech in English. The concept of weak forms will be introduced below. Second, we will be marking intonation groups, i.e. prosodic units that have a coherent intonation (e.g. rise, fall, fall-rise, rise-fall) and which, in speech, can end in a pause. We use the symbol | to indicate a minor group and the symbol || for a major group. For the sake of simplicity (and since we are transcribing hypothetical rather than actual speech), we assume minor groups after terms of address, at the end of a clause and between items which are listed, and we use the double bar to indicate the end of a sentence, regardless of its function (declarative, interrogative, imperative and exclamatory). The utterance *John, if I were you, I would give it a second chance* would therefore be transcribed (in GA) as follows:

  [ˈdʒɑːn | ɪf aɪ w(ə)r ˈjuː | (ˈ)aɪ wəd ˈgɪv ɪt ə ˈsɛkənd ˈtʃæns ||]
- We will be introducing the happY vowel [i], the inflUence vowel [u] and the GA consonant [ţ] in this section.
- Finally, the words chosen for the exercises will generally be more challenging; this is often due to the fact that they are of foreign (e.g. French, Latin or Greek) origin and that they tend to be longer.

Before we start transcribing, however, we have to look at two more theoretical questions that are crucial if we want to transcribe speech at an advanced level. First, we need to know how closely our transcription is to represent actual speech. As we said in the *Foundations* section, transcription is always an abstraction, no matter how much detail we include. The question that naturally arises from this fact is, of course, how much detail (and which details) we should include at this stage. Second, even if we have chosen a certain level of transcription depth, there remain enough cases in actual pronunciation that allow for variation. Some speakers, for example, would insert a [t] between [n] and [s] when they pronounce the word *dance*. Are we to represent this in transcription? What about the first vowel in the word *economic*? Some speakers use [iː] here, others [ɛ], and none of these forms seem to be inherently more prestigious than the other. Questions like these are often a matter of convention, and, accordingly, we will deal with them under the heading 'Transcription conventions and transcription tolerance'.

Transcription depth

Many scholars distinguish three types of transcription: phonemic transcription on the one hand and broad and narrow phonetic transcription on the other. (Please note that the term *phonetic transcription* is also used generically, covering all kinds of transcriptions of speech sounds.) To exemplify the difference between the three, we will use the first sentence of the passage *The North Wind and the Sun*, which is also employed by the International Phonetic Association to illustrate all kinds of accents (compare, for example, IPA 1999). The variety we will use for illustration here is RP.

> The North Wind and the Sun were disputing which was the stronger, when a traveller came along wrapped in a warm cloak.

Phonemic transcription is the most abstract of the three. As the name suggests, it only represents phonemes and does not display the result of phonological processes like assimilation, elision, weakening etc. Thus, allophones are not transcribed, either. Since the exact number of phonemes in a given accent and the underlying phonemic form of a word is sometimes a matter of dispute, many textbook writers limit their illustrations of phonemic transcription to a few clear examples. I must therefore point out that the following transcription may not find favour with all phonologists; however, the point here is not so much to make a theoretical statement about the underlying forms of words as to illustrate what a phonemic transcription might look like. I will assume that the happY and inflU-ence vowels are allophones (and are thus not represented), a decision that probably most phonologists will be happy with. I will also assume that the schwa is not a phoneme but an allophone of English[1] because (a) it can hardly ever be used to distinguish meaning, (b) it is normally restricted to unstressed syllables and (c) it is sometimes in free variation with other sounds, particularly [ɪ] and [ʊ] (cf. Chomsky & Halle 1968: 110–26, Wells 1982: 165, Giegerich 1992: 246f. and Roach 2000: 131). I will finally take it that there is the phoneme /r/ in words where it can potentially 'surface' (i.e. appear in actual speech before a vowel; cf. Giegerich 1992: 301–305). Note that phonemic transcription is enclosed in slashes: //. As outlined above, we use a single line (|) to indicate a minor intonation group (typically at the clause level) and a double line (‖) for sentences.

1 Note, however, that some transcribers recognise this status of schwa, yet still use it in 'phonemic transcription'.

/ði: nɔ:θ wɪnd ænd ði: sʌn wɜ:r dɪspju:tɪŋ wɪtʃ wɒz ði: strɒŋgɛr | wɛn ɛɪ trævɛlɛr kɛɪm ɛɪlɒŋ ræpt ɪn ɛɪ wɔ:m kləʊk ||/

You can see that this transcription is far removed from actual pronunciation. No speaker of any form of Received Pronunciation would pronounce the word *the* as [ði:] all the time or use three full vowels in the word *traveller*. Nor would anyone start the word *attempt* with the diphthong [ɛɪ], and a word-final [r] (as in *were*, *stronger*, *traveller*) would only be pronounced in non-rhotic accents like RP when the word that immediately follows begins with a vowel. Understood this way, phonemic transcription is an interesting academic exercise, but it is of little use for those who aim at transcribing actual speech.

At the other end, we find the **narrow phonetic transcription**. Here, we can include as much detail as we like (or as the transcription system allows us to). Narrow transcription is used, for example, to transcribe the speech of an actual individual (rather than a pre-defined model). Phonetic transcription (both of the broad and the narrow type) is enclosed in square brackets. Here is an example of a fictitious RP speaker.

[ðə ˈnɔ̝:θ ˌwɪ̃nd ə̃n ðə ˈsʌ̃n wə dɪsˈpju:tɪ̃ŋ ˈwɪtʃ wəz ðə ˈstɹɒ̃ŋgə | wɛ̃n ə ˈtɹævələ ˌkʰɛẽm əˈlɒ̃ŋ ˈɹæpt ɪ̃n ə ˌwɔ̝̃:m ˈkləʊk ||]

You will see immediately that this transcription differs greatly from the first one:

- It includes stress marks both for primary and secondary stress.
- It displays all the reduced vowels.
- It uses the symbol [ɹ] rather than [r] to represent the exact nature of the 'r'-sound in RP. Also, in this transcription, the [ɹ] only remains before vowels. Similarly, the THOUGHT vowel is represented by [ɔ̝:], using a diacritical symbol together with the more traditional notation [ɔ:]. This symbol indicates that the vowel is slightly higher than cardinal vowel 6. This notation is more precise since the actual place of articulation of RP THOUGHT is in between the cardinal vowels 6 and 7.
- Some of the allophones are represented. The raised [ʰ] following the plosive [k] in *came* indicates aspiration. This means that a short puff of air is released between the plosive and the following vowel. The slight nasalisation that occurs in vowels before nasal consonants ([m, n, ŋ]) is indicated by a tilde on the vowels (as in [ɪ̃]). In theory, many other diacritics could be used to indicate, for example, syllabicity, degree of lip rounding or voicing.

Narrow phonetic transcription is useful for many areas of applied linguistics, such as dialectology, sociolinguistics and forensic linguistics, when we want to transcribe *actual* speech and *actual* speakers with all their individual features. The fidelity of a narrow transcription is limited, among other things, by the ability of the transcriber to discriminate sounds, the purpose of transcription and the transcription system itself (cf. section C).

In parts A and B of this book, however, we do not transcribe actual speech. We want to represent the 'common core', i.e. a pronunciation that is specific enough to include some details that are important for foreign language teaching, for example, but general enough to allow for some minor variation. What we need, then, is a transcription of intermediate depth. For this purpose, we transcribe all the phonemes and the major allophones of the accent in question. 'Major allophones' here can be taken to refer to those varieties of a phoneme that are distinct enough to be recognised by native speakers of the respective accent. Speakers of German, for example, have no difficulty in telling the palatal fricative [ç] (*ich-laut*) from the uvular fricative [χ] (*ach-laut*), even though the two sounds are in complementary distribution and thus allophones of one phoneme. Dictionaries of German therefore transcribe these two sounds using two different symbols. For English, we include the schwa, the happY vowel and the inflUence vowel under the heading of 'major allophones', a decision that is in line with most modern dictionaries. What we arrive at is the so-called **broad phonetic transcription**, and this is what it looks like:

> [ðə ˈnɔːθ ˌwɪnd ənd ðə ˈsʌn wə dɪsˈpjuːtɪŋ ˈwɪtʃ wəz ðə ˈstrɒŋgə | wɛn ə ˈtrævələ ˌkɛɪm əˈlɒŋ ˈræpt ɪn ə ˈwɔːm ˈkləʊk]

This is the kind of transcription we aim at in this section, even though we neglect secondary stress for most exercises. The exact details of the transcription conventions will be discussed in the next section.

Transcription conventions and transcription tolerance

For the transcription of English, there is no universally acknowledged standard. Even when professionals transcribe written texts (and, of course, more so when they transcribe actual spoken language), the results may deviate due to the exact target norm and the transcription depth chosen, but also due to conventions. We have already discussed the question of symbols chosen for DRESS, SQUARE, FACE and the 'r'-sound as well as the target norms in section A. In this section, we will briefly introduce some of the conventions used in this book in those cases that allow for variation even within a defined target variety.

If you transcribe the word *beginning*, you will probably not hesitate to identify the stressed vowel in the second syllable as KIT. You also know that the suffix *-ing* starts with the same vowel. The question, however, is what we do with the vowel in the first syllable. Is it KIT, too, yielding a word with three identical vowels, or is it more centralised, and we would thus have to transcribe it as [ə]? Similarly, do we have to regard the vowel in the suffix *-ful* (as in *beautiful*) as FOOT, or is it schwa? We cannot give any definitive answer here since speakers themselves vary, and *beginning* and *beautiful* are not isolated cases.

Transcribers have been aware for some time now that short high vowels are sometimes in free variation with schwa when they occur in unstressed syllables. The three dictionaries introduced in the *Foundations* section of this book deal with this problem in different ways. The LPD and the EPD list one variety as a primary form and repeat the unstressed syllable with the other vowel as an alternative pronunciation. The ODP, on the other hand, employs non-IPA symbols ('barred' [ɪ] and [ʊ]) to mark the same phenomenon. In this book, we will enclose alternative pronunciations in parentheses. *Beginning* and *beautiful* would therefore be transcribed as [b(ɪ/ə)ˈgɪnɪŋ] and [ˈbju:t(ɪ/ə)f(ʊ/ə)l]. The same technique is used to display alternatives that involve two full vowels. The noun *subject*, for example, would be transcribed as [ˈsʌbdʒ(ɛ/ɪ)kt]. In some exceptional cases this also holds for consonants, as in the word *Portuguese*, which can either be pronounced with a medial [-tj-] or the assimilated form [-tʃ-].

Variation, however, is often not just a question of two alternative sounds.

- Sometimes a schwa in an unstressed syllable may not be pronounced at all. This is particularly true if it is preceded by an alveolar plosive and followed by /n/ or /l/. If the schwa is elided in these cases, the plosive is usually released either through the nose (nasal release) or alongside the tongue (lateral release). Thus, *pardon* would be transcribed as [ˈpɑ:dn] and *riddle* as [ˈrɪdl], and this is how we transcribe cases like these. This rule, however, does not hold if the plosive itself is preceded by /n/. *London* and *sentence*, for example, retain the schwa in the unstressed syllable. This is an interesting exception since it constitutes one of those rare instances in English where a phoneme exerts an influence on a sound with which it does not have any direct contact.
- In many other cases the use of schwa is a matter of style or the degree of attention paid to pronunciation. Sometimes the decision whether or not one uses a schwa results in a word having two different numbers of syllables. The pronunciation of *police*, for example, will normally be [pəˈli:s]. In rapid speech, however, it is not uncommon to drop the schwa, thus creating the monosyllabic word [pli:s]. Similarly, the GOAT diphthong is often reduced to schwa in unstressed syllables. The first syllable in *progressive* may either be [prəʊ] or [prə]. Whenever the use or non-use of a vowel appears to be a matter of style, we enclose it in brackets.
- CURE is generally transcribed as [ʊə] for British English; for some speakers, however, *sure* and *shore* would be homophones, i.e. they merge CURE and THOUGHT and pronounce both as [ɔ:]. Similarly, some speakers monophthongise SQUARE ([ɛ:]) and even words like *fire* and *power* ([a:]). In the cases of CURE

and SQUARE, these pronunciations are widely accepted; thus, you can take them as alternatives to the transcription used here. The monophthongisation of [aɪə] and [aʊə], however, is not regarded as standard.

- We do not usually transcribe assimilated forms. Some speakers, for example, would pronounce /n/ before /g/ or /k/ as [ŋ], so that *ungrateful* would be realised as [ˌʌŋˈgrɛɪtf(ə/ʊ)l].
- Similarly, in cases where a nasal is followed by a voiceless plosive or fricative (as in *fence* or *length*), some speakers would insert a plosive which has the same place of articulation as the nasal. Thus, *fence* would be pronounced [fɛnts] and *length* [lɛŋkθ]. These insertions are, however, not represented here.
- Since GA allows for more variation, it also is harder to define. As we saw in section A, this is particularly true for the back region of the vowel space. Many linguists now also seem to include the MARRY set in their description of GA, i.e. words in which /æ/ is raised to [ɛ] before /r/, even though not all Americans follow this pattern. For our purposes, however, we assume this raising pattern when we transcribe GA.

You can see that, in this book, we aim at the representation of careful educated speech, which nonetheless allows for some variation. The representation of stress is generally restricted to primary stress except for in an exercise which specifically deals with the question of stress (B5).

Weak forms

One typical feature of English pronunciation is that a number of words exist in two distinct forms: a **strong form** (or **citation form**) with a full vowel, which is used

- for citation ('The correct word to use here is "than".'),
- for special emphasis ('You *must* take your medicine!'),
- to indicate contrast ('This book isn't *from* Mary, it's *for* Mary!'),
- at the end of sentences or clauses ('What are you looking at?'), with the exception of pronouns ('He looked at them.'),
- often in singing,

and a **weak form** with a weakened vowel (or a syllabic consonant, cf. the second syllable of [ˈrɪdl], 'riddle', which does not contain a vowel), which is used in normal connected speech; it is always unstressed. Weakening is typical of function words like pronouns, prepositions and conjunctions, but it also affects the unstressed syllables of many content words, albeit in a less predictable way. The vowel used in weak forms is typically schwa (as in [bət], 'but'). In some cases, there is a choice between [ə] and [ɪ] (as in the first syllable of *beginning*). Other words have [i], notably the pronouns *he*, *she*, *we* and the days of the week (*Sunday, Monday* etc.) or [u] (e.g. *who*). Here are some general rules:

- At the beginning of a sentence or a clause, function words that can have a weak form may either be stressed (then retaining their strong form) or unstressed (and are then used as weak forms): 'Are they coming?' may be pronounced as [ˌɑː ðɛɪ ˈkʌmɪŋ ‖] or [ə ðɛɪ ˈkʌmɪŋ ‖].
- All auxiliary verbs which are written with contracted 'not' (like *mustn't, weren't, isn't, hasn't*) must be stressed and therefore cannot have the weak form.
- Several function words do not have a weak form at all, e.g. *down, off, on, then, through, up, when.*
- The auxiliaries *had, has, have, do* and *does* do not have weak forms when they are used as full verbs. But derivations of BE may be weak even when they are used lexically (as a full verb): *There* [wəz] *an accident.*
- If a word acts as a demonstrative (as in 'I don't want *that* book!'), it is strong.
- In question tags, the verb is stressed (therefore retaining its strong form) and the pronoun unstressed: *I'm not late, ˈam I?*
- Words that have a weak form and start with /h/ (*he, him, who* etc.) can usually drop this sound, but not at the beginning of a clause or when they are stressed.

Below you will find a list of highly frequent words (mostly function words) in alphabetical order which potentially have a weak form and the way they are transcribed in this section. Note that some scholars may have slightly deviating notions of the appropriate forms.

	Weak form(s)	**Comments/examples**
a, an	[ə], [ən]	*a good book, an awesome book*
am	[əm], [m]	*Nor am I. I'm looking forward to seeing you.*
and	[ənd]	*John and Mary*
are	[ə]/[(ə)r] [(ə)r]	before a consonant: *My ancestors are Scottish.* before a vowel: *We're able to do that.*
as	[əz]	*Jane is as tall as Sue.*
at	[ət]	*Look at that!*

be	[bi]	*You must be joking.*
because	[bɪˈk(ɒ/ə)z]/ [bɪˈk(ʌ/ɔː/ɑː/ə)z]	The distribution of weak vs. strong form is somewhat idiosyncratic with this word. Note that *because* is one of the few words of English that can have a stressed schwa.
been	[b(iː/ɪ)n]/[bɪn]]	*I've been waiting here for a while.*
but	[bət]	*I like cheese but not milk.*
can	[k(ə)n]	*What can we do?*
could	[kəd]	*I could have sworn he was there.*
-day	[di]	*Sunday, Monday* ... Also *yesterday*, but not *today*
do	[də] [du]	before consonant: *How do you like it?* before vowel: *Do all of you want to take part?*
does	[d(ə)z]	*When does he arrive?*
for	[fə]/[f(ə)r] [f(ə)r]	before a consonant: *for the doctor* before a vowel: *for a week*
from	[fr(ə)m]	*a letter from my aunt*
had	[d] [(h)əd]	after vowels: *I'd seen her before!* elsewhere: *Kate had gone home.*
has	[əz] [s] [z]	after sibilants: *George's come home.* after other voiceless sounds: *Pete's come home.* after other voiced sounds: *Sue's come home.*
have	[v] [(h)əv]	after vowels: *I've seen her!* elsewhere: *What have you done?*
he	[hi]	*Did he find you?*
her	[(h)ə]/[(h)(ə)r]	*Please send her my regards.*
him	[(h)ɪm]	*They gave him a round of applause.*

his	[(h)ɪz]	*Take his umbrella.*
is	[ɪz] [s] [z]	after sibilants: *The bus is coming.* after other voiceless sounds: *That's fine.* after other voiced sounds: *Where's the paper?*
just$_{\text{ADV}}$	[dʒəst]	*Can I just show you something?*
me	[mi]	*Tell me what you think about that.*
must	[məst]	*You must tell me the truth.*
of	[əv] [ə]	*for the fun of it, the captain of the team,* sometimes before a consonant: *a pint of stout*
or	[ɔː]/[(ə)r]	weak form only in GA: *Is your car red or blue?*
Saint	[s(ə)nt]	weak form only in RP: *Saint John*
shall	[ʃ(ə)l]	*I shall ring them up.*
she	[ʃi]	*Does she like it?*
should	[ʃ(ə)d]	*That's what we should do.*
Sir	[sə]/[s(ə)r]	*Sir Winston*
some	[s(ə)m]	as a determiner before uncountable nouns and countable nouns in the indefinite plural: *We'd like some cheese. We met some interesting people in Venice.*
than	[ð(ə)n]	*Cathy is older than Alice.*
that	[ðət]	as a conjunction or relative pronoun: *She thought that it might help. The girl that won the prize is only twelve.*
the	[ðə] [ði]	before a consonant: *in the morning* before a vowel: *in the evening*
their	[ðɛə]/[ð(ə)r]	weak form mostly in GA: *people in their late twenties*

them	[ð(ə)m]	*I sent them a letter.*
there	[ðə]/[ð(ə)r]	*Will there be enough for all of us?*
to (into, onto)	[tə] [t(u/ə)]/[tə]	before a consonant: *I want to see you.* before a vowel: *I wanted to ask you.*
us	[əs] [s]	*They gave us a lift.* *Let's do it.*
was	[wəz]	*Pamela was cooking. There was no water.*
we	[wi]	*When we went to London ...*
were	[wə]/[w(ə)r]	*The fans were cheering and shouting.*
who	[hu]	as a relative pronoun: *the people who are singing*
will	[(ə)l]	*I'll help you.*
would	[d] [əd] [wəd]	after a vowel: *I'd do it if I were you.* after a consonant: *It'd work.* *She would like it.*
you	[jə] [ju]	before a consonant: *When you heard it, did you laugh?* before a vowel: *I would like to invite you all.*
you'll	[j(u/ə)l]	*You'll never guess who I met last week.*
your	[jə]/[j(ə)r]	*I like your shirt.*
you're	[jə]/[j(ə)r]	*When you're young, the world seems open to you.*

The happY and the inflUence vowel

These two vowels are allophones which are distinct enough to be treated in their own right. The keyword 'happY' was introduced by Wells, and since no one has ever come up with a word for the [u] sound, 'inflUence' seems a reasonable enough addition. Scholars do not always agree when these allophones are used, but the rules below may be regarded as widely accepted.

Traditionally, the word *city* is transcribed as [ˈsɪtɪ] (for RP), and this is still the way some people (particularly older people from higher social classes in England) would pronounce it. However, if you pronounce the word *city* (or *whisky*) like most British or American people do today, you will realise that the vowels in the two syllables are not the same. They are both short, of course, but they have a noticeably different quality: while the first vowel clearly retains its KIT features, the second is about as decentralised as FLEECE, but shorter (which you can see if you compare the two vowels in *easy* or *treaty*). Most modern lexicographers account for this fact by using the symbol [i] at the end of these words, thus transcribing *city* as [sɪti]/[sɪt̬i]. The happY vowel is used in the following cases:

- in unstressed word-final positions (*happy, lucky, embassy, hobby* ...).
- if any of these words forms the basis for a morphological process (inflection, derivation, compounding); thus *happier, happiness* and *happy-go-lucky* all have a happY vowel. If, however, the suffix is *-ly* (as in *happily*), the base has final KIT.
- Word-medially, unstressed short high front vowels are raised to happY if they precede a vowel. The word *theology*, for example, has two happY vowels, one in the first and one in the last syllable. This is also true for prefixes. *React* has happY, whereas *recall* has KIT (cf. exercise B13).
- We also use the happY vowel for the weak forms of the words *he*, *she*, *we*, *me*, *be;* and for *the* if the next word begins with a vowel.

The word *bikini* has all three of the front high vowels in the order KIT, FLEECE and happY. Try to make sure that you do not confuse the sound sequence [iə] with [ɪə] in RP. Whereas the former straddles two syllables (as in *Austria*), the latter is a centring diphthong that forms the nucleus of only one syllable (as in *austere*). Here the word *inferior* can serve as an illustration: the second syllable has a NEAR diphthong while the third has a happY vowel which is followed by schwa.

A parallel phenomenon to the happY vowel can be found in the back region of the vowel quadrilateral. Here, a short but decentral [u] appears in certain contexts. Since, however, we do not find a short high back vowel in word-final position (*continue* is a possible exception), inflUence vowels are much less common than happY vowels. We find them:

- word-medially, at the end of an unstressed syllable if the next syllable begins with a vowel (as in *jaguar*, *situation* and *throughout*),
- in the weak forms of *do*, *you* and *to* before a pause or if the next word starts with a vowel and *who* in all weak-form contexts.

Practice

Exercise B1. Weak form or strong form? (☑)

Look at the following sentences and determine whether the underlined word is weak or strong; in some cases, either form is possible. Unless there is evidence to the contrary, assume an unmarked, neutral context. You do not need to transcribe the words, but try to provide a short explanation for your decision.

Sentence	WF/SF/ either	Explanation
Would you like <u>some</u> cake?		
Yes, I <u>would</u>.		
I don't know <u>them</u>.		
He <u>does</u> it without complaining.		
There <u>was</u> no water in that place.		
You <u>must</u> never forget that.		
You <u>mustn't</u> tell anybody.		
A ride on the suspension railway is a <u>must</u> when you visit Wuppertal.		
What did <u>he</u> say?		
We aren't walking much longer, <u>are</u> we?		
<u>Some</u> like it hot.		
That was <u>some</u> match yesterday!		
She <u>was</u> walking along the shore.		
I'm not going to the party <u>because</u> I don't like the music.		
I believe <u>that</u> the earth was created.		
Look at <u>that</u> man!		
I found the box over <u>there</u>.		
Where does <u>she</u> live?		
'You're not listening!' 'Oh, yes, we <u>are</u> listening!'		
How <u>do</u> you <u>do</u>?		
<u>Can</u> I come in?		

Exercise B2. happY, KIT, inflUence or FOOT? (☑)

Decide how the underlined vowel is realised in each case by ticking the appropriate field. You do not need to transcribe the whole word.

	happY	KIT	inflUence	FOOT
India				
the other thing				
annual				
seminar				
patriot				
easiest				
easiest				
evacuate				
Vienna				
qualification				
piano				
serious				
population				
universe				
valuable				
she (WF)				
funnily				

Exercise B3. Homophones 3 (☑)

Here is another set of homophones; this time they are a bit trickier.

1. [aɪl] a) ________________ b) ________________
2. [ˈbɛri] a) ________________ b) ________________
3. [sɛnt] a) ________________ b) ________________
   c) ________________
4. [pɛə]/[pɛr] a) ________________ b) ________________
5. [kjuː] a) ________________ b) ________________
   c) ________________
6. [dɪˈzɜːt]/[dɪˈzɜːrt] a) ________________ b) ________________
7. [fɛə]/[fɛr] a) ________________ b) ________________
8. [fluː] a) ________________ b) ________________
9. [ˈaɪdl] a) ________________ b) ________________
10. [θruː] a) ________________ b) ________________
11. [wɔː]/[wɔːr] a) ________________ b) ________________
12. [djuː]/[duː] a) ________________ b) ________________
13. [kiː] a) ________________ b) (RP) ________________
14. [dʒiːnz] a) ________________ b) ________________

Exercise B4. [t] or [t̬] (GA)? (☑)

Each of the following words or phrases has the phoneme /t/ in it. In American English, /t/ has two major allophones: [t] and [t̬] (which is sometimes referred to as 't flap'). [t̬] is used when /t/ stands

- between two vowels,
- between /r/ and a vowel (as in *party*) or
- between a vowel and a syllabic /l/ or /r/ (e.g. *glottal*, *bitter*),

but in any case only if the second vowel is not stressed; thus, *atom* has [t̬], while *atomic* has [t]. In the sequence /nt/ plus vowel or syllabic /r/ (e.g. *printer*), the /t/ may be deleted. Tick the appropriate box (you do not need to transcribe the words).

	[t]	[t̬]	[(t̬)]
bottle			
active			
atom			
atomic			
bright			
brighter			
Italy			
Italian			
center			
linguistics			
stigmatization			
advantage			
advantageous			
hit it			
heating			
winter			
inter city			
capital			
melted			

Exercise B5. Stress 1: Proper nouns and compounds (☑)

The stress pattern of compounds and similar constructions in English is complex and full of exceptions. (For a brief overview, see e.g. Collins & Mees 2008: 127–129 or Dretzke 2008: 82–84.) Usually, the first element is stressed, as in ˈ*textbook,* ˈ*home-sick,* ˈ*eating apple* or ˈ*showdown.* This is sometimes referred to as 'early stress' and generally true if the compound is written as one word. 'Late stress', on the other hand, with the main stress on the second element, occurs typically, but not exclusively, in the following cases:

- If the first element describes the material of the whole entity (cf. ˌ*apple* ˈ*pie* vs. ˈ*apple tree*; ˌ*paper* ˈ*bag* vs. ˈ*paperwork*). Note, however, that compounds with *juice* and *cake* always have early stress.
- If the first element or the whole compound describes a location, such as a country, town or other place (cf. *Russian rou*ˈ*lette,* ˌ*Paddington* ˈ*Station,* ˌ*Hyde* ˈ*Park* etc.). This is also true for all kinds of roads except those that have *Street* as their second element (cf. ˌ*Fifth* ˈ*Avenue,* ˌ*School* ˈ*Road*; but: ˈ*School Street*).
- If the compound forms an adjective (as in ˌ*old-*ˈ*fashioned*). Notice, however, that these compounds are usually subject to stress shift (cf. exercise B 19) when they are followed by a noun (*an* ˈ*old-fashioned* ˈ*lady*).
- If the first element contains a number (*a* ˌ*fifty-*ˌ*fifty* ˈ*chance*)

Transcribe the following words and see if you can work out the main stress of the constructions below. In this exercise you may also indicate secondary stress, using the symbol ˌ. For example, *twenty-dollar bill* would be transcribed as [ˌtwɛn(t̬)i dɑːl(ə)r ˈbɪl] for GA.

1. apple pie	2. Russian roulette	3. Trafalgar Square
4. New York	5. Church Road	6. Church Street
7. fruit salad	8. a fifty-pound note	9. user-friendly
10. man-made	11. waterproof	12. proof-reader
13. greenhouse	14. a green house	15. the White House
16. paper bag	17. orange juice	18. bottom line
19. cotton wool	20. Hyde Park	21. English teacher

Exercise B6. Mid and high front vowels (☑)

Each of the following words contains one of the sounds [iː], [i], [ɪ], [ɪə]/[ɪr], [ɛ] or schwa in the position underlined. Sometimes the choice depends on the accent (RP vs. GA); in many cases more than one sound is possible. Which would you choose?

1. ancestor	2. egoist	3. serious
4. stories	5. plenary	6. economics
7. captain	8. analysis, analyses	9. theory
10. really	11. grenade	12. inferiority
13. evolution	14. Kenya	15. eco-friendly
16. medieval	17. discrepancy	18. inherent
19. explain	20. explanation	21. breath, breathe

Exercise B7. Academic English 1: Phonetics (☑)

The major reason that makes academic English more difficult to transcribe than 'ordinary' English lies in the lexical items that are either part of the respective disciplines or reflect a more formal style. The following passage is the summary of an article that argues for the use of the epsilon symbol [ɛ] in the DRESS set (Schmitt 2007: 321). Transcribe the passage, paying attention to weak forms and sentence stress. Note that, in the context of connected speech, not all content words receive sentence stress. The exact degree to which they are stressed depends on various factors such as the speed of delivery and the attention paid to what is being spoken. For example, the words *paper* and *fact* in the second sentence may be stressed in careful speech, but they will not usually receive as much stress as *need* and *many*. Thus, some of the decisions made in this and other exercises which contain connected speech may be debatable. – Did you know that, at least in RP, there are two fundamentally different pronunciations for *epsilon*?

> In this article, I will argue for the use of the epsilon symbol in the lexical DRESS set (which includes words like *step, ready, said, shelf* etc.) for RP. The need for this paper arises from the fact that many, but by no means all, dictionaries and linguistic treatises employ the [e] symbol and that this symbol is neither the most accurate nor a particularly useful one, especially for foreign learners of English. An examination of current usage and its historical rationale (or lack thereof) is followed by articulatory and perceptual evidence for the DRESS vowel being close to the third cardinal vowel, more practical arguments and a discussion of the issues raised.

Exercise B8. [z] or [s]? (2) (☑)

Another set of [z] vs. [s] words. This time, there are several words that can have either the voiced or the voiceless fricative.

1. useful
2. crisis
3. crises
4. else
5. release
6. Glasgow
7. because
8. dangerous
9. crescent
10. conversation
11. paradise
12. absurd
13. abuse$_V$
14. abuse$_N$
15. series
16. newspaper
17. opposite
18. precise
19. increase$_V$
20. increase$_N$
21. Tuesday

Exercise B9. Base allomorphy (☑)

The following pairs of words all display base allomorphy, i.e. the base changes due to the affix that is attached. Transcribe each of the forms.

1. explain, explanation
2. explain, explanatory
3. know, knowledge
4. finite, infinite
5. please, pleasant
6. pronounce, pronunciation
7. prevail, prevalence
8. admire, admirable
9. excel, excellent
10. famous, infamous
11. south, southern
12. manager, managerial
13. prefer, preferable
14. suffice, sufficient

Exercise B10. Homophones 4 (@)

1. [lɛd] (RP) a) ________________ b) ________________
2. [ˈflaʊə]/[flaʊər] a) ________________ b) ________________
3. [mɪst] a) ________________ b) ________________
4. [mɔːnɪŋ]/[mɔːrnɪŋ] a) ________________ b) ________________
5. [saɪd] a) ________________ b) ________________
6. [gəˈrɪlə] a) ________________ b) ________________
7. [ˈhɛrəʊɪn]/[ˈhɛroʊən] a) ________________ b) ________________
8. [wɪtʃ] a) ________________ b) ________________
9. [pɔː]/[pɔːr] a) ________________
   b) (RP option, GA) ________________________________
   c) (RP option, GA option) ________________________________
   d) (RP) ________________________________
10. [swiːt] a) ________________ b) ________________
11. [sɔː]/[sɔːr] a) ________________ b) ________________
    c) (RP) ____________
12. [tʃuːz] a) ________________ b) ________________
13. [sɔːd]/[sɔːrd] a) ________________ b) ________________
14. [rəʊd]/[roʊd] a) ________________ b) ________________

Exercise B11. Low and mid front vowels (☑)

Transcribe the following words, each of which contains any of [æ], [ɛ], [ɛə]/[ɛr], [ɛɪ] or simply schwa. Again, in some cases more than one sound is possible.

1. f<u>ai</u>ry
2. f<u>e</u>rry
3. st<u>a</u>tus
4. c<u>a</u>pable
5. c<u>a</u>rriage
6. th<u>ei</u>r
7. <u>a</u>xis
8. ag<u>ai</u>n
9. extraordin<u>a</u>ry
10. s<u>ai</u>d
11. s<u>a</u>d
12. volunt<u>a</u>ry
13. m<u>a</u>rry
14. M<u>a</u>ry
15. m<u>e</u>rry
16. K<u>a</u>ren
17. <u>a</u>moral
18. necess<u>a</u>ry
19. <u>a</u>te
20. S<u>a</u>rah
21. prim<u>a</u>rily

Exercise B12. Text: Through the Looking-Glass (☑)

Lewis Carroll's *Alice's Adventures in Wonderland* and its sequel, *Through the Looking-Glass*, are quite popular with linguists as these works challenge some orthodox linguistic views. The following passage is a discussion between Alice and Humpty Dumpty, which contains several nonsense words. As we said before, the correspondence between spelling and sound is notoriously unreliable in English. In this case, however, we can (or have to) assume that the letters are used to reflect their prototypical pronunciation. Take the word *Jabberwocky*. Initial <j>s are almost always pronounced [dʒ] in English (as in *joy, jungle* etc.) – so there is no problem here. The next letter <a> can be pronounced in a number of ways, among them [æ] (as in *fat*), [ɛɪ] (*fate*) or [ɑː] (*father*). If, however, it is followed by a double consonant (as in this case), it is typically [æ] if it is preceded by a consonant (*hammer, ladder, cattle*). As you transcribe the passage (Carroll 1993: 206f.), try to determine (or at least guess) the most probable pronunciation of the nonsense words in this fashion.

> 'You seem very clever at explaining words, sir,' said Alice.
>
> 'Would you kindly tell me the meaning of the poem "Jabberwocky"?'
>
> 'Let's hear it,' said Humpty Dumpty. 'I can explain all the poems that ever were invented – and a good many that haven't been invented just yet.'
>
> This sounded very hopeful, so Alice repeated the first verse:
>
> > "Twas brillig, and the slithy toves
> > Did gyre and gimble in the wabe:
> > All mimsy were the borogoves,
> > And the mome raths outgrabe."
>
> 'That's enough to begin with,' Humpty Dumpty interrupted: 'there are plenty of hard words there. "*Brillig*" means four o'clock in the afternoon – the time when you begin *broiling* things for dinner.'
>
> 'That'll do very well,' said Alice: 'and "*slithy*"?'
>
> 'Well, "*slithy*" means "lithe and slimy". "Lithe" is the same as "active". You see it's like a portmanteau – there are two meanings packed up into one word.'

Exercise B13. The prefix *re-* (☑)

The pronunciation of the prefix *re-* (as in *rearrange*) depends on two factors: a) its meaning and b) the first sound of the base.

- It is pronounced [riː] when its meaning is 'again' (as in *redistribute*). In these cases it receives secondary stress, and sometimes the prefix is attached to the base with a hyphen (as in *re-dial*). If the prefix is pronounced [riː], the base is usually free (i.e. it could stand alone).
- In all other cases, the pronunciation is either [ri] or [r(ɪ/ə)].[2]

[2] Please note that in the third edition of the LPD, these prefixes have been "simplified" (Wells 2008: xiii) and are uniformly represented as [i].

- It is [ri] if the base starts with a vowel (as in *react*; notice that *react* does not mean 'act again' but 'respond'.). There are, however, only very few words that follow this pattern (mostly derivatives of *react*).
- It is [r(ɪ/ə)] if the base starts with a consonant (as in *recall*; *recall* here does not mean 'call again' but 'remember').

In either of these latter cases, *re-* is not stressed, and the base may be bound (i.e. does not exist by itself, as in *receive*).

Notice that the spelling <re-> in itself is not a guarantee that we are dealing with a prefix (cf. *realise, rebel*) and that there are some exceptions to these rules; for example, *re-* is pronounced [rɛ] in words like *recommend* or *represent*. Transcribe the following words, allocating them to the correct column. In some of the cases, *re-* may have two different pronunciations, depending on its meaning.

	[riː-]	[ri-]	[r(ɪ/ə)-]
release			
reaction			
re-read			
recount			
return			
rebuild			
reiterate			
re-import			
revival			
require			
recycle			
reusable			
remove			
reduce			
reflect			
reunion			
recover			
recharge$_V$			
repay			
reply			
resign			
reform			

Exercise B14. Medley 5 (☑)

The medleys in this section of the book are heavy stuff. Many of the words (particularly in the medleys 6 and 7) are from Latin, Greek or other foreign languages and are thus considered to be 'hard words' (cf. Leisi & Mair 1999: 48–77), even by native speakers.

1. thesis	2. vehicle	3. veggie burger
4. vary	5. ache	6. appropriate$_A$
7. bowl	8. bury	9. genuine
10. euro	11. translate	12. rationality
13. human	14. guerrilla	15. positive
16. exciting	17. actually	18. breathes
19. senior	20. preferable	21. iron

Exercise B15. Low vowels (☑)

Each of the following words contains one of the TRAP, STRUT, LOT or BATH vowels in their stressed syllable. Which is it? (In a few cases, GA speakers use a different vowel altogether.)

1. worry	2. want	3. front
4. bother	5. body	6. gone
7. drastic	8. yacht	9. frontier
10. aunt	11. comfort	12. fathom
13. chance	14. thorough	15. common
16. transitive	17. Glasgow	18. draught
19. won	20. graph	21. accomplish

Exercise B16. Alternative pronunciations (☑)

It is not uncommon for any accent to have a few words whose pronunciation may vary largely due to personal preference rather than situational or social context. This exercise contains several words that have alternative pronunciations either in British (RP) or American English (GA). As you transcribe these alternatives, also try to guess which one is the more common one.

1. sure (RP) a) ________ b) ________

2. data RP: a) ________ b) ________
GA: a) ________ b) ________

3. sorry (GA) a) ________ b) ________

4. schedule (RP) a) ________ b) ________
c) ________ d) ________

5. migraine (RP) a) ________ b) ________

6. envelope (RP) a) ________ b) ________

7. garage RP: a) ________ b) ________
c) ________
GA: a) ________ b) ________

8. patronise (GA) a) ________ b) ________

9. either RP: a) ________ b) ________
GA: a) ________ b) ________

10. issue (RP) a) ________ b) ________
c) ________

11. sandwich (RP) a) ________ b) ________

12. cigarette RP: a) ________ b) ________
GA: a) ________ b) ________

13. citizen (GA) a) ________ b) ________

14. ate (RP) a) ________ b) ________

Exercise B17. Low and mid back vowels (☑)

Some speakers of German find it particularly difficult to distinguish LOT and THOUGHT vowels, even if their target accent is RP. The reason is that they perceive (for reasons discussed in section C) and produce both LOT and THOUGHT with the same quality (around cardinal vowel 6, as in German *doch*), and they just lengthen it slightly for THOUGHT. As a result, the vowels in compounds like *corner shop* differ in quantity but not in quality when they are pronounced by Germans. The following words all contain one of the vowels [ɒ]/[(ɑː/ɔː)], [ɔː] or [əʊ]/[oʊ]. Sometimes, as usual, there is more than one option.

1. also	2. sausage	3. altogether
4. stroll	5. because	6. cause
7. erotic	8. rhotic	9. halt
10. false	11. often	12. enforce
13. job	14. exalt	15. exaltation
16. wasp	17. project$_N$	18. response
19. involve	20. know	21. knowledge

Exercise B18. Academic English 2: Dialectology (@)

The following passage is adapted from a modern introductory textbook on English linguistics (Mair 2008: 159).

> The results of dialectological research are often published in dialect atlases. These are based on linguistic fieldwork with local informants and offer large numbers of maps. In the production of such maps, the first step is usually to mark the localities investigated for their preferred variants. For example, a few hundred British informants could be asked about whether they pronounce the vowel in *come* as /ʊ/ or /ʌ/. Usually, the responses will not be distributed arbitrarily. There will be regional clusters, around which it is possible to draw lines – isoglosses (from the Greek for "same speech"). The more isoglosses run parallel or in close proximity, the sharper the corresponding dialect boundary is felt to be.

Exercise B19. Stress 2: Stress shift (☑)

English is somewhat exceptional in that it has quite a number of words with variable stress, depending either on their context or their syntactic class. Thus, for example, numbers above twelve and many adjectives have a secondary stress before the primary stress (e.g. *unhappy* as [ˌʌnˈhæpi]). When these words are followed by a noun, the secondarily stressed syllable receives the main stress of the word, while the syllable which used to have the main stress is not stressed at all. Thus, in the phrase *an unhappy child*, the main stress of the adjective is now on the first syllable (for more information see Davis 2002: 68f.).

Other words exist both as verbs and as nouns or adjectives (e.g. *abstract*, *rebel* etc.). In these cases, the verbs are sometimes distinguished from the nouns/ adjectives in that they are stressed on the second syllable, whereas the non-verbal forms are stressed on the first syllable.

Transcribe the following words and determine their main stress. We disregard secondary stress here since the underlined words may be secondarily stressed with regard to another word.

1. My sister turned thirteen last week.	2. There were thirteen candles on her cake.
3. There's a new Chinese restaurant in the neighbourhood.	4. But the owner doesn't look Chinese to me.
5. Do you think our sales will increase?	6. Yes, but the increase will be rather small.
7. Some restaurants offer a free refill for drinks.	8. This means that you can refill your glass as often as you like.
9. Let's meet tomorrow afternoon.	10. We could have an old-fashioned afternoon tea.
11. I suspect they will not find the criminal.	12. They've already got one suspect, but he's got an alibi.
13. Our company is planning to conduct a survey.	14. We're going to survey consumers under the age of 15.
15. We want to meet in Hyde Park,	16. more precisely at Hyde Park Corner.
17. We tried to transfer the money to your account.	18. It didn't work, though. The transfer was unsuccessful.
19. The Smiths have moved in next door.	20. From now on, we will have rather famous next-door neighbours.
21. There are still some remains of the Berlin Wall in Berlin.	

Exercise B20. High back vowels (☑)

Each of the words below contains one of the following: [uː], [u], [ʊ] or [ʊə]/[ʊr].

1. jewel	2. Europe	3. fluent
4. truant	5. urine	6. sure
7. valuable	8. crusade	9. July
10. continue	11. continual	12. continuous
13. wool	14. poor	15. during
16. dual	17. duel	18. good
19. tourism	20. plural	21. your (SF)

Exercise B21. Medley 6 (☑)

1. journal	2. didactic	3. tangible
4. analysis	5. vacuum	6. paradigm
7. suite	8. whereas	9. nee, née
10. brooch	11. attorney	12. grievous
13. fugitive	14. jewellery	15. stigmati(s/z)ation
16. occur	17. explanatory	18. psycholinguistics
19. atheistic	20. au pair	21. advantageous

Exercise B22. Funny you should say this: Homophone jokes 1 (☑)

The following jokes are probably not of a calibre that makes you want to share them with your friends, but that's not the point here. The point is that all of these jokes rely on homophones, and you will fail to understand the joke if you miss one of the meanings. See if you can make out the pun. If not, look at the "translation" in the key section. The variety used for these jokes is RP. Why does the last joke only work in RP but not in GA?

1. [waɪ ɪz ˈsɪks əˈfrɛɪd əv ˈsɛvən ‖ bɪkɒz ˈsɛvən ˈɛɪt ˈnaɪn ‖]

   ____

2. [wɒts ˈblæk ənd ˈwaɪt ən ˈrɛd ɔːl ˈəʊvə ‖ ə ˈnjuːzpɛɪpə ‖]

   ____

3. [wɒt də jə ˈkɔːl ə ˈdɪə wɪð nəʊ ˈaɪz ‖ ˈnəʊaɪˈdɪə ‖]

   ____

4. [ə ˈmæn ɪz ˈlɒkt ɪn ə ˈprɪzən sɛl wɪð nəʊ ˈdɔːz ɔː ˈwɪndəʊz | ˈdʒʌst ə ˈtɛɪbl ‖ ˈhaʊ dəz hi gɛt ˈaʊt ‖ hi ˈrʌbz hɪz ˈhændz ʌntɪl ðɛə ˈsɔː | hi ˈkʌts ðə ˈtɛɪbl ɪn ˈhɑːf wɪð ðə ˈsɔː | ˈtuː ˈhɑːvz mɛɪk ə ˈhəʊl ‖ hi ˈpʊts ðə ˈhəʊl ɪn ðə ˈwɔːl ənd klaɪmz ˈaʊt ‖]

   ____

   ____

   ____

   ____

   ____

   ____

Exercise B23. Text: Limericks (☑, ☑, @)

Limericks are always favourites with those who practise and teach transcription, not least for their little intricacies like metre (which may cause otherwise unstressed words to be stressed) or puns. Here's a selection. Transcribe them as you would read them.

1. One Saturday morning at three
   A cheesemonger's shop in Paree
   Collapsed to the ground
   With a thunderous sound
   Leaving only a pile of de brie.

2. It's a favourite project of mine
   A new value of pi to assign.
   I would fix it at three
   For it's simpler, you see
   Than three point one four one five nine.

3. There was a young man of Japan
   Whose limericks never would scan.[3]
   When they asked him, why?
   He said, with a sigh,
   'It's because I always try to get as many words into the last line as I possibly can.'

[3] 'Scan' here means 'to conform to a metrical pattern'.

Exercise B24. Frequently mispronounced words 1 (☑)

The following words are frequently mispronounced by learners of English. See if you can work out the correct pronunciation. (For a general description of the pronunciation difficulties that German-speaking learners of English have, see e.g. Eckert & Barry 2005 or Dretzke 2008: 180–210)

1. conversation	2. marriage	3. pressure
4. indigenous	5. Caribbean	6. prestigious
7. separate$_A$	8. towards	9. condolence
10. interaction	11. record$_V$	12. legislate
13. determine	14. identify	15. deviate$_V$
16. Japanese	17. Arabic	18. variable
19. opposite	20. bilingual	21. apparent

Exercise B25. Text: Jokes (☑)

Transcribe the following jokes.

1. A pregnant woman from Dublin was involved in a terrible car accident and went into a deep coma. After nearly six months, she wakes up and sees that she is no longer pregnant. Frantically, she asks the doctor about her baby. The doctor replies, 'Ma'am, you had twins! A boy and a girl. The babies are fine. Your brother from Galway came in and named them.' The woman thinks to herself, 'Oh no, not my brother! He's a clueless idiot.'

   Expecting the worst, she asks the doctor, 'Well, what's my daughter's name?' 'Denise', says the doctor. The new mother is somewhat relieved. 'Wow, that's not a bad name. I like it.' Then she asks, 'What's the boy's name?' 'Denephew'.

2. An Englishman, an Irishman and a Scotsman went into a pub for a pint. After being served, a fly landed in each of their beers and got caught in the creamy heads. The Englishman pushed his pint away from him in disgust and proceeded to order another one. The Irishman simply fished the offending fly out with his finger and proceeded to drink his pint as if nothing had happened. The Scotsman, eyes wide with anger, grabbed the fly and held it over his beer, shouting, 'Spit it out! Spit it out!'

Exercise B26. RP vs. GA (☑)

A number of words display distinct differences depending on which side of the Atlantic they are used. These differences cannot be predicted on the basis of general phonological rules (like, for example, the 'medial-t voicing' in General American), but depend on the lexeme itself. See if you can transcribe the more common pronunciation for both British and American English. The variation may show up on the segmental level (the vowels or consonants used), or it may depend on a different stress pattern; thus, please indicate stress as well. In some cases, the two varieties are a matter of preference (i.e. they are not used exclusively in either Britain or the US).

1. address_N	2. figure	3. schedule
4. thorough	5. mobile	6. vitamin
7. laboratory	8. either	9. progress_N
10. potato	11. vase	12. Z (as letter)
13. semi-	14. leisure	15. clerk
16. inquiry	17. buoy	18. rather
19. shone	20. secretary	21. suggest

Exercise B27. Frequently mispronounced words 2 (@)

1. indicator	2. migrant	3. knowledge
4. southern	5. interesting	6. obligatory
7. criteria	8. informative	9. humorous
10. phenomenon	11. category	12. inference
13. ethnic	14. vary	15. precisely
16. sincerity	17. adolescent	18. interpret
19. communicative	20. legitimacy	21. deficient

Exercise B28. Text: Psalm 23 (☑)

The following are the first four verses of the famous Psalm 23, taken from a revised version of the classical King James translation ('New King James Version'). Remember, as you transcribe, that the speed of delivery is probably slower and that, therefore, more words are likely to be pronounced as strong forms.

1 The LORD is my shepherd; I shall not want.

2 He makes me to lie down in green pastures;

He leads me beside the still waters.

3 He restores my soul;

He leads me in the paths of righteousness

For His name's sake.

4 Yea, though I walk through the valley of the shadow of death,

I will fear no evil;

For You are with me;

Your rod and Your staff, they comfort me.

Exercise B29. Text: Interview (☑)

The following is an excerpt of an interview I conducted in Scotland a while ago. Actually, it is a 'tidied-up', edited version of it since it does not contain several of the features that are typical of spontaneous speech, such as overlaps, false starts, hesitation particles ('erm'), some of the feedback signals, additional information on extralinguistic behaviour ('laughter') and so on. In addition, some minor grammatical revisions have been made. Transcribe the interview *as if* it had taken place in RP or GA. (*Inter* denotes my contributions, *Inf* the informant's.) If you would like to know how the interview actually sounded, consult section C, where the same excerpt is discussed in the context of 'ear transcription'. Bear in mind that your transcription is meant to represent spontaneous conversation.

1	Inter	Do you think there's any particular dialect that represents Scotland
2		best, where you would say, 'Okay, this is how Scottish people
3		speak', or 'This is the most typical Scottish dialect or accent'?

Inf	Possibly, I mean, Glasgow, it's the well known one across the world, I suppose, but I would prefer somewhere like the middle, like Inverness, Perth, because it's a sort of normal toned-down version, but it's still got the Scottish accent ...
Inter	Yeah, exactly, yeah.
Inf	in it, yeah
Inter	That's interesting, that's an interesting statement here. Do you have any favourite dialects or accents here in Scotland? I mean you've mentioned ... what was it? Inverness and Perth?
Inf	Well ...
Inter	I mean people that you enjoy listening to most just because of their accents or dialects?
Inf	Probably the Western Isles a bit, I mean I can laugh at the jokes that come from the Glasgow ones, but I think it can be very hard to make out, you know, for me and then possibly even worse for foreigners or even the English.
Inter	So you would say your favourite accent would be Western Isles?
Inf	Well it's got a lilt, and I like to, yeah, probably like hearing that.
Inter	Is there any dialect or language you don't particularly like here in Scotland, where you'd say, 'Mm it's not very pleasant to listen to'?
Inf	No, not really. I think maybe the Aberdonians, it's quite difficult to make out.
Inter	Yeah. Is it just difficult or is it unpleasant to you?
Inf	Well, I don't know, I never really thought about Scottish accents, but I don't particularly like the Birmingham accent in England because it's too ... it's a drone, it's a ...
Inter	The Brum.
Inf	it sounds very ... yeah. I don't particularly like that, but I haven't really thought about the Scottish accents as being grating.

33	Inter	Sorry?
34	Inf	I don’t find any of the Scottish accents grating.
35	Inter	‘Grating’, what does that mean?
36	Inf	Getting on your nerves, you know, grating, you know?
37	Inter	Okay, okay, ah yeah. Is that a Scottish term? Never heard of it.
38	Inf	Probably just mine!
39	Inter	How would you describe your own dialect or accent?
40	Inf	Well ...
41	Inter	I mean not just now, but when you talk to friends or to your family?
42 43 44 45 46	Inf	Well, there are certain words that I use that probably my husband that comes from Orphir doesn’t use, and that’s because I was brought up in Sanday, and there are certain words that come from every parish here. If I hear myself on the answering machine, I don’t like it.
47	Inter	All right?
48	Inf	I think I’m pretty broad if I’m relaxed, I’m pretty broad spoken.

Exercise B30. Funny you should say this: Homophone jokes 2 (@)

Here’s another set of homophone jokes, this time transcribed in GA. NB: Joke 2 relies on a near-homophone.

1. [tuː ˈhʌnt̬ərz ət̬ ə hʌnt̬ərz ˈmiːt̬ɪŋ || hæv ju ˈɛvər ˈhʌnt̬əd ˈbɛr || noʊ | aɪ ˈɑːlwɛɪz ˈhʌnt wɪθ maɪ ˈkloʊðz ɑːn ||]

   ____

   ____

2. [ˈfrɛndli ˈbiːvər tə ˈtriː | ɪts bɪn ˈnaɪs ˈnɔːɪŋ ju ||]

   ____

3. [ˈɛɪθiɪzm ɪz ə nɑːn ˈprɑːfət ɔːrgənɪˈzɛɪʃn ||]

   ____

Exercise B31. Proper nouns 1 (☑)

Students of English will come across many proper nouns whose pronunciation cannot be directly inferred from the spelling. Here are some of those you are likely to encounter. NB: Some of these words have more than one pronunciation in RP.

1. Aristotle	2. Michigan
3. Leicestershire	4. Portuguese
5. Spurgeon	6. McDonald
7. Greenwich (district of London)	8. February
9. Sioux	10. Thames (river in London)
11. Levis	12. Rolls-Royce
13. Edinburgh	14. Calais

Exercise B32. Text: Pygmalion (RP) (☑)

The following two passages are taken from the play that every phonetician knows: George Bernard Shaw's *Pygmalion*, which tells the story of Professor Higgins, a phonetician, who tries to turn the 'common' flower(-selling) girl Eliza into a Lady by teaching her to speak with an upper-class accent (Shaw 1957: 21, 9; reproduction courtesy of the Society of Authors).

The first scene is taken from the beginning of Act II, set in Higgins' laboratory, just after he has introduced his new friend, Colonel Pickering, to his phonetic equipment. The next excerpt is an example of dialect writing, a short discourse between 'The Flower Girl' (Eliza) and 'The Mother' in which Shaw attempted to represent Eliza's London dialect, even using the symbol 'ə' in the spelling (a 'translation' in standard orthography is provided). We cannot be entirely sure which pronunciation Shaw had in mind in each case, but we can assume that he used the rules of English orthography to represent his idea of Cockney. Try to translate the dialect writing into phonetic transcription. If you find this difficult, you may consult a description of Cockney (e.g. Wells 1982 (volume 2), ch. 4.2.), or you can listen to Eliza's representation in the musical *My Fair Lady*, which is based on *Pygmalion*. Since the play is set in London, a British transcription only is provided for this exercise.

HIGGINS [*as he shuts the last drawer*] Well, I think that's the whole show.

PICKERING. It's really amazing. I haven't taken half of it in, you know.

HIGGINS. Would you like to go over any of it again?

PICKERING [*rising and coming to the fireplace, where he plants himself with his back to the fire*] No, thank you: not now. I'm quite done up for this morning.

HIGGINS [*following him, and standing beside him on his left*] Tired of listening to sounds?

PICKERING. Yes. It's a fearful strain. I rather fancied myself because I can pronounce twenty-four distinct vowel sounds; but your hundred and thirty beat me. I can't hear a bit of difference between most of them.

HIGGINS [*chuckling, and going over to the piano to eat sweets*] Oh, that comes with practice. You hear no difference at first; but you keep on listening, and presently you find they're all as different as A from B.

THE MOTHER. How do you know that my son's name is Freddy, pray?

THE FLOWER GIRL. Ow, eez yə-ooa san, is e? Wal, fewd dan y' də-ooty bawmz a mather should, eed now bettern to spawl a pore gel's flahrzn then ran awy athaht pying. Will yə-oo py me f'them?

[Oh, he's your son, is he? Well, if you'd done your duty (bound) as a mother should, he'd know better (than) to spoil a poor girl's flowers and then run away without paying. Will you pay me for them?]

Exercise B33. Language terms (@)

The following are terms that are particularly relevant for language students.

1. metaphor	2. euphemism
3. covert (prestige)	4. interlanguage
5. articulatory	6. diglossia
7. parenthesis	8. dictionary
9. participle	10. plural
11. pronunciation	12. ellipsis, ellipses
13. diphthong	14. genre

Exercise B34. Proper nouns 2 (☑)

1. Chicago
2. Geoff
3. Gloucester
4. Gaelic
5. Niagara Falls
6. Boheme
7. Sean
8. Arkansas
9. Celtic
10. Connecticut
11. Cajun
12. Louisiana
13. Hebrew
14. Heligoland (stress!)

Exercise B35. Medley 7 (☑)

1. hypocrite
2. heuristic
3. illocution
4. haphazard
5. occurrence
6. hierarchy
7. xerox
8. pedagogy
9. archipelago
10. lieutenant
11. affricate
12. posthumously
13. antitheses
14. enthusiasm
15. miscellaneous
16. suffice
17. subsequent
18. accumulate
19. aesthetic
20. journalist
21. simultaneous

C Transcribing actual speech

Background

What we have done so far in this book is to transcribe written words or texts into a form that is meant to represent an average standard-like speech form. We did not require any native speakers to pronounce these words or read out these texts for us, but relied entirely on our knowledge of the accent chosen. Many of the more applied disciplines of linguistics, however, such as dialectology, sociolinguistics or speech pathology, operate in a significantly different way. Linguists working in these fields start out with actual speech and try to describe it as accurately as possible. In this section, we will look at the question of how we can tackle actual speech data.

'Ear transcription' is a much more demanding task than transcribing some more or less well-defined, abstract accent. First, you need a deeper understanding of the mechanisms that are at work in speech production (articulatory phonetics), and you may need to expand your repertoire of IPA symbols. Second, when we try to work out what a person actually says (rather than what we think this person says), our perception (and consequently our transcription) is influenced by quite a number of factors that are irrelevant when we do 'eye transcription' (cf. Cucchiarini 1993, chs. 3–4). The most important factor is certainly our own mother tongue, but there are also other reasons why our perception is not objective. Thus, it is vital that we understand these factors. Once we have grasped the basic articulatory and cognitive facts, we need to develop strategies how we can capture and transcribe unfamiliar sounds. Finally, the data have to be interpreted in order to describe the accent under investigation. These are, in a nutshell, the points we shall be looking at in the *Background* section before we try to transcribe real speech.

Phonetic knowledge relevant for ear transcription

One of the first things we need when we want to transcribe actual speech is a thorough understanding of how sounds are produced, i.e. of articulatory phonetics. This involves, for example, an appreciation of the active and passive articulators in our mouth and, at an advanced level, a knowledge of the different airstreams (pulmonic, glottalic, velaric), the role of the phonatory system (what happens in the throat) and of secondary articulation. (For a practical introduction, try Collins & Mees 2008.) This knowledge should eventually lead to a 'perceptual conquest of the articulatory space', i.e. the raising of an awareness of the processes in your own mouth (and beyond) that are involved in the creation of sounds. This is essential since you need to relate the sounds you hear to articulatory settings and then these articulatory settings to specific symbols.

Students who analyse new varieties will probably come across sounds that they have never encountered before.[1] Unless you want to become competent in the description of all the languages of the world, however, phonetic training at this stage may concentrate on the peculiarities of the group of accents you are going to investigate. If your primary interest is in English (or if, at least, you are going to operate within the context of Indo-European languages), you do not, for example, need to learn how to distinguish different tones as you would if you were dealing with Chinese or Igbo accents. Neither do you have to learn many 'exotic' consonants (remember that our sounds, particularly the dental fricatives, may be just as exotic to speakers of other languages). But you should, for example, understand the general concept of 'retroflex consonants' since in some Asian varieties of English speakers curl back their tongue with various (mostly alveolar) consonants. More importantly, you should be able to distinguish the different realisations of the 'r'-sounds, since it is here that we find a lot of variation across the 'Englishes' worldwide. The following are the most common r's, their corresponding symbols and some typical accents that make use of them:

- [ɹ] marks the post-alveolar approximant that we find in modern RP.
- [ɻ] stands for the retroflex approximant, a similar sound as the approximant just mentioned but with the tip of the tongue slightly curled back. An example of an English variety with a retroflex /r/ would be Irish English. American English /r/ is also commonly described as retroflex.[2]
- [ɾ] represents an alveolar flap, i.e. there is only one short contact between the tip of the tongue and the alveolar ridge. Many speakers of Scottish English use this variety. If there is repeated contact between tongue and alveolar ridge, the sound is referred to as an alveolar trill, and the symbol employed would be [r].
- [ʁ] stands for a voiced uvular fricative, which is the standard realisation of /r/ in most German accents. It is also the defining feature of the 'Northumbrian burr', which was used in the northeast of England but seems to be dying out now.
- [ʋ] is a labiodental approximant (do not confuse the symbol with the high back vowel [ʊ]). This sound is increasingly found in some south-east English accents for /r/, particularly in London.

---

1 A useful internet site, already mentioned in the *Foundations* section, with all the sounds of the IPA is http://www.paulmeier.com/ipa/charts.html.

2 Trudgill & Hannah 2002: 40, however, state that this retroflexion is merely an acoustic impression which is achieved, for many Americans, by the "humping up of the body of the tongue rather than actual retroflexion."

- Some speakers also employ noticeably devoiced varieties of /r/, especially after voiceless plosives (as in *price*); when this happens, we can use the diacritical mark [̥] together with the respective /r/ symbol (e.g. [ɹ̥]).

Finally, it is important to know how speech sounds are combined in actual speech. They may, depending on the context, be altered (e.g. assimilated, devoiced etc.), elided, or new sounds may be added. In other words, it is a good idea to have an understanding of basic phonological processes. Knowing all these 'physical' facts, however, is not enough if we want to transcribe actual speech. Ear transcription depends to a large extent on the transcriber's perception of the sounds (i.e. on psychological factors), and this perception is subject to a number of influences we will look at now.

Factors that influence auditory perception

As a matter of fact, we still have a rather limited understanding of the interaction between hearing and mind, and even less of an understanding of how phonetic perception can be trained. The first and most important point is that, without any further training, we tend to hear and interpret the sounds of a foreign language or accent along the lines of our own **mother tongue**. When we acquire our first language, we develop a habit of discriminating the sounds we hear according to their potential to alter the meaning of words in our own language (the phonemic principle). Apparently, the acquisition of this skill starts even before birth and is more or less completed when a child is only about ten months old.[3] After this, whatever stretch of spoken noise arrives at our ear is broken up according to the patterns of our mother tongue. Later on, as adults, we cannot simply switch this mechanism off when we hear a new variety with a different sound system. This is the reason why, for example, Germans find it hard to distinguish between the English DRESS and the TRAP vowel. German has a vowel that is virtually identical with DRESS (English *bet* and German *Bett* sound pretty much the same), but it does not have a vowel in the low to mid-low region where TRAP is located. Consequently, when speakers of German hear the sound [æ], their phonemically trained perception allocates it to the vowel slot closest to it, and that is /ɛ/. There have been many studies with artificially modified sounds that support the idea that people tend to interpret sounds in terms of these 'slots' and that intermediate sounds are not usually heard as 'in between' but as belonging to one of the nearby phonemes (the pioneering study is Liberman et al. 1957). This is referred to as 'categorical perception'. An interesting point here is that

3 Cf. Eimas et al. 1971, Gut 2009: 200f., Ohala 2008, Strange & Shafer 2008: 155. Obviously it is not possible to ask infants which sounds they have just heard and how they interpret them. If you are interested in finding out how even newborn babies perceive sounds, read Ohala 2008 for an overview.

we find it much more difficult to identify sounds as different that are rather similar to sounds from our own system than sounds that are completely dissimilar. Germans, for example, usually have no problem perceiving the dental fricatives (/ð/, /θ/) as different from their own sounds, even though they may have problems producing them. The more subtle differences between the 'English' /uː/ and the 'German' /uː/ ('shoe' vs. 'Schuh'), however, usually go unnoticed.

Sound perception is not just a matter of the phonemic inventory of one's mother tongue. Allophonic variation in either the listener's or the speaker's accent may also cause perceptual problems. To give an example: speakers of British English commonly distinguish between two realisations of the phoneme /l/: a 'clear' and a 'dark' one. If your own language or even your own native accent of English does not make this distinction, you are unlikely to perceive this *allophonic* difference in somebody else's speech even though you may have the phoneme /l/ as part of your *phonemic* inventory.

Apparently, even the phonological rules of one's mother tongue may influence the perception of foreign sounds. Speakers of German, for example, regularly replace English monophthongs with what appears to be the closest equivalent in their mother tongue. Thus, English *fee* sounds like *Vieh*, *luck* like *Lack* and *got* like *Gott*. There is, however, one exception. The RP THOUGHT vowel is, in terms of articulation, exactly midway between the vowel in German *Sohn* (/oː/) and that in *So̱nne* (/ɔ/). When it comes to pronouncing THOUGHT words, though, Germans tend to employ a lengthened variant of the *Sonne* vowel rather than the one in *Sohn*. For example, *bought* is pronounced with a quality which is more or less identical with the vowel in *Sonne* (close to cardinal vowel 6), but longer, and *not* like the German word *Boot*. This is doubly surprising since (a) this involves the manipulation (the lengthening) of a native sound and (b) it leaves a German sound with a similar function (the long vowel phoneme /oː/ as opposed to the shorter /ɔ/) unused. Which explanation is strong enough to account for this unexpected behaviour? My own theory goes like this: When German-speaking pupils learn English, they usually acquire an accent which displays features of both British and American English, even though their teacher may clearly adhere to one of the two. This intermediate accent typically includes occasional, but not regular medial-/t/ voicing, a British-like [ɑː] (or [aː]) pronunciation of BATH words and rhoticity. Thus, learners realise the /r/ in the word *floor*, and they also realise that it is clearly a consonant. In German, however, consonantal /r/s in coda position are only possible after short vowels (as in *wirr*, *hart*, *Kordel*); after long vowels (as in *nur, sehr, vier*), standard ('High') German employs a vocalic realisation of the /r/ ([ɐ]). Since THOUGHT is phonetically located between the two German 'o' phonemes, this phonological rule of German may tip the balance for German pupils to interpret the vowel in THOUGHT as corresponding to their /ɔ/, even though they hear that it is longer, and lengthen it accordingly.

Phonotactic restrictions (i.e. the question of which phoneme combinations are possible) in the listener's phonological system are another problem when it comes to interpreting new accents (cf. Strange & Shafer 2008: 163). German, for instance, does not have many words with the phoneme cluster /ŋg/ (*Tango* would be one exception). English, on the other hand, has quite a few of them (e.g. *angle*, *jungle*, *longer*, *longest*). A native speaker of German listening to English is likely to not notice the realisation of /g/ in these words. This is particularly true for cognates like *finger*, *hunger* or *England* since these words are so close – in pronunciation *and* in meaning – to what speakers of German know from their own language.

As you can see, the listener's mother tongue plays an important role, probably *the* most important role, in the phonetic interpretation (and therefore, potentially, in the transcription) of actual speech. One linguist even concluded that "the narrow transcriptions of the phoneticians do not tell us so very much about the actual dialectal realizations of the phonemes, but tell us more about the fieldworkers themselves, about their native pronunciations and about their confusion when coming to new regions." (Ringaard in Cucchiarini 1993: 5) If this were the end of the story, if there were no point in trying to overcome our 'perceptual grid' when, for example, we learn a new language, then ear training would be of no avail. In fact, however, there is hope:

> [A]dult listeners are able to demonstrate good perceptual differentiation of speech stimuli differing in phonetically-relevant acoustic parameters, whether or not those acoustic cues differentiate phonological categories in their native language. That is, despite years of employing learned patterns of selective perception and integration, adults can access those language-general processing abilities that they were born with. However, under more cognitively demanding conditions, listeners revert to their (automatic) language-specific patterns of perception. (Strange & Shafer 2008: 166)

Thus, it *is* possible to re-train our ear (or, rather, the cognitive perception of the speech sounds we encounter), and a good starting point is to get to know the phonology of our own accent so that we can develop an awareness of the listening strategies we acquired when we were young.

Our mother tongue may easily be the most important factor that determines our perception of speech; it is, however, not the only one. Another important element is the fact that, in everyday conversations, we do not usually pay so much attention to *how* something is said as to the content of the message. In other words, we practice **semantic hearing**. Normal listening is always a combination of bottom-up and top-down processes: Sounds and sound sequences arrive at our ear, are analysed according to our own phonological system, and the results are quickly matched with our mental lexicon and our encyclopaedic knowledge. This allows us to process and even reconstruct imperfect utterances. Under the appropriate circumstances, a sound sequence like [əɹaʊnəˈfʊʔbɔ] can easily be interpreted as 'a round of football', especially if it is preceded by a syntactic structure like 'and then we played'. Even as trained phoneticians, we can hardly do without semantic hearing:

> The transcriber [...] has learned to listen analytically but he will never succeed in doing so without the help of semantic listening. Even the extremely good trained transcriber cannot simply listen analytically, because the two kinds of information processing of the human mind, i.e. data-driven and conceptually driven processing are unalterably bound up with each other. (Vieregge 1987: 9)

As phoneticians, however, we need to be retrained to listen beyond *what* was actually said to *how* it was said. In current British English speech, for example, the sound string [jə] can stand for *you* ('When you cross the road'), *your* ('I enjoy your friendship') and *you're* ('When you're young'). 'Native listeners' of these sequences will easily identify them (even if they cannot label the differences) as a personal pronoun, a possessive article or a combination of pronoun and verb. And yet, the phonetic form may be exactly the same in all three cases.

Thus, our interpretation will always also be influenced by our **familiarity with the accent or language** in question. We must, on the other hand, be careful not to be misguided by our **expectancy**. Once we know a particular accent, it is easy to hear something into a speech sequence that is not there – or miss something that is. It is particularly easy to fall into this trap if we have listened to a single speaker for a while. If you have interpreted a phoneme in his/her speech twenty times in a particular way, you are quite likely to interpret it in the same way when it occurs for the twenty-first time, even though this time it may be realised in a slightly different way. Thus, **transcription duration**, too, can have an influence on the result. This is also true because transcribing actual speech is a very demanding task. Loss of concentration may lead to overgeneralisations in the interpretation. On the other hand, as we have just seen, the (semantic and phonetic) comprehension of a particular accent increases with time. It might therefore be a good idea to employ a two-step procedure when we have to transcribe texts which are more difficult to understand: first, we have to comprehend the content of the message. Then we might go back and listen to what was actually said (i.e. which sounds a speaker produced) rather than what we thought was said.

Even the **phonetic context** of the individual sounds influences their perception. Generally, it is easier to identify vowels in a CVC setting than the same vowel in isolation (cf. Reetz & Jongman 2009: 256). Vowels that are followed by obstruents (plosives, fricatives, affricates, as in *brick*) seem to be easier to interpret than those that are followed by sonorants (e.g. *bring*; cf. König 1988: 172). Apparently, in the interpretation of vowels, we use transitional information from neighbouring sounds as well (e.g. assimilation). A similar case can be made for the interpretation of some consonants. For plosives, it seems to be the voice onset time (VOT; the time that passes from the release of a plosive to the beginning of the vibration of the vocal folds) that helps us to distinguish voiced and voiceless sounds (e.g. [biː] vs. [piː]).

Spelling and the symbols used for transcription (e.g. IPA) are factors that may provide false clues. When they start transcribing, for example, some students insist that words like *write* have an initial [w]. **Background noise** influences the perception of sounds in that it is much harder for non-native speakers to ignore it than for native speakers (cf. Strange & Shafer 2008: 168). Finally, the kind of **training** that transcribers receive will have an influence on their listening (and, subsequently, their transcription). In an experiment, Ladefoged demonstrated that the same vowels were interpreted differently by different transcribers in accordance with their particular educational background (Cucchiarini 1993: 56).[4]

From theory to practice: Analysing unfamiliar sounds

Once you have developed an understanding of articulatory phonetics, common phonological processes and the psychological side of hearing, it is essential to develop a general strategy to analyse sounds that are unfamiliar to you. The best way is usually that you start from a sound you know and whose articulatory features you can describe. Then imitate the new sound. Shift between the two sounds and observe how you have to change your articulation to arrive at the new sound. Do you have to raise or lower your tongue, shift it to the front or back or curl it? Do you have to round your lips? Is there any difference in voicing? In Scotland, for example, you may come across somebody who speaks about *Loch Ness*, using a sound in *Loch* that reminds you of the fricative you find in the German word *Loch*. And yet, the realisation is not exactly the same. If you use the uvular fricative ([χ]) that you know from German as a starting point and move in the direction of the new sound, observing yourself as you do so, you will probably realise that you move your tongue slightly forward, but not so much that it sounds like the fricative in German *ich*. You can now use the IPA table to find out which symbol is used for this sound. Since, in terms of place of articulation, the Scottish sound is between the uvular [χ] and the palatal [ç], it must be velar, and since, like the German sounds, it is both voiceless and a fricative, the appropriate symbol is [x]. You can even test this analysis. You know that the sounds [k], [g] and [ŋ] are velars. The only difference is that their *manner* of articulation is different. If you use the place of one of these sounds and produce a fricative in the same position, you will once again arrive at [x]. This example shows how to combine a general phonetic knowledge about the realisation of

4 For a state-of-the-art overview of research methods and models of L2 perception, see Strange & Shafer 2008.

sounds (in this case place and manner of articulation of consonants) and your own linguistic background in analysing new sounds.

When we produce vowels, there is (by definition) no relevant contact between two articulators. The air can escape unimpeded, modified only by the position of the tongue, the lips and the soft palate (determining the nasality of the vowel, which we disregard for the moment). The articulation of vowels, therefore, takes place in a continuum of three dimensions: tongue height, the front-back position of the tongue and lip rounding. Of the three, the latter is mostly regarded as dichotomous (if at all) within one accent, i.e. we do not have to distinguish more than two degrees of lip rounding phonemically. Consequently, the subtle differences between tongue positions across accents and their description may present more of a problem. The general strategy for their identification, however, is similar to the one described above.

First of all, establish reference vowels that you can use to compare the vowels you hear. These vowels can for instance be your own vowels, i.e. those of your mother tongue. A good description of your accent may help you locate them in the vowel quadrilateral, but be aware that these descriptions usually refer to some standard-like or typical pronunciation which you may or may not share. A reliable source for major international varieties of English is Trudgill & Hannah 2002. If your mother tongue is German, the following diagram lists the positions for some of the vowel phonemes of High German (cf. Kohler 1999. There are more vowels in German, but for illustrative purposes we only represent these eight):

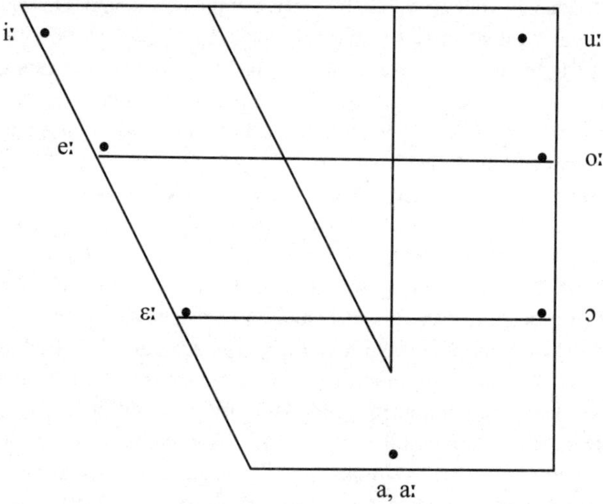

There are no official standard lexical sets for German, but the following words may serve the same purpose:

iː	eː	ɛː	a	aː	ɔ	oː	uː
dienen	dehnen	Dänen	Kamm	kam	Rotte	rote	Rute

As you can see, six of the vowel phonemes are more or less identical with cardinal vowels.[5] This is by no means a common situation. Most languages have their vowels scattered all over the quadrilateral, with a general tendency towards peripheral positions (compare, for example, IPA 1999). (If Daniel Jones had been German, he would probably have been accused of bias.) But this distribution gives speakers of (standard) German an invaluable advantage when it comes to identifying vowels within the IPA framework in the high, mid-high and mid-low regions. Use these six vowels as perceptual anchor points to identify foreign vowels. If you integrate schwa into your strategy, you can easily say that, for example, a new vowel is in between cardinal vowels 6 and 7 or that it is slightly centralised from cardinal vowel 2. However, in the low region, speakers of German quickly lose their bearings. Yes, German has the two /a/ phonemes (which differ in length rather than quality), but most speakers of German fail to realise that the English TRAP vowel is different from DRESS – unless they have specifically learned this. If you integrate the RP TRAP and BATH vowels (or GA TRAP and PALM) into your perceptual paradigm, you can cover almost all of Jones's first set of cardinal vowels. And you can even go beyond this: the German vowel phonemes [yː] (as in *Bühne*), [øː] (*lösen*) and [œ] (*können*) give you an idea of what rounded front vowels sound like. Note, however, that their position is not identical with cardinal vowels 9, 10 and 11; each of the rounded vowels is more centralised and slightly more open than their unrounded counterpart.

Alternatively (especially if you speak a language other than German), you may take the cardinal vowels as a starting point. You can find reliable guides on the internet at

> http://www.let.uu.nl/~audiufon/data/e_cardinal_vowels.html (an original recording of Daniel Jones himself from 1956!)

or at

> http://www.paulmeier.com/ipa/charts.html.

Once you have established your own reference points in the vowel quadrilateral, use them in the comparison of authentic vowels:

---

5 Some speakers of German do not distinguish /eː/ and /ɛː/ and pronounce words like *Käse* with /eː/. Dialect speakers may have different places of articulation altogether. Thus, before you use the strategy outlined, make sure that you know where your own vowels lie.

a) Listen to the new vowel.

b) Try to imitate it.

c) Compare with one or two neighbouring vowels of your accent. While you are doing this, observe how you have to move your tongue to get from a similar (or even any other) vowel in your accent to the position of the new vowel. For example, if you think that the starting point of the MOUTH diphthong you have heard is slightly higher than the one you are used to from RP or GA, test this hypothesis against schwa. If you are unsure, use a third vowel to locate the new vowel.

d) Finally, check for differences in lip rounding and nasalisation.

Analysing unknown languages

If you are going to work among a group of speakers whose language is not genetically related to your own, your challenge will be much greater. This is particularly true if, for example, the language uses tone to differentiate phonemes (unless you speak a tone language yourself), or if the language you are studying has not yet been described, i.e. if you only partially understand the words and the structure of that language. In this case, you can start out with little more than guesswork, based on your experience with the languages you know and your expertise in phonetics and phonology. Vieregge (1987: 37) summarises the difficulties as follows:

> Transcribing unknown languages narrowly without further auxiliary means is basically impossible. Note that neither of the two kinds of listening, i.e. analytic and semantic listening, can serve for making a narrow transcription of the unknown language in question. [...] All [the transcriber] can do is make an "impressionistic transcription" in order to get a global impression of the utterances in question.

The reason for this is that as transcribers of an unknown language, we cannot be sure which sound distinctions are phonologically relevant in that language. It seems, however, that the statement above goes a bit too far. The IPA distinguishes just over 80 consonants symbolically. These represent the consonant groups found so far in the languages of the world. (I use the term 'consonant group' here since the actual realisation of the sound may be slightly different from language to language.) In most languages it is enough to use one symbol (or set of symbols) for any distinct consonant sound. This is also in line with the International Phonetic Association's policy to assign, as far as possible, a distinct symbol to each phoneme of a given language (see IPA 1999:159). In a limited number of cases we need to distinguish two phonemes for a group of sounds that is only represented by one (basic) symbol, e.g., as was already mentioned in the *Foundations* section, in Chinese, which uses /p/ and /pʰ/ distinctively. In rare cases, this number of distinctive sounds per symbol may go up to four, but these are extremes. Generally, therefore, we can assume that the number of consonant phonemes in each of the slots created by the 'place of articulation – manner of articulation – voicing' matrix created by the IPA is limited to one or two at the most for any one language. Thus, the theoretically almost infinite number of sounds that humans could produce using their vocal apparatus boils down in practice to a still considerable, yet manageable number of sounds. Or, in other words, the potential total diversity of sounds is restricted by the universal features we find in the languages of the world.

Many linguists also recommend transcribing nonsense words. These 'words' represent an arbitrary sound combination and may include foreign sounds (e.g. [ŋgʉɾʂ̩i]; compare, for example, Ashby 2007: 1658), but have no meaning. Since transcribers cannot rely on semantic listening to support their analysis and since the phonosyntactic structure may or may not comply with any language they know, the trainees have to rely on what they know about articulatory phonetics – and on that alone.

However, it is also important not to restrict the training material to arbitrarily combined but isolated sound sequences:

> Until recently, most studies of non-native phonetic perception have employed materials in which nonsense syllables or real words are produced and presented in isolation (i.e., in a citation-form style of speech), rather than in continuous speech contexts (phrases or sentences). Again, it has been well established that the acoustic parameters differentiating phonetic segments differ substantially as a function of this difference in speech style (e.g., Strange et al. 2007). Thus, studies using citation-form materials may not yield results that are easily generalizable to real-world situations in which perceivers are usually listening to and trying to comprehend continuous speech. (Strange & Shafer 2008: 163)

Thus, after a period in which ear trainees have familiarised themselves with the general principles of articulation and become accustomed to a wide variety of sounds, it is probably a good idea to include more natural (i.e. continuous) speech data in the training process.

Data interpretation

Once they have analysed the sounds of a particular variety phonetically, linguists need to interpret them phonologically (i.e. according to the role they play in the accent under investigation). What are the phonemes of this variety, which allophones can you find, and what rules relate the latter to the former? If you have a second, similar accent (a reference variety), you can compare these two varieties on four different levels (cf. Collins & Mees 2008: 150–152): the systemic, the lexical, the distributional and the realisational level. To do this, you have to ask yourself the following questions:

1. **Systemic variation**. Are there sets of words where one variety has only one phoneme that splits into two in the other variety, or two that merge into one? A typical example from English is relevant for the difference between Northern English and RP: whereas RP distinguishes between STRUT and FOOT (a minimal pair would be *luck* and *look*), these two merge into Northern English /ʊ/ (or something similar). An example which works the other way round would be Scottish English. Some speakers employ a contrast between /w/ and /ʍ/, the latter being a voiceless /w/ used in words that have a <wh> in the spelling. Thus, words like *wear* and *where* or *Wales* and *whales* are minimal pairs. In this case, and seen from the perspective of RP, there is a split.

2. **Lexical variation**. Do you find differences in the lexical distribution of the phonemes? In other words, is there a set of words that has one phoneme in one accent but different phoneme in another accent? A typical example for English would be the BATH words (like *staff* or *example*) that have /ɑː/ in RP but /æ/ in GA.

3. **Distributional variation**. If you find the same phoneme in both varieties, are there rules that lead to a different distribution of the allophones? The most obvious distinction here is, of course, that between rhotic and non-rhotic accents: Whereas all the /r/s are pronounced in the former, this is only the case before vowels with the latter. Another typical example would be the case of clear vs. dark /l/: While RP has a complementary (allophonic) distribution of these sounds, other accents may only employ the clear (e.g. Irish English) or only the dark variant (e.g. New Zealand English).

4. **Realisational variation**. Finally, even if the distribution of sounds is the same, there are usually some more or less noticeable differences in the realisation of phonemes between accents. This question is particularly relevant for vowels (both monophthongs and diphthongs). The FACE diphthong, for example, is considerably wider in, say, Australian English than in RP. Another good way of distinguishing English accents, as was mentioned above, is to look at how the phoneme /r/ is realised (e.g. as a retroflex, tap etc.).

The limitations of ear transcription

Is objective transcription ever possible for humans? The answer is, probably not. First, there are inherent limitations. Since actual speech always constitutes a continuum, transcription, no matter how 'narrow' or precise, will always be an abstraction.[6] Duranti (1997: 161) remarks:

6 For the question of validity and reliability in transcription see Vieregge 1986.

> [T]ranscription is a *selective* process, aimed at highlighting certain aspects of the interaction for specific research goals; [...] there is no *perfect* transcript in the sense of a transcript that can fully recapture the total experience of being in the original situation, but there are better transcripts, that is, transcripts that represent information in ways that are (more) consistent with our descriptive and theoretical goals [...].

Second, people are not machines which record sounds unemotionally and without any mental processes. As we have seen, there are many factors that influence the transcription of a section of speech, among them the native language and experience of the transcriber, the speech style of the informant and the length of the utterance. It has even been shown that the transcriptions of scholars who were trained in different traditions differed systematically (Ladefoged 1960). Port (2002) remarks:

> There are no perfect phoneticians among either adults or infants. No adult listener can come close to correctly recognizing all phonetic sounds in all languages. Nor has anyone ever claimed that they could – nor that anyone else could. This includes such famous experts in impressionistic transcription as Daniel Jones and Kenneth Pike.[7]

There is even one study that suggests that auditory perception is at least to some degree a gift. Using established techniques like nonsense words and substitutions for her ear-training, Patricia Ashby compared the transcription of her students over a period of about six months. She expected an improvement in the identification success rate from a mid-course assessment after 12 weeks to the final assessment after 24 weeks, but the results remained pretty much the same. She concludes (2007: 1660; emphasis in the original):

> The fact that the total ***range*** of results [...] remained largely constant across the three different tests and two levels of difficulty – at all stages, there were individuals scoring full marks and others scoring nothing – suggests that some learners may be more predisposed towards becoming phoneticians than others. This finding hints at an innate capacity which may not be shared by everyone.

After looking in some detail at the differences between ear transcription and eye transcription, let us now go on to do some practical work.

---

7 Kenneth Pike (1912–2000) was renowned for his ability to deal with linguistic field data. He became particularly popular through his public demonstrations in which he analysed and 'learned' a new language by listening to a native speaker and imitating his/her sounds.

Practice

Exercise C1. Casual speech (☑)

What you transcribed in the first parts of this book was (potentially) natural but careful speech, such as is found, for example, in lectures, when reading a text or in more formal conversation. When talking casually, however, people pay less attention to their actual pronunciation. As a result, they may 'drop' sounds, merge them or make them more similar to each other. In some cases, they may also insert an extra sound into their speech. In phonology, these processes are referred to as elision, coalescence, assimilation and epenthesis/intrusion. Read the following sentences and phrases in a very casual, yet native-like way; then transcribe your own speech.

1. Would you hold this?	2. You can keep it.
3. fish and chips	4. the effects of that
5. She jumped up and down.	6. Tell him!
7. the next day	8. Look at that man!
9. That's correct.	10. Good night!
11. Get them!	12. India and Pakistan
13. Perhaps I should leave.	14. Come on, do it!

Exercise C2. Words with non-canonical speech sounds (☑)

When it comes to transcribing interjections or imitations of words of foreign origin, the symbols used for the phonemes and major allophones of a language are usually not sufficient. Examples 1 and 2 are interjections. Look up the symbols you don't know, and then try to imitate the sounds. Which interjections are they, and how are they normally represented in writing? Number 3 is the short form of a village in North Wales, as it is pronounced in Welsh (the full name is actually one of the longest place names in the world). Again, look up the sounds you don't know and try to pronounce the word. How, do you think, will English speakers (who don't speak Welsh and thus will only use their native inventory) pronounce it? The words in numbers 4–6 work the other way round. They are represented in their conventional spelling. Imitate these words, try to localise the place of articulation and identify the manner and (if necessary) the voicing, rounding and airstream (egressive vs. ingressive). Then turn to the overview of the IPA symbols in the back cover of this book and see if you can find the appropriate symbols.

1. [ɸː] or [pɸː]
2. [ɯɪə] or [jʌx] (both interjections are used to express the same feeling!)
3. Llanfairpwllgwyngyll [ˌɬanvaiɾ puːɬ ˈgwïn gïɬ]
4. Loch Ness (the famous lake in Scotland)
5. tut-tut (interjection to show disapproval, produced by sucking in air)
6. Chopin, chanson, Mont Blanc (transcribe these words as they are pronounced by speakers of English who imitate French)

Exercise C3. Locating the German 'vocalic r' (☑)

The German phonological system contains a sound that we refer to as the 'vocalic r', i.e. a vowel-like realisation of the phoneme /r/ (sometimes also referred to as 'r schwa'). We find it after most long vowels (as in *Bier*, *Tür*, *sehr*, *Friseur*, *Bär*, *Ohr*, *Schur*; in some accents also after [aː] as in *Haar*) and as a realisation of final <er> as in *Bäcker*. Locate the position of this allophone with the help of the strategies outlined above. Use the vowels whose position you know and observe how you have to move your tongue to arrive at this sound. Hint: the vowel is in the low region of the quadrilateral, so you might want to relate it to the vowels you know there.

Analysing Interview Data

Below you will find the interview from section B again, this time in a less tidied-up version. It is first represented in conventional standard spelling and then in phonetic transcript. 'Inter' stands for my contributions, 'Inf' for the informant's. Double slashes (//) indicate overlap.

You can find the whole interview (and listen to it) on the *Scottish Corpus of Text and Speech* (www.scottishcorpus.ac.uk/corpus/search/document.php?documentid =1412). This excerpt is from 1:32 to 4:45.

Inter:	Do you think there's any particular dialect that represents Scotland best, where you would say, 'Okay, this is how S- well Scottish people speak', or 'This is the, the most typical Scottish dialect or accent'?

Inf:	Possibly, I mean, possibly Glasgow, it's the well-known one across the world I suppose but ehm I would prefer that somewhere like the middle, like oh Inverness, Perth, that was because it's a sort of normal ehm toned down version, but it's still got the Scottish sort of accent
Inter:	//Yeah, exactly, mm//, yeah.
Inf:	//in it// yeah.
Inter:	That's interesting, that's an interesting statement here. Do, do you have any favourite dialects or accents here in Scotland? I mean you've mentioned eh what was it? Inverness and Perth?
Inf:	Well
Inter:	I mean people that you enjoy listening to most just because of their accents or dialects?
Inf:	Probably the Western Isles a bit, ehm, I mean I can laugh at the, the jokes that comes from the Gal- the Glasgow ones, but ehm I think it can be very hard to make out, you know, for, for me an then probab- possibly even worse for foreigners or even the English.
Inter:	So ah you would say your favourite accent would be Western Isles in Scotland?
Inf:	Well it's got a lilt, and I like to, yeah, probably like hearing that.
Inter:	Ehm is there any dialect or language you don't particularly like here in Scotland, where you'd say, 'Mm it's not very pleasant to listen to'?
Inf:	Ehm, no not really I think maybe the Aberdonians do, it's quite difficult to make out, it's
Inter:	Yeah. Is it just difficult or is it unpleasant to you?
Inf:	Well, I ca- I don't know, I never really thought about Scottish accents but I don't particularly like the Birmingham accent in England because it's too, it's a drone, it's a
Inter:	//The Brum.//
Inf:	//it sounds very// yeah, I don't, I don't particularly like that but I have not really thought about the Scottish accents as being grating.
Inter:	Sorry?

Inf:	I don't find any o the Scottish accents grating.
Inter:	m-m. 'Grating', what does that mean?
Inf:	Getting on your nerves, you know, grating, you know?
Inter:	Okay, okay, ah yeah. Is, is that a Scottish term? Never //heard of it//.
Inf:	//Probably just// mine!
Inter:	How would you describe your own dialect or accent?
Inf:	Well
Inter:	I mean w- not just now but when you talk to friends or to your family?
Inf:	Well there's certain words that I use that probably me husband that comes from Orphir doesn't use, and that's because I was brought up in Sanday, and there's certain words comes from every parish here. Ehm, if I hear myself on the answering machine, I don't like it ehm
Inter:	All right?
Inf:	I, I think I'm pretty broad if I, if I'm relaxed, I'm pretty broad spoken.

The following rules have been applied in the phonetic transcription of the text:

- The transcription depth is meant to be similar to that in Part B. However, we do transcribe prominent glottal plosives (stops). Since the variety under investigation is still unanalysed (i.e. we cannot yet know exactly what the phonemes and allophones of this speaker are), we a) have to use our background knowledge of English, and b) we transcribe the sounds as closely as possible to the actual pronunciation. However, for most of the time anyway, we refrain from using diacritics. Length marks are allocated more or less impressionistically. Intonation groups and stress are also marked.
- The phoneme /r/ is transcribed according to its actual realisation.
- Ordinary feedback signals (*yeah, uh-huh, m-m* etc.) are not always transcribed to ease the readability of the text.
- Para-verbal behaviour (like blowing out air and laughter) is not represented either, since this exercise focuses on the accent of the speaker(s), not on their communicative behaviour.

What we get looks something like the following:

Inter:	dju θɪŋk ðɛəz ɛni | pəˈtɪkjələ | daɪəlɛkt ðɛt ɹɛpɹɪzɛnts skɒtlənd ˈbɛst ‖ wɛ jə wəd sɛɪ əkɛɪ ðɪs ɪs | haʊ s wɛl skɒtɪʃ piːpl ˈspiːk ‖ ɔ ðɪs ɪs ðə ðə məʊst ˈtɪpɪkl | ˈskɒtɪʃ | ˈdaɪəlɛkt ɔɹ ˈæksnt ‖
Inf:	pɔsəbli | aɪ miːn pɔsəbli ˈglaːsgoː | ɪs ðə wɛl noːn wan əkɹɔs zə ˈwɛɾld | w ˈsəpoːs | bat ɛːm | ˈaɪ wʊd prɪfɛə ðət samwɛ laɪk | ðə ˈmɛdl laɪk o | ɛnvɛɾˈnɛs | ˈpɛəθ | ðət wəz | bɪkəz dəts ə sət ə ˈnɔʁməl | ɛm ˈtoːn ˈdoːn | ˈvɛəʃn bat ɪtstɪl gɔt ðə ˈskɔtɪʃ | ˈɑːksɛnt |
Inter:	//ja ɪgˈzæktli ‖// mː ja‖
Inf:	//ˈɛn ɛt ‖// jɛə‖
Inter:	ðæts ˈɪntɹɛstɪŋ | ðæts ən ɪntɹɛstɪŋ ˈstɛɪtmənt hɪə ‖ də djə hæv ɛni ˈfɛɪvɹət | ˈdaɪəlɛkts ɔɹ ˈæksənts hɪə ɪn skɒtlənd ‖ aɪ mɪn | jəv ˈmɛnʃnt | ə wɒ ˈwɒz ɪt | ɪnvəˈnɛs | ɛnd | ①ˈpɛɾθ‖
Inf:	ˈwɛl
Inter:	a mɪn piːpl ðæt ju ɪnˈdʒɔɪ lɪsənɪŋ tu məʊst dʒəst bɪkɔz əv ðɛə | ˈæksəns ‖ ɔ ˈdaɪəlɛkts ‖
Inf:	prɔbəbli ðə wɛstən ˈaɪlz ə ˈbɛt | ɛm | a min aɪ ˈkɛːn laːf ət ðə | ðə ˈtʃoːks ðət kamz fə ðə gæl ðə ˈglaːsgoː wanz | bat em | aɪ θɪŋk ɪt ˈkɛːn bi ˈvɛɾi haː tə mɛɪk ˈuːt ‖ jə noː ‖ ˈfəɾ | fə ˈmiː ɛn dɛn prɔbəb ˈpɔsəbli iːvn wɔʂ fə | ˈfɔɾənəʂ ɔɾ | iːvn ðə ˈɛŋglɪʃ ‖
Inter:	soʊ əː | ju wəd sɛɪ jə ˈfɛɪvəɹət | ˈæksənt wʊd bi ˈwɛstən aɪlz | ɪn ˈskɒtlənd ‖
Inf:	wɛl ɪts gɒʔ ə ˈlɛlt ‖ ənd a laɪk tə | ˈjɛa | prɔbəbli laɪk ˈhiːrən dæt ‖
Inter:	əm ‖ ɪs ðə ɛni ˈdaɪəlɛkt ɔ læŋgwɪdʒ jʊ ˈdəʊnt pətɪkjʊləli laɪk | hi ɪn skɒʔlənt ‖ wɛə jʊd sɛɪ ˈm | ɪs nɒt vɛɹi ˈplɛznt tu lɪsn tu ‖
Inf:	ˈhːɛːm ‖ ˈno nɔt ɹiːli a θɪŋk mɛbi ðɪ æbəˈdoːniəns du ‖ ɛst kwaɪ ˈdɛfɛkəlt tə mɛɪk uːt ‖ ɪs
Inter:	jɛ ‖ ɪz ɪt dʒəs | ˈdɪfikəlt ɔɹ ɪz ɪt | ②ˈʌnplɛzən tə ju ‖
Inf:	ˈwɛl | a ka a doːnt noː aɪ nɛvə ɹiːli θɔːt əbuːt ˈskɔtɪʃ aksənts bat aɪ ˈdoːnt pətɪkjəli laɪk ðə ˈbɛrmɪŋhəm aksənt ɪn ˈɪŋglənd | bəkəs

	ɛts ˈtuː ɛts ə ˈdɹoːn | ɛts ə
Inter:	//ðə ˈbrʌm ‖//
Inf:	//ɪt saʊndz vɛɾi// jɛə ‖ a ˈdoːn a ˈdoːn pətɪkjəli laɪk ˈða ‖ bat hæv nə ɾiːli ˈθɔːt əbut ðə skɔtɪʃ æksəns | æz ˈbiən ˈɡɾeːtən ‖
Inter:	ˈsɒɹɪ ‖
Inf:	a doːnt faɪnd ɛni ɔv ðə ˈskɔtɪʃ aksəns ˈɡɾeːtən ‖
Inter:	mm ‖ ˈɡɾeːtən | wə dəz ðæ miːn ‖
Inf:	ɡɛtn ɔn jə ˈnɛːvz | jə noː | //ˈɡɾeːtn | jə noː ‖//.
Inter:	//əkɛɪ əkɛɪ ‖// a ja ‖ ɪs ɪs ðæ ə ˈskɒtɪʃ tɜːm ‖ //nɛvə ˈhɜːd əv ɪt ‖//
Inf:	//prɔbli dʒəs// ˈmaɪn ‖
Inter:	haʊ wʊd jə | dɪskraɪb jəɹ ˈəʊn | ˈdaɪəlɛkt ɔɹ ˈæksnt ‖
Inf:	ˈwɛːl |
Inter:	aɪ mɪn w ˈnɒ dʒəs naʊ | bə wɛn jə tɔːk tə ˈfɹɛndz ɔ tə jə ˈfæmli ‖
Inf:	wɛl ðə s̬ɛtn wɛdz ðət aɪ ˈjuːz | ˈðæt | prɔbli mi ˈhazbənd ðət kams fm ˈɔːfa daznt juːs ‖ æn ðæts bɪkɔz a wəz brɔːt ap ɛn ˈsaːndi ‖ æn ðɛs̬ɛtn wɛds kamz fə ˈɛvɾi paːɾɪʃ ˈhiɐ ‖ ɛːm | ɛf a hiə masɛlf ɔn ðə | ˈaːnsəɾɪn məʃiːn | a doːnt ˈlaɪk ɛt ‖ ɛm |
Inter:	ɔː ˈɹaɪt ‖
Inf:	aɪ aɪ θɪŋk am prɪʔi ˈbrɔːd ‖ ɛf a ɛf am rəˈlakst am prɪʔi brɔːd | spoːkən‖

Exercise C4. Reading transcribed speech

In class, allocate a few lines of the informant's contributions to each student (the tutor of the course can read all the *Inter* sections). Take a few minutes to prepare your lines, and then read the interview aloud. You may disregard the overlap and read each line by itself. Then listen to the actual excerpt. Is it as you expected? If not, what is different, and why?

If you want to do any of the following exercises, you can either listen to the interview directly from the website, or you can download the file (using the button with the speaker and the arrow at the bottom of the page). The sound file comes as an mp4, but you can convert it to mp3 (or several other formats) using a freeware multimedia converter.

Exercise C5. Transcribing actual speech data

Listen to the excerpt of the interview. Choose a small portion of the excerpt, and try to transcribe it yourself, using the guidelines above. Then compare it with the transcription given in the book. You should not be surprised to find some differences since even the transcriptions of trained phoneticians do not always agree (and I am not making any claims that mine represents the ultimate truth). However, if you do find major differences, are they systematic? If so, what might be the reason? Alternatively, you can first work with a partner who transcribes the same passage. Compare your transcriptions and discuss any differences you notice. You may need to go back to the actual recording to test whose interpretation is more valid. Then compare your final result with the transcription in this book.

Exercise C6. Analysing authentic data 1: Vowels (☑)

Characterise the realisation and distribution of the vowels in the informant's accent, paying special attention to the KIT, FACE, GOAT, TRAP, NURSE and MOUTH sets.

Exercise C7. Analysing authentic data 2: Consonants (☑)

- Is the informant's accent rhotic or non-rhotic? What can you say about the realisation of the phoneme /r/?
- In which contexts do you find the retroflex fricative [ʂ]? (Hint: In Orcadian English, [ʂ] is an allophone with a regular and therefore predictable distribution.)
- Are there any other non-RP consonantal features in the speaker's accent?

Exercise C8. Analysing authentic data 3: Intonation (☑)

Orcadians are popularly said to have a 'sing-song intonation' or a 'lilt'. Can you give evidence of this folk-linguistic impression? Pay particular attention to the underlined words in phrases like "Birmingham accent in England" (l. 29), "my husband that comes from Orphir" (l. 43f.) "brought up in Sanday" (l. 44f.) or various other instances in the remainder of the interview. How can you describe this intonation pattern?

Exercise C9. Analysing authentic data 4: Lexis and grammar (☑)

- In two cases, the actual pronunciation of this informant (a) seems to be very far removed from Standard English and (b) does not agree with patterns that we find elsewhere in this section of the interview. Thus, it seems more appropriate to assume a different lexeme or affixation pattern altogether. Can you give an example?
- Can you detect any other non-standard grammatical features?

Exercise C10. Analysing authentic data 5: Idiosyncrasies (☑)

Can you comment on my pronunciation of the words which are preceded by the symbols ① and ②? What might have been the reason for these choices?

Exercise C11. Analysing authentic data 6: Doing your own research project

Download the whole interview from the web and listen to it.

- Do you notice any change in the informant's accent as the interview progresses? Can you give evidence for your claim? What might be the reasons for this change? The interviewee's own statement in line 48f. gives a clue to one of the reasons.
- There is at least one consonantal feature that is typical of some Scottish accents that we have not discussed yet. Listen particularly to the passage from 'Well, it's maybe just me own opinion, but ...' to '... what would they decide?' (10:28 – 10:53) What is it? What can you say about the distribution of this feature?

Exercise C12. The Speech Accent Archive

There is a very useful internet site that contains a host of recordings of first, second and foreign language speakers of English. The *Speech Accent Archive* (http://accent.gmu.edu/) offers hundreds of speech samples from all over the world. You can choose speakers according to various social (e.g. age, sex) and linguistic (e.g. substratum) backgrounds, with biographical information being provided. Most of the recordings are narrowly transcribed so that you can practise both your listening and transcription skills and acquaint yourself with many forms of World English at the same time. Note, however, that some transcriptions may be debatable.

Key

Section A

A1. Standard Lexical Sets

A moth is not a moth in mother,	LOT STRUT
Nor both in bother, broth in brother.	GOAT LOT LOT STRUT
And here is not a match for there,	NEAR SQUARE
Nor dear and fear for bear and pear.	NEAR NEAR SQUARE SQUARE
And then there's dose and rose and lose –	GOAT GOAT GOOSE
Just look them up – and goose and choose,	GOOSE GOOSE
And cord and word and card and ward,	THOUGHT NURSE BATH THOUGHT
And font and front and word and sword,	LOT STRUT NURSE THOUGHT
And do and go and thwart and cart –	GOOSE GOAT THOUGHT BATH
Come, come, I've hardly made a start!	
A dreadful language? Man alive!	
I'd mastered it when I was five!	

For American English, replace

- LOT for the words *moth*, *bother* and *broth* (but not for *font*) by CLOTH,
- THOUGHT for the words *cord*, *ward*, *sword* and *thwart* by NORTH,
- and BATH for the words *card* and *cart* by START.

A2. Words with [iː]

deep	[diːp]	receipt	[r(ɪ/ə)ˈsiːt]
people	[ˈpiːpl]	Eve	[iːv]
eagle	[ˈiːgl]	equal	[ˈiːkwəl]
mean	[miːn]	agree	[əˈgriː]
knee	[niː]	idea (GA)	[aɪˈdiːə]
believe	[b(ə/ɪ)ˈliːv]	Z (GA)	[ziː]

A3. Words with [ɪ]

hit	[hɪt]	women	[ˈwɪmən]
build	[bɪld]	biscuit	[ˈbɪskɪt]
wind	[wɪnd]	bushes (RP)	[ˈbʊʃɪz]
miss	[mɪs]	Miller	[ˈmɪlə]
ring	[rɪŋ]	singer	[ˈsɪŋə]/[ˈsɪŋər]
riddle	[ˈrɪdl]	business	[ˈbɪzn(ə/ɪ)s]

A4. Words with [ɛ]

end	[ɛnd]	friend	[frɛnd]
men	[mɛn]	bless	[blɛs]
sweat	[swɛt]	cleanse	[klɛnz]
tell	[tɛl]	Thames	[tɛmz]
get	[gɛt]	says	[sɛz]
deaf	[dɛf]	Carol (GA)	[ˈkɛr(ə)l]

A5. Words with [æ]

man	[mæn]	jazz	[dʒæz]
sad	[sæd]	wax	[wæks]
camp	[kæmp]	carrot (RP)	[ˈkærət]
thanks	[θæŋks]	bath (GA)	[bæθ]
apple	[æpl]	dance (GA)	[dæns]
Brad	[bræd]	master (GA)	[ˈmæst(ə)r]

A6. Words with [ʌ]

must	[mʌst]	onion	[ˈʌnjən]
one	[wʌn]	thunder	[ˈθʌndə]/[ˈθʌnd(ə)r]
son	[sʌn]	tongue	[tʌŋ]
sun	[sʌn]	mother	[ˈmʌðə]/[ˈmʌð(ə)r]
other	[ˈʌðə]/[ˈʌð(ə)r]	courage (RP)	[ˈkʌrɪdʒ]
colo(u)r	[ˈkʌlə]/[ˈkʌl(ə)r]	thorough (RP)	[ˈθʌrə]

A7. Words with [ɑː]

palm [pɑːm]
schwa [ʃwɑː]
star [stɑː]/[stɑːr]
card [kɑːd]/[kɑːrd]
bath (RP) [bɑːθ]
laugh (RP) [lɑːf]
dance (RP) [dɑːns]
branch (RP) [brɑːnʃ]
stop (GA) [stɑːp]
solve (GA) [sɑːlv]
Tom (GA) [tɑːm]
watch (GA) [wɑːtʃ]

A8. Words with [ɒ] (RP)

shot [ʃɒt]
lock [lɒk]
song [sɒŋ]
want [wɒnt]
object$_{N}$ [ˈɒbdʒ(ɛ/ɪ)kt]
John [dʒɒn]
modern [ˈmɒdən]
honest [ˈɒn(ɪ/ə)st]
porridge [ˈpɒrɪdʒ]
orange [ˈɒr(ɪ/ə)ndʒ]
pocket [ˈpɒkɪt]
chocolate [ˈtʃɒkl(ɪ/ə)t]

A9. Words with [ɔː]

door [dɔː]/[dɔːr]
shore [ʃɔː]/[ʃɔːr]
north [nɔːθ]/[nɔːrθ]
boring [ˈbɔːrɪŋ]
brought [brɔːt]
caution [ˈkɔːʃ(ə)n]
clause [klɔːz]
Chaucer [ˈtʃɔːsə]/[ˈtʃɔːs(ə)r]
long (GA) [lɔːŋ]
boss (GA) [bɔːs]
offer (GA) [ˈɔːf(ə)r]
across (GA) [əˈkrɔːs]

A10. Words with [uː]

new [njuː]/[n(j)uː]
fruit [fruːt]
soon [suːn]
glue [gluː]
juice [dʒuːs]
lose [luːz]
Ruth [ruːθ]
taboo [t(ə/æ)ˈbuː]
union [ˈjuːnjən]
queue [kjuː]
UK [juːˈkɛɪ]
smooth [smuːð]

A11. Words with [ʊ]

cook	[kʊk]	wool	[wʊl]
wood	[wʊd]	cushion	[ˈkʊʃ(ə)n]
push	[pʊʃ]	wolf	[wʊlf]
full	[fʊl]	sugar	[ˈʃʊgə]/[ˈʃʊgər]
should (SF)	[ʃʊd]	woman	[ˈwʊmən]

A12. Words with [ɜː]/[ɜːr]

turn	[tɜːn]/[tɜːrn]	nerve	[nɜːv]/[nɜːrv]
verb	[vɜːb]/[vɜːrb]	murder	[ˈmɜːdə]/[ˈmɜːrd(ə)r]
heard	[hɜːd]/[hɜːrd]	urge	[ɜːdʒ]/[ɜːrdʒ]
worth	[wɜːθ]/[wɜːrθ]	person	[ˈpɜːs(ə)n]/[ˈpɜːrs(ə)n]
worse	[wɜːs]/[wɜːrs]	Wordsworth	[ˈwɜːdzwɜːθ]/ [ˈwɜːrdzwɜːrθ]

A13. Words with [ə]

sofa	[ˈsəʊfə]/[ˈsoʊfə]	diet	[ˈdaɪət]
about	[əˈbaʊt]	nation	[ˈnɛɪʃ(ə)n]
dealer	[ˈdiːlə]/[ˈdiːl(ə)r]	pleasure	[ˈplɛʒə]/[ˈplɛʒ(ə)r]
comma	[ˈkɒmə]/[ˈkɑːmə]	palace	[ˈpæl(ə/ɪ)s]
teacher	[ˈtiːtʃə]/[ˈtiːtʃər]	professor	[prəˈfɛsə]/[prəˈfɛs(ə)r]

A14. Words with [aɪ]

fight	[faɪt]	choir	[ˈkwaɪə]/[ˈkwaɪ(ə)r]
knife	[naɪf]	tiger	[ˈtaɪgə]/[taɪg(ə)r]
sigh	[saɪ]	decide	[d(ɪ/ə)ˈsaɪd]
write	[raɪt]	science	[ˈsaɪəns]
fire	[ˈfaɪə]/[ˈfaɪ(ə)r]	island	[ˈaɪlənd]

A15. Words with [aʊ]

shout	[ʃaʊt]	house	[haʊs]
browse	[braʊz]	flower	[ˈflaʊə]/[ˈflaʊ(ə)r]
south	[saʊθ]	trousers	[ˈtraʊzəz]/[ˈtraʊz(ə)rz]
crowd	[ˈkraʊd]	mountain	[ˈmaʊnt(ɪ/ə)n]
power	[ˈpaʊə]/[ˈpaʊ(ə)r]	however	[haʊˈɛvə]/[haʊˈɛv(ə)r]

A16. Words with [ɛɪ]

name	[nɛɪm]	bacon	[ˈbɛɪk(ə)n]
steak	[stɛɪk]	nature	[ˈnɛɪtʃə]/[ˈnɛɪtʃ(ə)r]
came	[kɛɪm]	obey	[ə(ʊ)ˈbɛɪ]/[(oʊ/ə)ˈbɛɪ]
wave	[wɛɪv]	station	[ˈstɛɪʃ(ə)n]
jail	[dʒɛɪl]	arrange	[əˈrɛɪndʒ]

A17. Words with [ɔɪ]

voice	[vɔɪs]	annoy	[əˈnɔɪ]
coin	[kɔɪn]	oyster	[ˈɔɪstə]/[ˈɔɪst(ə)r]
boy	[bɔɪ]	employ	[(ɪ/ɛ)mˈplɔɪ]
noise	[nɔɪz]	rejoice	[r(ɪ/ə)ˈdʒɔɪs]
moist	[mɔɪst]	soya	[ˈsɔɪə]

A18. Words with [əʊ]/[oʊ]

hole	[həʊl]/[hoʊl]	joke	[dʒəʊk]/[dʒoʊk]
don't	[dəʊnt]/[doʊnt]	ocean	[ˈəʊʃ(ə)n]/[ˈoʊʃ(ə)n]
rose	[rəʊz]/[roʊz]	okay	[əʊˈkɛɪ]/[oʊˈkɛɪ]
comb	[kəʊm]/[koʊm]	clothe	[kləʊð]/[kloʊð]
though	[ðəʊ]/[ðoʊ]	control	[kənˈtrəʊl]/[kənˈtroʊl]

A19. Words with [ɪə]/[ir]

ear	[ɪə]/[ir]	weird	[wɪəd]/[wird]
era	[ˈɪərə]/[ˈirə]	sincere	[sɪnˈsɪə]/[sɪnˈsir]
sheer	[ʃɪə]/[ʃir]	career	[kəˈrɪə]/[kəˈrir]
cheer	[tʃɪə]/[tʃir]	appear	[əˈpɪə]/[əˈpir]
beard	[bɪəd]/[bird]	persevere	[pɜːs(ɪ/ə)ˈvɪə]/[pɜːrsəˈvir]

A20. Words with [ʊə]/[ʊr]

sure	[ʃʊə]/[ʃʊr]	ensure	[(ɪ/ɛ)nˈʃʊə]/[(ɪ/ɛ)nˈʃʊr]
tour	[tʊə]/[tʊr]	Europe	[ˈjʊərəp]/[ˈjʊrəp]
poor	[pʊə]/[pʊr]	secure	[s(ə/ɪ)ˈkjʊə]/[s(ə/ɪ)ˈkjʊr]
cure	[kjʊə]/[kjʊr]	tourism	[ˈtʊərɪz(ə)m]/[ˈtʊrɪz(ə)m]
mature	[məˈtjʊə]/[məˈtjʊr]	plural	[ˈplʊərəl]/[ˈplʊrəl]

A21. Words with [ɛə]/[ɛr]

their	[ðɛə]/[ðɛr]	prayer	[prɛə]/[prɛr]
heir	[ɛə]/[ɛr]	scarce	[skɛəs]/[skɛrs]
air	[ɛə]/[ɛr]	upstairs	[ʌpˈstɛəz]/[ʌpˈstɛrz]
swear	[swɛə]/[swɛr]	unfair	[ʌnˈfɛə]/[ʌnˈfɛr]
where	[wɛə]/[wɛr]	mayor (RP)	[mɛə]

A23. Words with <o>

worry	[ˈwʌri]/[ˈwɜːri][1]	lorry	[ˈlɒri]/[ˈl(ɔː/ɑː)ri][1]
stomach	[ˈstʌmək]	once	[wʌns]
doctor	[ˈdɒktə]/[ˈdɑːkt(ə)r]	comfort	[ˈkʌmfət]/[ˈkʌmf(ə)rt]
onion	[ˈʌnjən]	oven	[ˈʌv(ə)n]
sponge	[spʌn(d)ʒ]	font	[fɒnt]/[fɑːnt]
front	[frʌnt]	wonder	[ˈwʌndə]/[ˈwʌnd(ə)r]

A24. Silent letters

The silent letters are underlined in each word.

1. should	[ʃʊd]	2. hymn	[hɪm]
3. sword	[sɔːd]/[sɔːrd]	4. hour	[ˈaʊə]/[ˈaʊ(ə)r]
5. psalm	[sɑːm]	6. write	[raɪt]
7. listen	[ˈlɪs(ə)n]	8. debt	[dɛt]
9. gnaw	[nɔː]/[n(ɔː/ɑː)]	10. heir	[ɛə]/[ɛr]
11. folk	[fəʊk]/[foʊk]	12. climb	[klaɪm]
13. build	[bɪld]	14. height	[haɪt]

Note that silent <e>s at the end of words are so frequent (as in *please, breathe, muse, close, write* etc.) that speakers of English pronounce the German car manufacturer *Porsche* as [pɔːʃ]/[pɔːrʃ]. Conversely, many German speakers pronounce *Nike* as [naɪk] in analogy to *Mike*, when, in fact, the English pronunciation is [ˈnaɪki].

---

[1] We have not introduced the sound [i] yet, so don't worry if you got it wrong.

A25. TRAP vs. DRESS

There are many minimal pairs of this kind. Here's a selection: man/men, sad/said, cattle/kettle, shall (SF)/shell, marry/merry (RP), latter/letter, g had (SF)/head, land/lend, tan/ten, bag/beg, pan/pen, lad/le(a)d, and (SF)/end, mass/mess, rant/rent, sacks/sex, sacked/sect, mat/met, lag/leg, salary/celery ... If you find it difficult to distinguish these two vowels, it may also help to remember words like *rectangle* or *academic* that contain both a TRAP and a DRESS vowel.

A26. Inflectional affixes 1 (-s/'s)

	[z]	**[s]**	**[ɪz]/[əz]**
Bob's	[bɒbz]/[bɑːbz]		
churches			[ˈtʃɜːtʃɪz]/[ˈtʃɜːrtʃəz]
hits		[hɪts]	
Sarah's	[ˈsɛərəz]/[ˈsɛrəz]		
buses			[ˈbʌsɪz]/[ˈbʌsəz]
misses			[ˈmɪsɪz]/[ˈmɪsəz]
plays	[plɛɪz]		
breaks		[brɛɪks]	
smashes			[ˈsmæʃɪz]/[ˈsmæʃəz]
Sue's	[suːz]		
knives	[naɪvz]		
lifts		[lɪfts]	
marks		[mɑːks]/[mɑːrks]	
stairs	[stɛəz]/[stɛrz]		
promises			[ˈprɒmɪsɪz]/[ˈprɑːməsəz]
presses			[ˈprɛsɪz]/[prɛsəz]
sings	[sɪŋz]		
helps		[hɛlps]	
climbs	[klaɪmz]		
shows	[ʃəʊz]/[ʃoʊz]		
Smith's		[smɪθs]	
Jones's			[ˈdʒəʊnzɪz]/[ˈdʒoʊnzəz][2]

2 The possessive form of proper nouns with final sibilants is not always entirely regular. Sometimes it is realized by a zero morph so that *Jones's* (or *Jones'*) is pronounced [dʒəʊnz], i.e. like the base form. Sometimes this even seems to be the preferred form, as in *Jesus' disciples*. Common nouns in the plural are regularly inflected without overt (phonetic) marking for possession (e.g. *the parents' duties*).

A27. Inflectional affixes 2 (-ed)

	[d]	[t]	[ɪd]/[əd]
selected			[səˈlɛktɪd]/ [səˈlɛktəd]
needed			[ˈniːdɪd]/[ˈniːdəd]
tran-scribed	[trænˈskraɪbd]		
missed		[mɪst]	
showed	[ʃəʊd]/[ʃoʊd]		
wanted			[ˈwɒntɪd]/ [ˈw(ɑː/ɔː)n(t̬)əd]
promised		[prɒmɪst]/ [prɑːmɪst]	
arranged	[əˈrɛɪndʒd]		
laughed		[lɑːft]/[læft]	
licked		[lɪkt]	
subdued	[səbˈdjuːd]/[səbˈd(j)uːd]		
decided			[d(ɪ/ə)ˈsaɪdɪd]
smoked		[sməʊkt]/[smoʊkt]	

A28. The dental fricatives: [ð] or [θ]?

1. month [mʌnθ] – 2. method [ˈmɛθəd] – 3. thread [θrɛd] – 4. breath [brɛθ] – 5. breathe [briːð] – 6. smooth [smuːð] – 7. with [wɪð]/[wɪθ][3] – 8. either [ˈaɪðə]/[iːðər] – 9. both [bəʊθ]/[boʊθ] – 10. thirteenth [θɜːtiːnθ]/[θɜːrtiːnθ][4] – 11. oath [əʊθ]/[oʊθ] – 12. oaths [əʊ(ðz/θs)]/[oʊ(ðz/θs)] – 13. bath [bɑːθ]/[bæθ] – 14. baths [bɑː(ðz/θs)]/[bæ(ðz/θs)] – 15. width [wɪ(d/t)θ][5] – 16. there [ðɛə]/[ðɛr] – 17. weather [wɛðə]/[wɛðər] – 18. north [nɔːθ]/[nɔːrθ]

---

3 According to Wells (2008), there is a clear preference in Britain for the voiced fricative (85%) and in America for the voiceless one (84%).

4 *Thirteenth* may be stressed on the first or the second syllable, depending on the context, cf. exercise B19.

5 *Width* is one of those very few cases where two final obstruents (plosives or fricatives) may not agree in voice (i.e. be both either voiced or voiceless).

A29. Homophones 1

1. [æd]	a) ad	b) add
2. [baɪ]	a) buy c) bye	b) by
3. [hɪə]/[hir]	a) hear	b) here
4. [haɪ]	a) hi	b) high
5. [nju:]/[nu:]	a) knew	b) new
6. [nəʊ]/[noʊ]	a) know	b) no
7. [rɛɪn]	a) rain	b) reign
8. [sʌn]	a) son	b) sun
9. [sti:l]	a) steal	b) steel
10. [ðɛə]/[ðɛr]	a) their	b) there
11. [mi:t]	a) meat	b) meet
12. [pi:s]	a) peace	b) piece
13. [wi:k]	a) weak	b) week
14. [si:]	a) sea	b) see

A30. Spot the mistake

Below you will find the correct transcription.

1. write [raɪt]	2. finger [ˈfɪŋgə]/[ˈfɪŋg(ə)r]
3. father [ˈfɑ:ðə]/[ˈfɑ:ð(ə)r]	4. honest [ˈɒn(ɪ/ə)st]/[ˈɑ:nəst]
5. kids [kɪdz]	6. biggest [ˈbɪg(ɪ/ə)st]
7. symbol [ˈsɪmbl]	8. know [nəʊ]/[noʊ]
9. word [wɜ:d]/[wɜ:rd]	10. professor [prəˈfɛsə]/[prəˈfɛs(ə)r]
11. just [dʒʌst]	12. ring [rɪŋ]
13. weather [ˈwɛðə]/[ˈwɛð(ə)r]	14. highlights [ˈhaɪlaɪts][6]

6 Note that both symbols of the PRICE diphthong needed correction here.

A32. Medley 2

1. build [bɪld]
2. pure [pjʊə]/[pjʊr]
3. slow [sləʊ]/[sloʊ]
4. teach [tiːtʃ]
5. these [ðiːz]
6. third [θɜːd]/[θɜːrd]
7. throat [θrəʊt]/[θroʊt]
8. trouble [ˈtrʌb(ə)l]
9. warm [wɔːm]/[wɔːrm]
10. thunder [ˈθʌndə]/[ˈθʌnd(ə)r]
11. size [saɪz]
12. rather [ˈrɑːðə]/[ˈrɑð(ə)r]
13. wealth [wɛlθ]
14. suppose [səˈpəʊz]/[səˈpoʊz]

A33. [z] or [s]? (1)

1. use$_{V}$ [juːz] – 2. use$_{N}$ [juːs] – 3. please [pliːz] – 4. result [r(ɪ/ə)ˈzʌlt] – 5. false [f(ɔː/ɒ)ls]/ [f(ɔː/ɑː)ls] – 6. difference [ˈdɪf(ə)rəns] – 7. house [haʊs] – 8. houses [ˈhaʊzɪz] – 9. of course [əv kɔːs]/[əv kɔːrs] – 10. cause [kɔːz]/[k(ɔː/ɑː)z] – 11. his [hɪz] – 12. example [(ɪ/ɛ)(g/k)ˈzɑːmpl]/[(ɪ/ɛ)gˈzæmpl] – 13. Miss [mɪs] – 14. Ms [m(ɪ/ə)z] – 15. excuse$_{N}$ [(ɪ/ɛ)ksˈkjuːs] – 16. excuse$_{V}$ [(ɪ/ɛ)ksˈkjuːz] – 17. close$_{A}$ [kləʊs]/[kloʊs] – 18. close$_{V}$ [kləʊz]/[kloʊz] – 19. loose [luːs] – 20. lose [luːz] – 21. this [ðɪs]

A35. Medley 3

1. worm [wɜːm]/[wɜːrm] – 2. suit [s(j)uːst]/[suːt] – 3. suggest [səˈdʒɛst]/[səgˈdʒɛst] – 4. tradition [trəˈdɪʃ(ə)n] – 5. process [ˈpr(əʊ/ɒ)s(ɛ/ɪ)s]/[ˈpr(ɑː/oʊ)s(ɛ/ə)s] – 6. business [ˈbɪzn(ɪ/ə)s] – 7. tension [ˈtɛnʃ(ə)n] – 8. view [vjuː] – 9. theatre [ˈθ(ɪə/iːə)tə]/[ˈθiːət̬(ə)r] – 10. often [ˈɒf(t)(ə)n]/[ˈɑːf(t)(ə)n] – 11. debt [dɛt] – 12. pressure [ˈprɛʃə]/[ˈprɛʃ(ə)r] – 13. pleasant [ˈplɛz(ə)nt] – 14. tomorrow [t(ə/ʊ)ˈmɒrəʊ]/[t(ə/ʊ)ˈm(ɑː/ɔː)roʊ]

A37. Medley 4

1. primitive [ˈprɪmɪtɪv]/[ˈprɪmɪt̬ɪv] – 2. ruin [ˈruːɪn] – 3. axis [ˈæksɪs] – 4. Switzerland [ˈswɪtsələnd]/[ˈswɪtsərlənd] – 5. strength [strɛŋθ] – 6. examine [(ɪ/ɛ)(g/k)ˈzæmɪn] – 7. equal [ˈiːkw(ə)l] – 8. superficial [s(j)uːpəˈfɪʃ(ə)l]/[suːpərˈfɪʃ(ə)l] – 9. courage [ˈkʌrɪdʒ]/[ˈkɜːrɪdʒ] – 10. transcribe [tr(æ/ɑː)nˈskraɪb] – 11. elegance [ˈɛl(ɪ/ə)g(ə)ns] – 12. universal [jʊn(ɪ/ə)ˈvɜːs(ə)l]/[jʊnəˈvɜːrs(ə)l] – 13. closure [ˈkləʊʒə]/[ˈkloʊʒ(ə)r] – 14. criticism [ˈkrɪtɪsɪz(ə)m]/[ˈkrɪt̬ɪsɪz(ə)m]

Section B

B1. Weak form or strong form?

Sentence	WF/SF/either	Explanation
Would you like some cake?	WF	*Some* is a determiner here.
Yes, I would.	SF	In final position, most words that can have weak forms are strong.
I don't know them.	WF	An exception to the above rule is pronouns, which are usually weak even in final position.
He does it without complaining.	SF	*Does* is used as a full/lexical verb here.
There was no water in that place.	WF	The forms of the lexeme BE are normally weak even when they are full verbs.
You must never forget that.	WF	No need for the strong form.
You mustn't tell any-body.	SF	Auxiliaries with contracted *not* are always strong.
A ride on the suspension railway is a must when you visit Wuppertal.	SF	*Must* is a noun in this case.
What did he say?	WF	No need for the strong form.
We aren't walking much longer, are we?	SF	In question tags, the verb is stressed and the pronoun unstressed.
Some like it hot.	SF	*Some* is a pronoun here.
That was some match yesterday!	SF	If *some* has the meaning 'remark-able' or 'unspecified' (as in *She's married to some politician*), it is usually stressed.
She was walking along the shore.	WF	*Was* is an auxiliary here.
I'm not going to the party because I don't like the music.	SF/WF	The use of SF/WF in *because* is largely dependent on the speaker and the formality of the situation.

I believe that the earth was created.	WF	*That* is a conjunction here.
Look at that man!	SF	*That* is a demonstrative here.
I found the box over there.	SF	Similarly, *there* is a demonstrative.
Where does she live?	WF	No need for the strong form.
'You're not listening!' 'Oh, yes, we are listening!'	SF	To express contrast, the auxiliary is stressed here.
How do you do?	WF, SF	*Do* is an auxiliary in the first and a full verb in the second case.
Can I come in?	SF/WF	Auxiliaries in initial position may be either stressed or unstressed. (Dretzke 2008: 107)

B2. happY, KIT, inflUence or FOOT?

	happY	KIT	inflUence	FOOT
India	☑			
the other thing	☑			
annual			☑	
seminar		☑		
patriot	☑			
easiest	☑			
easiest		☑ (or [ə])		
evacuate			☑	
Vienna	☑			
qualification		☑		
piano	☑			
serious	☑			
population				☑
universe		☑		

valuable			①	①
she (wf)	☑			
funnily		☑		

① The use of inflUence vs. FOOT here depends on whether or not the sound is followed by a schwa and, thus, on the number of syllables used in this word. The more frequent form is probably [ˈvæljʊbl] (with 3 syllables), but [ˈvæljuəbl] (4 syllables) is possible, too, especially in more careful speech. GA prefers [-jəb-].

B3. Homophones 3

1. [aɪl]	a) aisle	b) isle
2. [ˈbɛri]	a) berry	b) bury
3. [sɛnt]	a) cent c) sent	b) scent
4. [pɛə]/[pɛr]	a) pair	b) pear
5. [kjuː]	a) cue c) queue	b) Q
6. [dɪˈzɜːt]/[dɪˈzɜːrt]	a) desert (abandon)	b) dessert
7. [fɛə]/[fɛr]	a) fair	b) fare
8. [fluː]	a) flew	b) flu
9. [ˈaɪdl]	a) idle	b) idol
10. [θruː]	a) threw	b) through
11. [wɔː]/[wɔːr]	a) war	b) wore
12. [djuː]/[duː]	a) dew	b) due
13. [kiː]	a) key	b) (RP) quay
14. [dʒiːnz]	a) genes	b) jeans

B4. [t] or [t̬] (GA)?

	[t]	[t̬]	[(t̬)]
bottle		☑	
active	☑		
atom		☑	
atomic	☑		
bright	☑		
brighter		☑	
Italy		☑	
Italian	☑		
center			☑
linguistics	☑		
stigmat̬ization		☑	
advantage			☑
advantageous	☑		
hit it		☑	
heating		☑	
winter			☑
inter city		☑ (city)	☑ (inter)
capital		☑	
melted	①	①	

① Phoneticians do not agree whether or not /t/ is voiced after /l/ in American English, thus you will find both of these transcriptions.

B5. Stress: Proper nouns and compounds

1. apple pie [ˌæpl ˈpaɪ] – 2. Russian roulette [ˌrʌʃ(ə)n ru:ˈlɛt] – 3. Trafalgar Square [trəˌfælgə ˈskwɛə]/[trəˈfælg(ə)r ˈskwɛr] – 4. New York [ˌnju: ˈjɔ:k]/[ˌnu: ˈjɔ:rk] – 5. Church Road [ˌtʃ3:tʃ ˈrəʊd]/[ˌtʃ3:rtʃ ˈroʊd] – 6. Church Street [ˈtʃ3:tʃ stri:t]/[ˈtʃ3:rtʃ stri:t] – 7. fruit salad [ˌfru:t ˈsæləd] – 8. a fifty-pound note [ə ˌfɪfti paʊnd ˈnəʊt]/[ə ˌfɪfti paʊnd ˈnoʊt] – 9. user-friendly [ˌju:zə ˈfrɛndli]/[ˌju:z(ə)r ˈfrɛndli] – 10. man-made [ˌmæn ˈmɛɪd] – 11. waterproof [ˈwɔ:təpru:f]/[ˈw(ɔ:/ɑ:)t̬(ə)rpru:f] – 12. proof-reader [ˈpru:fri:də]/[ˈpru:fri:d(ə)r] – 13. greenhouse [ˈgri:nhaʊs] – 14. a green house [ə ˌgri:n ˈhaʊs] – 15. the White House[7] – 16. paper bag [ˌpɛɪpə ˈbæg]/[ˌpɛɪp(ə)r ˈbæg] – 17. orange juice [ˈɒr(ɪ/ə)ndʒ dʒu:s]/[ˈ(ɔ:/ɑ:)r(ɪ/ə)ndʒ dʒu:s] – 18. bottom line [ˌbɒtəm ˈlaɪn]/[ˌbɑ:t̬(ə)m ˈlaɪn] – 19. cotton wool [ˌkɒt(ə)n ˈwʊl]/[ˌkɑ:t(ə)n ˈwʊl] – 20. Hyde Park [ˌhaɪd ˈpɑ:k]/[ˌhaɪd ˈpɑ:rk] – 21. English teacher[8]

B6. Mid and high front vowels

1. ancestor [ˈæns(ɛ/ɪ)stə]/[ˈænsɛst(ə)r] – 2. egoist [ˈ(i:/ɛ)gəʊɪst]/[ˈ(i:/ɛ)goʊɪst] – 3. serious [ˈsɪəriəs]/[ˈsiriəs] – 4. Stories [ˈstɔ:riz] – 5. plenary [ˈpl(i:/ɛ)n(ə)ri] – 6. economics [(i:/ɛ)kəˈnɒmɪks]/[(i:/ɛ)kəˈnɑ:mɪks] – 7. captain [ˈkæpt(ɪ/ə/-)n]/[ˈkæpt(ə/-)n] – 8. analysis, analyses [əˈnæləsɪs], [əˈnæləsi:z] – 9. theory [ˈθ(ɪə/i:ə)ri]/[ˈθ(i:ə/ɪ)ri] – 10. really [ˈr(ɪə/i:)li]/[ˈr(i:/i:ə)li] – 11. grenade [gr(ɪ/ə)ˈnɛɪd] – 12. inferiority [ɪnfɪəriˈɒr(ɪ/ə)ti]/[ɪnfiriˈ(ɑ:/ɔ:)rət̬i] – 13. evolution [(i:/ɛ)vəˈl(j)u:ʃ(ə)n]/[ɛvəˈlu:ʃ(ə)n] – 14. Kenya [ˈk(ɛ/i:)njə] – 15. eco-friendly [ˈ(i:/ɛ)kəʊ frɛndli]/[ˈ(ɛ/i:)koʊ frɛndli] – 16. medieval [mɛd(i)ˈi:v(ə)l]/[m(i:/ɛ/ɪ)dˈi:v(ə)l] – 17. discrepancy [dɪsˈkrɛp(ə)nsi] – 18. inherent [ɪnˈh(ɛ/ɪə)r(ə)nt]/[ɪnˈh(i/ɛ)r(ə)nt] – 19. explain [(ɪ/ɛ)ksˈplɛɪn] – 20. explanation [ɛkspləˈnɛɪʃ(ə)n] – 21. breath, breathe [brɛθ] [bri:ð]

7 Interestingly, the stress pattern for this compound can differ between British and American English. While the Americans naturally interpret it as a compound (thus [ˈwaɪt haʊs]), the British alternate between the American pronunciation and an interpretation as Adj + Noun ([ˌwaɪt ˈhaʊs]).

8 The stress pattern here depends, of course, on the meaning. If the teacher teaches English as a subject, the pronunciation is [ˈɪŋglɪʃ ti:tʃə]/[ˈɪŋglɪʃ ti:tʃ(ə)r]; if, however, we refer to an English person who happens to be a teacher (of any subject), we have an Adj + N construction, thus [ˌɪŋglɪʃ ˈti:tʃə]/[ˌɪŋglɪʃ ˈti:tʃ(ə)r].

B7. Academic English 1: Phonetics

[ɪn ðɪs ˈɑ:tɪkl | aɪ w(ɪ/ə/-)l ˈɑ:gju: fə ðə ˈju:s əv ði (ɛpˈsaɪlən/ˈɛpsɪlən) sɪmbl ɪn ðə lɛksɪkl ˈdrɛs sɛt | wɪtʃ ɪnklu:dz ˈwɜ:dz laɪk ˈstɛp | ˈrɛdi | ˈsɛd | ˈʃɛlf (ɛ/ə)t sɛtrə | fər ɑ: ˈpi: || ðə ˈni:d fə ðɪs pɛɪp(ə)r əraɪzɪz frəm ðə fækt ðət ˈmɛni | b(ʌ/ə)t baɪ ˈnəʊ mi:nz ˈɔ:l | ˈdɪkʃ(ə)n(ə)riz ənd lɪŋgwɪstɪk ˈtri:tɪ(z/s)ɪz ɪmplɔɪ ði ˈi: sɪmbl ənd ðət ðɪs sɪmbl ɪz naɪðə ðə məʊst ˈækj(ʊ/ə)r(ə/ɪ)t nɔ:r ə pətɪkj(ʊ/ə)ləli ˈju:sf(ʊ/ə/-)l wʌn | ɪˈspɛʃ(ə)li fə ˈfɒr(ɪ/ə)n lɜ:nəz əv ɪŋglɪʃ || ən (ɪ/ɛ/ə)gzæmɪˈnɛɪʃ(ə)n əv ˈkʌr(ə)nt ˈju:(s/z)ɪdʒ ənd ɪts hɪsˈtɒrɪkl ræʃəˈn(ɑ:/æ)l | ɔ: ˈlæk ðɛərɒf | ɪz fɒləʊd baɪ ɑ:ˈtɪkj(ʊ/ə)lət(ə)ri ənd pəˈsɛp(t)ʃu(ə)l ˈɛvɪdəns fə ðə ˈdrɛs vaʊ(ə)l bi:ɪŋ ˈkləʊs tə ðə ˈθɜ:d ˈkɑ:dɪn(ə)l vaʊ(ə)l | mɔ: ˈpræktɪkl ɑ:gj(ʊ/ə)mənts ənd ə dɪsˈkʌʃn əv ði ˈɪ(ʃ/sj/ʃj)u:z rɛɪzd ||]

[ɪn ðɪs ˈɑ:rt̬ɪkl | aɪ w(ɪ/ə/-)l ˈɑ:rgju: f(ə)r ðə ˈju:s əv ði ˈɛpsəl(ɑ:/ə)n sɪmbl ɪn ðə lɛksɪkl ˈdrɛs sɛt | wɪtʃ ɪnklu:dz ˈwɜ:rdz laɪk ˈstɛp | ˈrɛdi | ˈsɛd | ˈʃɛlf (ɛ/ə)t sɛ(t̬ə/t)rə | f(ə)r ɑ:r ˈpi: || ðə ˈni:d f(ə)r ðɪs pɛɪp(ə)r əraɪzəz frəm ðə fækt ðət ˈmɛni | b(ʌ/ə)t baɪ ˈnoʊ mi:nz ˈɑ:l | ˈdɪkʃənɛriz ənd lɪŋgwɪstɪk ˈtri:t̬əsəz ɪmplɔɪ ði ˈi: sɪmbl ənd ðət ðɪs sɪmbl ɪz ni:ð(ə)r ðə moʊst ˈækj(ʊ/ə)r(ə/ɪ)t nɔ:r ə p(ə)rtɪkjəl(ə)rli ˈju:sf(ʊ/ə/-)l wʌn | ɪˈspɛʃ(ə)li f(ə)r ˈf(ɔ:/ɑ:)rən lɜ:rn(ə)rz əv ɪŋglɪʃ || ən (ɪ/ɛ/ə)gzæmɪˈnɛɪʃ(ə)n əv ˈkɜ:r(ə)nt ˈju:(s/z)ɪdʒ ənd ɪts hɪsˈt(ɑ:/ɔ:)rɪkl ræʃəˈnæl | (ɔ:/ə)r ˈlæk ðɛr(ʌ/ɑ:)v | ɪz fɑ:loʊd baɪ ɑ:rˈtɪkjələtɔ:ri ənd p(ə)rˈsɛp(t)ʃu(ə)l ˈɛvɪdəns f(ə)r ðə ˈdrɛs vaʊ(ə)l bi:ɪŋ ˈkloʊs tə ðə ˈθɜ:rd ˈkɑ:rdɪn(ə)l vaʊ(ə)l | mɔ:r ˈpræktɪkl ɑ:rgj(ʊ/ə)mənts ənd ə dɪsˈkʌʃn əv ði ˈɪʃu:z rɛɪzd ||]

B8. [z] or [s]? (2)

1. useful [ˈju:sf(ʊ/ə)l] – 2. crisis [ˈkraɪsɪs] – 3. crises [ˈkraɪsi:z] – 4. else [ɛls] – 5. release [r(ɪ/ə)ˈli:s] – 6. Glasgow [ˈgl(ɑ:/æ)(z/s)gəʊ]/ [ˈglæ(z/s)goʊ] – 7. because [b(ɪ/ə)ˈk(ɒ/ə)z]/[b(ɪ/ə)ˈk(ʌ/ɔ:/ɑ:)z] – 8. dangerous [ˈdɛɪndʒərəs] – 9. crescent [ˈkrɛ(z/s)(ə)nt]/[ˈkrɛs(ə)nt] – 10. conversation [kɒnvəˈsɛɪʃ(ə)n]/[kɑ:nvərˈsɛɪʃ(ə)n] – 11. paradise [ˈpærədaɪs]/[ˈpɛrədaɪ(s/z)] – 12. absurd [əbˈ(z/s)ɜ:d]/[əbˈ(s/z)ɜ:rd] – 13. abuse$_{V}$ [əˈbju:z] 14. abuse$_{N}$ [əˈbju:s] – 15. series [ˈsɪər(i:/ɪ)z]/[ˈsɪri:z] – 16. newspaper [ˈnju:(z/s)pɛɪpə]/[ˈn(j)u:zpɛɪp(ə)r] – 17. opposite [ˈɒpə(z/s)ɪt]/[ˈɑ:pə(z/s)ɪt] – 18. precise [pr(ɪ/ə)ˈsaɪs] – 19. increase$_{V}$ [ɪnˈkri:s] – 20. increase$_{N}$ [ˈɪnkri:s] – 21. Tuesday [ˈtju:zd(ɛɪ/i)]/[ˈt(j)u:zd(ɛɪ/i)]

B9. Base allomorphy

1. explain, explanation [(ɪ/ɛ)ks'plɛɪn], [ɛksplə'nɛɪʃ(ə)n]
2. explain, explanatory [(ɪ/ɛ)ks'plɛɪn], [(ɪ/ɛ)ks'plænət(ə)ri]/[(ɪ/ɛ)ks'plænətɔːri]
3. know, knowledge [nəʊ]/[noʊ], ['nɒlɪdʒ]/['nɑːlɪdʒ]
4. finite, infinite ['faɪnaɪt], ['ɪnf(ɪ/ə)n(ɪ/ə)t]
5. please, pleasant [pliːz], ['plɛz(ə)nt]
6. pronounce, pronunciation [prə'naʊns], [prənʌnsi'ɛɪʃ(ə)n]
7. prevail, prevalence [prɪ'vɛɪl], ['prɛvələns]
8. admire, admirable [əd'maɪə]/[əd'maɪ(ə)r], ['ædmərəbl]
9. excel, excellent [(ɪ/ɛ)k'sɛl], ['ɛks(ə)lənt]
10. famous, infamous ['fɛɪməs], ['ɪnfəməs] Note that, here, base allomorphy goes hand in hand with a change in meaning: *infamous* does not mean 'not famous' but 'famous for its bad qualities'.
11. south, southern [saʊθ], ['sʌð(ə)n]/['sʌð(ə)rn]
12. manager, managerial ['mæn(ɪ/ə)dʒə]/['mæn(ɪ/ə)dʒ(ə)r], [mænə'dʒɪəriəl]/[mænə'dʒiriəl]
13. prefer, preferable [pr(ɪ/ə)'fɜː]/[pr(ɪ/ə)'fɜːr], ['prɛf(ə)rəbl]
14. suffice, sufficient [sə'faɪs], [sə'fɪʃ(ə)nt]

B11. Low and mid front vowels

1. fairy ['fɛəri]/['fɛri] – 2. ferry ['fɛri][9] – 3. status ['stɛɪtəs]/['stæt̬əs] – 4. capable ['kɛɪpəbl] – 5. carriage ['kærɪdʒ]/['kɛrɪdʒ] – 6. their [ðɛə]/[ðɛr] – 7. axis ['æksɪs] – 8. again [ə'g(ɛ/ɛɪ)n]/[ə'gɛn] – 9. extraordinary [(ɪ/ɛ)k'strɔːd(ɪ/ə/-)n(ə/-)ri]/[(ɪ/ɛ)k'strɔːrd(ə/-)nɛri] – 10. said [sɛd] – 11. sad [sæd] – 12. voluntary ['vɒlənt(-/ə)ri]/['vɑːlɔntɛri] – 13. marry ['mæri]/['mɛri] – 14. Mary ['mɛəri]/['mɛri] – 15. merry ['mɛri] – 16. Karen ['kærən]/['kɛrən] – 17. amoral [(ɛɪ/æ)'mɒr(ə)l]/[ɛɪ'm(ɔː/ɑː)r(ə)l] – 18. necessary ['nɛs(ə/ɪ)s(ə/-/ɛ)ri]/['nɛs(ə/ɪ)sɛri] – 19. ate [(ɛɪ/ɛ)t]/[ɛɪt] – 20. Sarah ['sɛərə]/['sɛrə] – 21. primarily [(')praɪ(')m(ɛə/ɛ)r(ɪ/ə/-)li]/[(')praɪ(')mɛr(ə/-)li]

---

[9] The pronunciation of *fairy* and *ferry* is not exactly the same in GA; still, most transcribers use the same transcription for both.

B12. Text: Through the Looking-Glass

[jə si:m vɛri ˈklɛvər ət (ɪ/ɛ)ksˈplɛɪnɪŋ ˈwɜ:dz | ˈsɜ: | sɛd ˈælɪs||

w(ʊ/ə)d jə ˈkaɪndli ˈtɛl mi ðə ˈmi:nɪŋ əv ðə ˈpəʊ(ɪ/ə)m ˈdʒæbəwɒki ||

lɛts ˈhɪər ɪt | sɛd hʌm(p)ti dʌm(p)ti || aɪ kən (ɪ/ɛ)ksplɛɪn ˈɔ:l ðə ˈpəʊ(ɪ/ə)mz ðət ˈɛvə wər ɪnˈvɛntɪd | ənd ə ˈgʊd ˈmɛni ðət ˈhævnt b(i:/ɪ)n ɪnvɛntɪd dʒəst ˈjɛt ||

ðɪs saʊndɪd vɛri ˈhəʊpf(ʊ/ə)l | səʊ ælɪs r(ɪ/ə)ˈpi:tɪd ðə ˈfɜ:st ˈvɜ:s||

tw(ɒ/ə)z ˈbrɪlɪg | ənd ðə ˈslaɪði ˈtəʊvz

dɪd ˈ(g/dʒ)aɪər ənd ˈ(g/dʒ)ɪmbl ɪn ðə ˈwɛɪb |

ɔ:l ˈmɪmzi wə ðə ˈbɒrə(ʊ)gəʊvz |

ənd ðə ˈməʊm ˈr(æ/ɑ:)(θs/ðz) aʊtˈgrɛɪb ||

ðæts ɪˈnʌf tə b(ɪ/ə)ˈgɪn wɪð | hʌm(p)ti ɪntəˈrʌptɪd || ð(ɛ)ər ə ˈplɛnti əv ˈhɑ:d ˈwɜ:dz ðɛə || ˈbrɪlɪg mi:nz ˈfɔ:rə ˈklɒk ɪn ði ɑ:ftəˈnu:n | ðə ˈtaɪm wɛn jə b(ɪ/ə)ˈgɪn ˈbrɔɪlɪŋ ˈθɪŋz fə ˈdɪnə ||

ðætl ˈdu: vɛri ˈwɛl | sɛd ælɪs | ənd ˈslaɪði ||

wɛl | ˈslaɪði mi:nz ˈlaɪð ənd ˈslaɪmi || ˈlaɪð ɪz ðə sɛɪm əz ˈæktɪv || jə si: | ɪts laɪk ə pɔ:tˈmæntəʊ | ð(ɛ/ə)r ə ˈtu: ˈmi:nɪŋz pækt ˈʌp ɪntə ˈwʌn ˈwɜ:d ||]

[jə si:m vɛri ˈklɛvər ət (ɪ/ɛ)ksˈplɛɪnɪŋ ˈwɜ:rdz | ˈsɜ:r | sɛd ˈælɪs||

w(ʊ/ə)d jə ˈkaɪndli ˈtɛl mi ðə ˈmi:nɪŋ əv ðə ˈpoʊəm ˈdʒæb(ə)rwɑ:ki ||

lɛts ˈhir ɪt | sɛd hʌm(p)ti dʌm(p)ti || aɪ kən (ɪ/ɛ)ksplɛɪn ˈ(ɑ:/ɔ:)l ðə ˈpoʊəmz ðət ˈɛvər wər ɪnˈvɛn(t̬)əd | ənd ə ˈgʊd ˈmɛni ðət ˈhævnt bɪn ɪnvɛn(t̬)əd dʒəst ˈjɛt ||

ðɪs saʊndəd vɛri ˈhoʊpf(ʊ/ə)l | soʊ ælɪs r(ɪ/ə)ˈpi:t̬əd ðə ˈfɜ:rst ˈvɜ:rs||

tw(ʌ/ɑ:/ə)z ˈbrɪlɪg | ənd ðə ˈslaɪði ˈtoʊvz

dɪd ˈdʒaɪ(ə)r ənd ˈgɪmbl ɪn ðə ˈwɛɪb |

(ɔ:/ɑ:)l ˈmɪmzi wər ðə ˈb(ɑ:/ɔ:)r(ə/oʊ)goʊvz |

ənd ðə ˈmoʊm ˈr(æ/ɑ:)(θs/ðz) aʊtˈgrɛɪb ||

ðæts ɪˈnʌf tə b(ɪ/ə)ˈgɪn wɪθ | hʌm(p)ti ɪntəˈrʌptəd || ðɛr ə ˈplɛn(t̬)i əv ˈhɑ:rd ˈwɜ:rdz ðɛr || ˈbrɪlɪg mi:nz ˈfɔ:rə ˈklɑ:k ɪn ði æftərˈnu:n | ðə ˈtaɪm wɛn jə b(ɪ/ə)ˈgɪn ˈbrɔɪlɪŋ ˈθɪŋz fər ˈdɪnər ||

ðætl ˈdu: vɛri ˈwɛl | sɛd ælɪs | ənd ˈslaɪði ||

wɛl | ˈslaɪði mi:nz ˈlaɪð ənd ˈslaɪmi || ˈlaɪð ɪz ðə sɛɪm əz ˈæktɪv || jə si: | ɪts laɪk ə pɔ:rtˈmæntoʊ | ð(ɛ/ə)r ə ˈtu: ˈmi:nɪŋz pækt ˈʌp ɪntə ˈwʌn ˈwɜ:rd ||]

B13. The prefix *re-*

	[riː-]	[ri-]	[r(ɪ/ə)-]
release			[r(ɪ/ə)ˈliːs]
reaction		[riˈækʃ(ə)n]	
re-read	[ˌriːˈriːd]		
recount	[ˌriːˈkaʊnt]①		[r(ɪ/ə)ˈkaʊnt]①
return			[r(ɪ/ə)ˈtɜːn]/ [r(ɪ/ə)ˈtɜːrn]
rebuild	[ˌriːˈbɪld]		
reiterate		[riˈɪt(ə)reɪt]/ [riˈɪt̬(ə)reɪt]	
re-import	[ˌriɪmˈpɔːt]/ [ˌriɪmˈpɔːrt]		
revival			[r(ɪ/ə)ˈvaɪv(ə)l]
require			[r(ɪ/ə)ˈkwaɪə]/ [r(ɪ/ə)ˈkwaɪər]
recycle	[ˌriːˈsaɪkl]②		
reusable	[ˌriːˈjuːzəb(ə)l]		
remove			[r(ɪ/ə)ˈmuːv]
reduce			[r(ɪ/ə)ˈdjuːs]/ [r(ɪ/ə)ˈd(j)uːs]
reflect			[r(ɪ/ə)ˈflɛkt]
reunion	[ˌriːˈjuːniən]/ [ˌriːˈjʊnjən]		
recover	[ˌriːˈkʌvə]/ [ˌriːˈkʌv(ə)r]①		[r(ɪ/ə)ˈkʌvə]/ [r(ɪ/ə)ˈkʌv(ə)r]①
recharge$_V$	[ˌriːˈtʃɑːdʒ]/ [ˌriːˈtʃɑːrdʒ]		

repay	[ˌriːˈpɛɪ]①		[r(ɪ/ə)ˈpɛɪ]①
reply			[r(ɪ/ə)ˈplaɪ]
resign			[r(ɪ/ə)ˈzaɪn]
reform	[ˌriːˈfɔːm]/ [ˌriːˈfɔːrm]①		[r(ɪ/ə)ˈfɔːm]/ [r(ɪ/ə)ˈfɔːrm]①

① If the *re-* in *recount*, *recover* and *reform* means *count*, *cover* or *form again*, the prefix receives secondary stress and is pronounced [ˌriː]. If, however, the meaning of the base changes (even slightly), thus if *recount* means *tell a story*, *recover* means *get better* and *reform* means *make better*, the prefix is pronounced [r(ɪ/ə)].

② *Cycle* (as a verb) has two different meanings: in Britain, it usually means going by bicycle. In America, however, it can refer to going through a series of events. *Recycle*, of course, is related to the second meaning.

B14. Medley 5

1. thesis [ˈθiːsɪs] – 2. vehicle [ˈviː(ɪ/ə)kl]/[ˈviː(ək/hɪk)l] – 3. veggie burger [ˈvɛdʒibɜːgə]/[ˈvɛdʒibɜːrg(ə)r] – 4. vary [ˈvɛəri]/[ˈv(ɛ/æ)ri] – 5. ache [ɛɪk] – 6. appropriate$_A$ [əˈprəʊpriət]/[əˈproʊpriət] – 7. bowl [bəʊl]/[boʊl] – 8. bury [ˈbɛri] – 9. genuine [ˈdʒɛnjuɪn]/ [ˈdʒɛnju(aɪ/ɪ)n] – 10. euro [ˈjʊərəʊ]/[ˈjʊroʊ] – 11. translate [træn(s/z)ˈlɛɪt] – 12. rationality [ræʃ(ə)ˈnæl(ə/ɪ)ti]/[ræʃ(ə)ˈnælət̬i] – 13. human [ˈhjuːmən] – 14. guerrilla [gəˈrɪlə] – 15. positive [ˈpɒz(ə/ɪ/-)tɪv]/[ˈpɑːz(ət̬/t)ɪv] – 16. exciting [(ɪ/ɛ)kˈsaɪtɪŋ]/[(ɪ/ɛ)kˈsaɪt̬ɪŋ] – 17. actually [ˈæktʃ(u)əli] – 18. breathes [briːðz] – 19. senior [ˈsiːn(j/i)ə]/[ˈsiːnjər] – 20. preferable [ˈprɛf(ə)rəb(ə)l] – 21. iron [ˈaɪən]/[ˈaɪ(ə)rn]

B15. Low vowels

1. worry [ˈwʌri]/[ˈwɜːri] – 2. want [wɒnt]/[w(ɑː/ɔː)nt] – 3. front [frʌnt] – 4. bother [ˈbɒðə]/[ˈbɑːðər] – 5. body [ˈbɒdi]/[ˈbɑːdi] – 6. gone [gɒn]/[g(ɔː/ɑː)n] – 7. drastic [ˈdr(æ/ɑː)stɪk]/[ˈdræstɪk] – 8. yacht [jɒt]/[jɔːt] – 9. frontier [(ˈ)fr(ʌ/ɒ)n(ˈ)tɪə]/ [fr(ʌ/ɑː)nˈtir] – 10. aunt [ɑːnt]/[(æ/ɑː)nt] – 11. comfort [ˈkʌmfət]/[ˈkʌmfərt] – 12. fathom [ˈfæð(ə)m] – 13. chance [tʃɑːns]/[tʃæns] – 14. thorough [ˈθʌrə]/[ˈθɜːroʊ] – 15. common [ˈkɒmən]/[ˈkɑːmən] – 16. transitive [ˈtr(æ/ɑː)n(s/z)(ɪ/ə)tɪv]/ [ˈtræn(s/z)ət̬ɪv] – 17. Glasgow [ˈgl(ɑː/æ)(s/z)gəʊ]/[ˈglæ(s/z)goʊ] – 18. draught [drɑːft]/[dræft] – 19. won [wʌn] – 20. graph [gr(ɑː/æ)f]/[græf] – 21. accomplish [əˈk(ʌ/ɒ)mplɪʃ]/[əˈk(ɑː/ʌ)mplɪʃ]

B16. Alternative pronunciations

Below you will find the actual percentages of preference. The figures are taken from Wells 2008 and are based on five opinion polls carried out between 1988 and 2007. The most frequently used form is always listed first. Sometimes, however, the fact that a form is used more frequently does not mean that this will also be so in the future since the percentages may vary between age groups, too. For more details, consult the LPD.

1. sure (RP)		a) [ʃʊə] 54%	b) [ʃɔː] 46%
2. data	RP:	a) [ˈdɛɪtə] 92%	b) [ˈdɑːtə] 6%
	GA:	a) [ˈdɛɪt̬ə] 64%	b) [ˈdæt̬ə] 35%
3. sorry (GA)		a) [ˈsɑːri] 68%	b) [ˈsɔːri] 32%
4. schedule (RP)		a) [ˈʃɛd(j/ʒ)uːl] 70%	b) [ˈskɛd(j/ʒ)uːl] 30%
		c) [ˈ(ʃ/sk)ɛdjuːl] 79%	d) [ˈ(ʃ/sk)ɛdʒuːl] 21%
		Wells does not differentiate any further here.	
5. migraine (RP)		a) [ˈmiːgrɛɪn] 61%	b) [ˈmaɪgrɛɪn] 39%
6. envelope (RP)		a) [ˈɛnvələʊp] 78%	b) [ˈɒnvələʊp] 22%
7. garage	RP:	a) [ˈgærɑː(d)ʒ] 56% c) [gəˈrɑː(d)ʒ] 6%	b) [ˈgærɪdʒ] 38%
	GA:	a) [gəˈrɑːʒ] 52%	b) [gəˈrɑːdʒ] 48%
8. patronise (GA)		a) [ˈpɛɪtrənaɪz] 64%	b) [ˈpætrənaɪz] 36%
9. either	RP:	a) [ˈaɪðə] 87%	b) [ˈiːðə] 13%
	GA:	a) [ˈiːð(ə)r] 84%	b) [ˈaɪð(ə)r] 16%
10. issue (RP)		a) [ˈɪʃuː] 49% c) [ˈɪʃjuː] 21%	b) [ˈɪsjuː] 30%
11. sandwich (RP)		a) [ˈsæn(d)wɪdʒ] 53%	b) [ˈsæn(d)wɪtʃ] 47%
12. cigarette	RP:	a) [ˌsɪgəˈrɛt] 85%	b) [ˈsɪgərɛt] 15%
	GA:	a) [ˈsɪgərɛt] 65%	b) [ˌsɪgəˈrɛt] 35%
13. citizen (GA)		a) [ˈsɪt̬əz(ə)n] 64%	b) [ˈsɪt̬əs(ə)n] 36%
14. ate (RP)		a) [ɛt] 55%	b) [ɛɪt] 45%

B17. Low and mid back vowels

1. also [ˈɔːlsəʊ]/[ˈ(ɔː/ɑː)lsoʊ] – 2. sausage [ˈsɒsɪdʒ]/[ˈs(ɑː/ɔː)sɪdʒ] – 3. altogether [ɔːltəˈgɛðə]/[(ɔː/ɑːltəˈgɛðər) – 4. stroll [strəʊl]/[stroʊl] – 5. because [b(ɪ/ə)ˈk(ɒ/ə)z]/[b(ɪ/ə)ˈk(ʌ/ɔː/ɑː/ə)z][10] – 6. cause [kɔːz]/[kɔː/ɑːz] – 7. erotic [ɪˈrɒtɪk]/[ɪˈrɑːt̬ɪk] – 8. rhotic [ˈrəʊtɪk]/[ˈroʊt̬ɪk] – 9. halt [h(ɔː/ɒ)lt]/[h(ɔː/ɑː)lt] – 10. false [f(ɔː/ɒ)ls]/[f(ɑː/ɔː)ls] – 11. often [ˈɒf(t)(ə)n]/[ˈ(ɑː/ɔː)f(t)(ə)n] – 12. enforce [(ɪ/ɛ)nˈfɔːs]/[(ɛ/ɪ)nˈfɔːrs] – 13. job [dʒɒb]/[dʒɑːb] – 14. exalt [(ɪ/ɛ)(gˈz/kˈs)(ɔː/ɒ)lt]/[(ɪ/ɛ)gˈzɑːlt] – 15. exaltation [ɛ(gz/ks)(ɔː/ɒ)lˈtɛɪʃ(ə)n]/[ɛ(gz/ks)(ɔː/ɑː)lˈtɛɪʃ(ə)n] – 16. wasp [wɒsp]/[wɑːsp] – 17. project$_N$ [ˈprɒdʒ(ɛ/ɪ)kt]/ [ˈprɑːdʒ(ɛ/ɪ)kt] – 18. response [r(ɪ/ə)sˈpɒns]/[r(ɪ/ə)sˈpɑːns] – 19. involve [ɪnˈvɒlv]/[ɪnˈv(ɑː/ɔː)lv] – 20. know [nəʊ]/[noʊ] – 21. knowledge [ˈnɒlɪdʒ]/ [ˈnɑːlɪdʒ]

B19. Stress 2: Stress shift

1. [θɜːˈtiːn]/[θɜːrˈtiːn]	2. [ˈθɜːtiːn]/[ˈθɜːrt̬iːn]
3. [ˈtʃaɪniːz]	4. [tʃaɪˈniːz]
5. [ɪnˈkriːs]	6. [ˈɪnkriːs]
7. [ˈriːfɪl]	8. [riːˈfɪl]
9. [ɑːftəˈnuːn]/[æft(ə)rˈnuːn]	10. [ˈɑːftənuːn]/[ˈæft(ə)rnuːn]
11. [səsˈpɛkt]	12. [ˈsʌspɛkt]
13. [ˈsɜːvɛɪ]/[ˈsɜːrvɛɪ]	14. [səˈvɛɪ]/[sɜːrˈvɛɪ]
15. [haɪd ˈpɑːk]/[haɪd ˈpɑːrk]	16. [ˈhaɪd pɑːk]/[ˈhaɪd pɑːrk]
17. [trænsˈfɜː]/[trænsˈfɜːr]	18. [ˈtrænsfɜː]/[ˈtrænsfɜːr]
19. [nɛkst ˈdɔː]/[nɛkst ˈdɔːr]	20. [ˈnɛkst dɔː]/[ˈnɛkst dɔːr]
21. [ˈbɜːlɪn]/[ˈbɜːrlɪn], [bɜːˈlɪn]/[bɜːrˈlɪn]	

[10] The word *because* is quite unusual in that it can (as an alternative) have a stressed schwa.

B20. High back vowels

1. jewel ['dʒu:əl] – 2. Europe ['jʊərəp]/['jʊrəp] – 3. fluent ['flu:ənt] – 4. truant ['tru:ənt] – 5. urine ['jʊərɪn]/['jʊr(ɪ/ə)n] – 6. sure [ʃʊə]/[ʃʊr] – 7. valuable ['vælj(ʊ/ə/uə)bl]/['væljəbl] – 8. crusade [kru:'sɛɪd] – 9. July [dʒ(ʊ/ə/u:)'laɪ] – 10. continue [kən'tɪnj(u:/u)] – 11. continual [kən'tɪnjuəl] – 12. continuous [kən'tɪnjuəs] – 13. wool [wʊl] – 14. poor [pʊə]/[pʊr] – 15. during ['djʊərɪŋ]/['d(j)(ɜ:/ʊ)rɪŋ] – 16. dual ['dj(u:ə/ʊə)l]/['d(j)u:əl] – 17. duel ['dju:əl]/['d(j)u:əl] – 18. good [gʊd] – 19. tourism ['tʊərɪz(ə)m]/['tʊrɪz(ə)m] – 20. plural ['plʊər(ə)l]/['plʊr(ə)l] – 21. your (SF) [jʊə]/[jʊr]

If you use RP as your reference variety and you find it difficult to tell the diphthong [ʊə] from the vowel combination [u:ə], there are two strategies that may help you: first, and probably more importantly, you will find that for basically all [ʊə] forms, there is an alternative [ɔ:] pronunciation. Thus, for example, *during* might also be pronounced ['djɔ:rɪŋ] in RP whereas *duel* cannot be pronounced *[djɔ:l]. Secondly, there is always a syllable boundary between [u:] and schwa, whereas [ʊə] forms a centring diphthong and thus belongs to the same syllable. In the word *truant*, for example, the schwa belongs to the second syllable, in the word *urine* to the first.

B21. Medley 6

1. journal ['dʒɜ:n(ə)l]/['dʒɜ:rn(ə)l] – 2. didactic [d(ɪ/aɪ)'dæktɪk] – 3. tangible ['tændʒ(ɪ/ə)bl]/['tændʒəbl] – 4. analysis [ə'næl(ɪ/ə)sɪs] – 5. vacuum ['vækj(uə/u:/ʊ)m] – 6. paradigm ['pærədaɪm]/['pɛrədaɪm] – 7. suite [swi:t] – 8. whereas [w(ɛ)ər'æz]/[wɛr'æz] – 9. nee, née [nɛɪ] – 10. brooch [brəʊtʃ]/[br(oʊ/u:)tʃ] – 11. attorney [ə'tɜ:ni]/[ə'tɜ:rni] – 12. grievous [gri:vəs] – 13. fugitive ['fju:dʒ(ə/ɪ)tɪv]/['fju:dʒəṱɪv] – 14. jewellery ['dʒ(u:ə/u:/ʊə)lri] – 15. stigmati(s/z)ation [stɪgm(ə/ɪ)taɪ'zɛɪʃ(ə)n]/[stɪgməṱə'zɛɪʃ(ə)n] – 16. occur [ə'kɜ:]/[ə'kɜ:r] – 17. explanatory [(ɪ/ɛ)ks'plænətri]/[(ɪ/ɛ)ks'plænətɔ:ri] – 18. psycholinguistics [saɪkəʊlɪŋ'gwɪstɪks]/[saɪkoʊlɪŋ'gwɪstɪks] – 19. atheistic [ɛɪθi'ɪstɪk] – 20. au pair [əʊ 'pɛə]/[oʊ 'pɛr] – 21. advantageous [ædv(ə/æ)n'tɛɪdʒəs]

B22. Funny you should say this: Homophone jokes 1

1. Why is six afraid of seven? Because seven eight/ate nine.
2. What's black and white and read/red all over? A newspaper.
3. What do you call a deer with no eyes? No-eyed deer/No idea!
4. A man is locked in a prison cell with no doors or windows. How does he get out? He rubs his hands until they're sore. He cuts the table in half with the saw. Two halves make a whole. He puts the hole in the wall and climbs out.

'Sore' and 'saw' are, of course, homophones in RP, but not in GA.

B23. Text: Limericks

RP

1. [wʌn ˈsætəd(eɪ/i) ˈmɔːnɪŋ ət ˈθriː |
ə ˈtʃiːzmʌŋgəz ˈʃɒp ɪn pəˈriː ||
kəˈlæpstə ðə ˈgraʊnd |
wɪð ə ˈθʌndərəs ˈsaʊnd |
liːvɪŋ ˈəʊnli ə ˈpaɪl əv də ˈbriː ||]

2. [ɪts ə ˈfeɪvərət ˈprɒdʒ(ɛ/ɪ)kt əv ˈmaɪn |
ə njuː ˈvæljuː əv ˈpaɪ tu əˈsaɪn ||
aɪ w(ə/ʊ)d ˈfɪks ɪt ət ˈθriː |
fər ɪts ˈsɪmplə jə ˈsiː |
ðən ˈθriː pɔɪnt ˈwʌn fɔː wʌn faɪv ˈnaɪn ||]

GA

1. [wʌn ˈsæt̬(ə)rd(eɪ/i) ˈmɔːrnɪŋ ət ˈθriː |
ə ˈtʃiːzm(ʌ/ɑː)ŋg(ə)rz ˈʃɑːp ɪn pəˈriː |
kəˈlæpstə ðə ˈgraʊnd |
wɪθ ə ˈθʌndərəs ˈsaʊnd |
liːvɪŋ ˈoʊnli ə ˈpaɪl əv də ˈbriː ||]

2. [ɪts ə ˈfeɪvərət ˈprɑːdʒ(ɛ/ɪ)kt əv ˈmaɪn |
ə n(j)uː ˈvæljuː əv ˈpaɪ t(u/ə) əˈsaɪn |
aɪ w(ə/ʊ)d ˈfɪks ɪt ət ˈθriː |
fər ɪts ˈsɪmpl(ə)r jə ˈsiː |
ðən ˈθriː pɔɪnt ˈwʌn fɔːr wʌn faɪv ˈnaɪn ||]

B24. Frequently mispronounced words 1

1. conversation [kɒnvəˈseɪʃn]/[kɑːnv(ə)rˈseɪʃn] – 2. marriage [ˈmærɪdʒ]/[ˈmɛrɪdʒ] – 3. pressure [ˈprɛʃə]/[ˈprɛʃər] – 4. indigenous [ɪnˈdɪdʒ(ɪ/ə)nəs] – 5. Caribbean [(kær(ə/ɪ)ˈbiːən/kəˈrɪbiən)]/[(kɛr(ə/ɪ)ˈbiːən/kəˈrɪbiən)] – 6. prestigious [pr(ɛ/ə/ɪ)sˈtɪdʒəs]/[pr(ɛ/ə/ɪ)sˈt(iː/ɪ)dʒɛs] – 7. separate$_A$ [ˈsɛp(ə)r(ə/ɪ)t] – 8. towards [t(ə/ʊ/-)ˈwɔːdz]/[t(w)(ɔː/oʊ)rdz] – 9. condolence [kənˈdəʊləns]/ [kənˈdoʊləns] – 10. interaction [ɪntə(r)ˈækʃn]/[ɪn(t̬)(ə)rˈækʃn] – 11. record$_V$ [r(ɪ/ə)ˈkɔːd]/[rɪˈkɔːrd] – 12. legislate [ˈlɛdʒɪsleɪt] – 13. determine [d(ɪ/ə)ˈtɜːmɪn]/[d(ɪ/ə)ˈtɜːrmɪn] – 14. identify [aɪˈdɛnt(ɪ/ə)faɪ]/[aɪˈdɛn(t̬)(ɪ/ə)faɪ] – 15. deviate$_V$ [ˈdiːvieɪt] – 16. Japanese [dʒæpəˈniːz] – 17. Arabic [ˈærəbɪk]/[ˈɛrəbɪk] – 18. variable [ˈvɛəriəbl]/ [ˈv(ɛ/æ)riəbl] – 19. opposite [ˈɒpə(s/z)ɪt]/[ˈɑːpə(s/z)ɪt] – 20. bilingual [baɪˈlɪŋg(wə/juə)l] – 21. apparent [əˈp(æ/ɛə)rənt]/[əˈpɛrənt]

B25. Text: Jokes

RP

[ə ˈprɛgnənt ˈwʊmən frəm ˈdʌblɪn wəz ɪnˈvɒlvd ɪn ə ˈtɛrɪbl ˈkɑːr æksɪdənt | ənd ˈwɛnt ɪntu ə ˈdiːp ˈkəʊmə ‖ ɑːftə nɪəli ˈsɪks ˈmʌnθs | ʃi weɪks ˈʌp | ənd ˈsiːz ðət ʃi ɪz nəʊ lɒŋgə ˈprɛgnənt ‖ ˈfræntɪk(ə)li | ʃi ɑːsks ðə ˈdɒktər əbaʊt hə ˈbeɪbi ‖ ðə ˈdɒktə rɪˈplaɪz | ˈmæm | jə hæd ˈtwɪnz ‖ ə ˈbɔɪ ənd ə ˈgɜːl ‖ ðə ˈbeɪbiz ə ˈfaɪn ‖ jə ˈbrʌðə frəm ˈgɔːlweɪ keɪm ˈɪn ənd ˈneɪmd ðəm ‖ ðə ˈwʊmən ˈθɪŋks tə həˈsɛlf | ˈəʊ ˈnəʊ | ˈnɒt maɪ ˈbrʌðə ‖ hiz ə ˈkluːl(ə/ɪ)s ˈɪdiət ‖ (ɪ/ɛ)ksˈpɛktɪŋ ðə ˈwɜːst | ʃi ɑːsks ðə ˈdɒktə | ˈwɛl | ˈwɒts maɪ ˈdɔːtəz ˈneɪm ‖ d(ə/ɛ)ˈniː(z/s) | sɛz ðə ˈdɒktə ‖ ðə njuː ˈmʌðər ɪz sʌmwɒt r(ɪ/ə)ˈliːvd ‖ ˈwaʊ | ˈðæts nɒt ə ˈbæd ˈneɪm ‖ aɪ ˈlaɪk ɪt ‖ ˈðɛn ʃi ˈɑːsks | ˈwɒts ðə ˈbɔɪz ˈneɪm ‖ dəˈnɛ(f/v)juː ‖] ①

[ən ˈɪŋglɪʃmən | ən ˈaɪrɪʃmən ənd ə ˈskɒtsmən wɛnt ɪntu ə ˈpʌb fər ə ˈpaɪnt ‖ ɑːftə biːɪŋ ˈsɜːvd | ə ˈflaɪ ˈlændɪd ɪn iːtʃ əv ðə ˈbɪəz ənd gɒt ˈkɔːt ɪn ðə ˈkriːmi ˈhɛdz ‖ ði ˈɪŋglɪʃmən ˈpʊʃt hɪz ˈpaɪnt əˈweɪ frəm hɪm ɪn dɪsˈgʌst | ənd prəˈsiːdɪd tu ˈɔːdər ənʌðə wʌn ‖ ði ˈaɪrɪʃmən sɪmpli ˈfɪʃt ði əˈfɛndɪŋ ˈflaɪ ˈaʊt wɪð hɪz ˈfɪŋgər ənd prəˈsiːdɪd tə ˈdrɪŋk hɪz ˈpaɪnt əz ɪf ˈnʌθɪŋ həd ˈhæp(ə)nd ‖ ðə ˈskɒtsmən | ˈaɪz ˈwaɪd wɪð ˈæŋgə | ˈgræbd ðə ˈflaɪ ənd ˈhɛld ɪt əʊvə hɪz ˈbɪə | ˈʃaʊtɪŋ | ˈspɪt ɪt ˈaʊt ‖ ˈspɪt ɪt ˈaʊt‖] ②

GA

[ə ˈprɛgnənt ˈwʊmən fr(ə)m ˈdʌblɪn wəz ɪnˈvɑːlvd ɪn ə ˈtɛrɪbl ˈkɑːr æksɪdənt | ənd ˈwɛn(t̬) ɪntu ə ˈdiːp ˈkoʊmə ‖ æftər nirli ˈsɪks ˈmʌnθs | ʃi weɪks ˈʌp | ənd ˈsiːz ðət ʃi ɪz noʊ l(ɔː/ɑː)ŋgər ˈprɛgnənt ‖ ˈfræn(t̬)ɪk(ə)li | ʃi æsks ðə ˈdɑːkt(ə)r əbaʊt hər ˈbeɪbi ‖ ðə ˈdɑːkt(ə)r rɪˈplaɪz | ˈmæm | jə hæd ˈtwɪnz ‖ ə ˈbɔɪ ənd ə ˈgɜːrl ‖ ðə ˈbeɪbiz ər

ˈfaɪn ‖ jər ˈbrʌð(ə)r frəm ˈg(ɑː/ɔː)lweɪ keɪm ˈɪn ənd ˈneɪmd ðəm ‖ ðə ˈwʊmən ˈθɪŋks tə hərˈsɛlf | ˈoʊ ˈnoʊ | ˈnɑːt maɪ ˈbrʌð(ə)r ‖ hiz ə ˈkluːl(ə/ɪ)s ˈɪdiət ‖ (ɪ/ɛ)ksˈpɛktɪŋ ðə ˈwɜːrst | ʃi æsks ðə ˈdɑːkt(ə)r | ˈwɛl | ˈwɑːts maɪ ˈdɔːt̬(ə)rz ˈneɪm ‖ d(ə/ɛ)ˈniː(z/s) | sɛz ðə ˈdɑːkt(ə)r ‖ ðə nuː ˈmʌð(ə)r ɪz sʌmw(ʌ/ɑː)t r(ɪ/ə)ˈliːvd ‖ ˈwaʊ | ˈðæts nɑːt ə ˈbæd ˈneɪm ‖ aɪ ˈlaɪk ɪt ‖ ˈðɛn ʃi ˈæsks | ˈwɑːts ðə ˈbɔɪz ˈneɪm ‖ dəˈnɛ(f/v)juː ‖] ①

[ən ˈɪŋglɪʃmən | ən ˈaɪrɪʃmən ənd ə ˈskɑːtsmən wɛn(t̬) ɪntu ə ˈpʌb fər ə ˈpaɪnt ‖ æftər biːɪŋ ˈsɜːrvd | ə ˈflaɪ ˈlændəd ɪn iːtʃ əv ðə ˈbirz ənd gɑːt ˈkɑːt ɪn ðə ˈkriːmi ˈhɛdz ‖ ði ˈɪŋglɪʃmən ˈpʊʃt hɪz ˈpaɪnt əˈweɪ frəm hɪm ɪn dɪsˈgʌst | ənd prəˈsiːdəd tə ˈɔːrd(ə)r ənʌð(ə)r wʌn ‖ ði ˈaɪrɪʃmən sɪmpli ˈfɪʃt ði əˈfɛndɪŋ ˈflaɪ ˈaʊt wɪθ hɪz ˈfɪŋg(ə)r ənd prəˈsiːdəd tə ˈdrɪŋk hɪz ˈpaɪnt əz ɪf ˈnʌθɪŋ həd ˈhæp(ə)nd ‖ ðə ˈskɑːtsmən | ˈaɪz ˈwaɪd wɪθ ˈæŋg(ə)r | ˈgræbd ðə ˈflaɪ ənd ˈhɛld ɪt oʊv(ə)r hɪz ˈbir | ˈʃaʊt̬ɪŋ | ˈspɪt̬ ɪt̬ ˈaʊt ‖ ˈspɪt̬ ɪt̬ ˈaʊt‖] ②

① This joke is sometimes also placed in other localities. The point is that the brother's accent has to be one that replaces the dental fricatives by plosives. In Ireland, speakers from all over the Republic may use alveolar [t, d] or dental [t̪, d̪] plosives where RP employs [θ, ð], but since Dublin is the capital as well as the largest and the most cosmopolitan city, joke tellers feel that its inhabitants speak the variety that is closest to international standards. Galway, on the other hand, lies in the west of Ireland and represents a more rural community with speakers of broader and – for many people – less socially desirable dialects.

② Depending on their disposition, some joke tellers reverse the roles of the Scotsman and the Irishman.

B26. RP vs. GA

1. address$_N$ [əˈdrɛs]/[ˈædrɛs] – 2. figure [ˈfɪgə]/[ˈfɪgj(ə/ʊ/-)r] – 3. schedule [ˈʃɛdjuːl]/ [ˈskɛdʒuːl] – 4. thorough [ˈθʌrə]/[ˈθɜːroʊ] – 5. mobile [ˈməʊbaɪl]/[ˈmoʊbl] – 6. vitamin [ˈvɪtəmɪn]/[ˈvaɪt̬əmɪn] – 7. laboratory [ləˈbɒrət(ə)ri]/[ˈlæbrətɔːri] – 8. either [ˈaɪðə]/[ˈiːð(ə)r] – 9. progress$_N$ [ˈprəʊgrɛs]/[ˈprɑːgrɛs] – 10. potato [pəˈteɪtəʊ]/[pəˈteɪt̬oʊ] – 11. vase [vɑːz]/[veɪ(s/z)] – 12. Z (as letter) [zɛd]/[ziː] – 13. semi- [sɛmi]/[sɛmaɪ] – 14. leisure [ˈlɛʒə]/[ˈliːʒ(ə)r] – 15. clerk [klɑːk]/[klɜːrk] – 16. inquiry [ɪnˈkwaɪ(ə)ri]/[ˈɪnkwəri] – 17. buoy [bɔɪ]/[ˈbuːi] – 18. rather [ˈrɑːðə]/[ˈræð(ə)r] – 19. shone [ʃɒn]/[ʃoʊn] – 20. secretary [ˈsɛkrət(ə)ri]/[ˈsɛkrətɛri] – 21. suggest [səˈdʒɛst]/[səgˈdʒɛst]

B28. Text: Psalm 23

RP

1 [ðə ˈlɔːd ɪz maɪ ˈʃɛpəd |
ˈaɪ ˈʃæl ˈnɒt ˈwɒnt ||

2 hi ˈmɛɪks mi tə laɪ ˈdaʊn ɪn ˈgriːn ˈpɑːstʃəz ||
hi ˈliːdz mi bɪsaɪd ðə ˈstɪl ˈwɔːtəz ||
3 hi rɪˈstɔː(rə)z maɪ ˈsəʊl ||
hi ˈliːdz mi ɪn ðə ˈpɑː(ðz/θs) əv ˈraɪtʃəsn(ə/ɪ)s |
f(ə/ɔː) hɪz ˈnɛɪmz ˈsɛɪk ||
4 ˈjɛɪ | ðəʊ aɪ ˈwɔːk θruː ðə ˈvæli (ə/ɒ)v ðə ˈʃædəʊ əv ˈdɛθ |
aɪ wɪl ˈfɪə nəʊ ˈiːv(ɪ/ə/-)l |
fɔː ˈjuː (ɑː/ə) ˈwɪð ˈmi(ː) ||
jʊə ˈrɒd (æ/ə)nd jʊə ˈstɑːf | ˈðɛɪ ˈkʌmfət mi ||]

GA

1 [ðə ˈlɔːrd ɪz maɪ ˈʃɛpərd |
ˈaɪ ˈʃæl ˈnɑːt ˈw(ɑː/ɔː)nt ||

2 hi ˈmɛɪks mi tə laɪ ˈdaʊn ɪn ˈgriːn ˈpæstʃ(ə)rz ||
hi ˈliːdz mi bɪsaɪd ðə ˈstɪl ˈw(ɔː/ɑː)t̬ərz ||
3 hi rɪˈstɔːrz maɪ ˈsoʊl ||
hi ˈliːdz mi ɪn ðə ˈpæ(ðz/θs) əv ˈraɪtʃəsn(ə/ɪ)s |
f(ə/ɔː)r hɪz ˈnɛɪmz ˈsɛɪk ||
4 ˈjɛɪ | ðoʊ aɪ ˈw(ɔː/ɑː)k θruː ðə ˈvæli (ə/ʌ/ɑː)v ðə ˈʃædoʊ əv ˈdɛθ |
aɪ wɪl ˈfir noʊ ˈiːv(ɪ/ə/-)l |
fɔːr ˈjuː (ɑː/ə)r ˈwɪθ ˈmi(ː) ||
jʊr ˈrɑːd (æ/ə)nd jʊr ˈstæf | ˈðɛɪ ˈkʌmf(ə)rt mi ||]

B29. Text: Interview

RP

1	Inter:	də jə ˈθɪŋk ðɛəz ɛni pəˈtɪkj(ʊ/ə)lə ˈdaɪəlɛkt ðət rɛprɪˈzɛnts ˈskɒtlənd
2		ˈbɛst | wɛə jə wəd ˈsɛɪ | əʊˈkɛɪ | ˈðɪs ɪz haʊ ˈskɒtɪʃ ˈpiːpl
3		ˈspiːk | ɔː ˈðɪs ɪz ðə ˈməʊst ˈtɪpɪkl ˈskɒtɪʃ ˈdaɪəlɛkt ɔːr ˈæksənt ‖
4	Inf:	ˈpɒsəbli | aɪ miːn ˈgl(ɑː/æ)(s/z)gəʊ | ɪts ðə ˈwɛl ˈnəʊn ˈwʌn əkrɒs ðə
5		ˈwɜːld | aɪ səpəʊz | b(ʌ/ə)t ˈaɪ wəd prɪˈfɜː sʌmwɛə laɪk ðə ˈmɪdl |
6		laɪk ɪnvəˈnɛs | ˈpɜːθ | bɪk(ɒ/ə)z ɪts ə sɔːt əv ˈnɔːm(ə)l
7		ˈtəʊnˈdaʊn ˈvɜː(ʃ/ʒ)n | b(ʌ/ə)t ɪt ˈstɪl gɒt ðə ˈskɒtɪʃ ˈæksənt
8	Inter:	jɛə | ɪgˈzæktli | jɛə‖
9	Inf:	ɪn ɪt | jɛə‖
10	Inter:	ðæts ˈɪntr(ɛ/ə)stɪŋ | ðæts ən ˈɪntr(ɛ/ə)stɪŋ ˈstɛɪtmənt hɪə ‖ də jə hæv
11		ɛni ˈfɛɪv(ə)rət ˈdaɪəlɛkts ɔːr ˈæksənts hɪə ɪn ˈskɒtlənd ‖ aɪ miːn |
12		jəv ˈmɛnʃnt | wɒt w(ɒ/ə)z ɪt | ɪnvəˈnɛs ənd ˈpɜːθ‖
13	Inf:	wɛl
14	Inter:	aɪ miːn piːpl ðət ju ɪnˈdʒɔɪ ˈlɪsənɪŋ tu ˈməʊst ˈdʒʌst
15		bɪk(ɔː/ə)z əv ð(ɛ)ər ˈæksənts ɔː ˈdaɪəlɛkts ‖
16	Inf:	prɒbəbli ðə wɛstən ˈaɪlz ə bɪt | aɪ miːn aɪ (ˈ)k(æ/ə)n ˈlɑːf ət ðə
17		ˈdʒəʊks ðət kʌm frəm ðə ˈgl(ɑː/æ)(s/z)gəʊ ˈwʌnz | b(ʌ/ə)t aɪ ˈθɪŋk ɪt kən
18		bi vɛri ˈhɑːd tə ˈmɛɪk ˈaʊt | jə nəʊ | fə ˈmi ənd ðɛn ˈpɒsəbli iːvn
19		ˈwɜːs fə ˈfɒrənəz ɔːr iːvn ði ˈɪŋglɪʃ ‖
20	Inter:	səʊ jə wəd sɛɪ jə ˈfɛɪvərət ˈæksənt wəd bi wɛstən ˈaɪlz ‖
21	Inf:	wɛl | ɪts gɒt ə ˈlɪlt | ənd aɪ ˈlaɪk tə | jɛə | prɒbəbli laɪk hɪərɪŋ ˈðæt ‖
22	Inter:	ɪz ð(ɛ)ər ɛni ˈdaɪəlɛkt ɔː ˈlæŋgwɪdʒ jə ˈdəʊnt pətɪkj(ʊ/ə)ləli ˈlaɪk | hɪər
23		ɪn ˈskɒtlənd | wɛə jəd sɛɪ | ˈm | ɪts ˈnɒt vɛri ˈplɛznt tə ˈlɪsn tu ‖

Inf:	ˈnəʊ | nɒt ˈrɪəli ‖ aɪ ˈθɪŋk mɛɪbi ði æbəˈdəʊniənz | ɪts ˈkwaɪt ˈdɪfɪkəlt tə ˈmɛɪk ˈaʊt ‖
Inter:	jɛə ‖ ɪz ɪt dʒʌst ˈdɪfɪkəlt ɔːr ɪz ɪt ʌnˈplɛzəntə ju ‖
Inf:	wɛl | aɪ ˈdəʊnt ˈnəʊ | aɪ ˈnɛvə rɪəli ˈθɔːt əbaʊt skɒtɪʃ ˈæksənts | b(ʌ/ə)t aɪ ˈdəʊnt pətɪkj(ʊ/ə)ləli laɪk ðə ˈbɜːmɪŋhəm ˈæksənt ɪn ˈɪŋglənd | bɪk(ɔː/ə)z ɪts ˈtuː ɪts ə ˈdrəʊn | ɪts ə
Inter:	ðə ˈbrʌm ‖
Inf:	ɪt saʊndz vɛri | jɛə ‖ aɪ ˈdəʊnt pətɪkj(ʊ/ə)ləli laɪk ˈðæt | b(ʌ/ə)t aɪ hævnt rɪəli ˈθɔːt əbaʊt ðə ˈskɒtɪʃ ˈæksənts əz biɪŋ ˈgrɛɪtɪŋ ‖
Inter:	ˈsɒri ‖
Inf:	aɪ ˈdəʊnt faɪnd ɛni əv ðə ˈskɒtɪʃ ˈæksənts ˈgrɛɪtɪŋ ‖
Inter:	ˈgrɛɪtɪŋ | wɒt dəz ðæt ˈmiːn ‖
Inf:	gɛtɪŋ ɒn jə ˈnɜːvz | jə nəʊ | ˈgrɛɪtɪŋ | jə nəʊ ‖
Inter:	əʊˈkɛɪ əʊˈkɛɪ | ɑː ˈjɛə ‖ ɪz ðæt ə ˈskɒtɪʃ ˈtɜːm ‖ nɛvə ˈhɜːd əv ɪt ‖
Inf:	prɒbəbli dʒʌst ˈmaɪn ‖
Inter:	haʊ w(ə/ʊ)d jə dɪskraɪb jər ˈəʊn ˈdaɪəlɛkt ɔːr ˈæksənt ‖
Inf:	wɛːl |
Inter:	aɪ miːn nɒt dʒʌst ˈnaʊ | b(ʌ/ə)t wɛn jə tɔːk tə ˈfrɛndz ɔː tə jə ˈfæm(ə)li ‖
Inf:	wɛl ð(ɛ)ərə sɜːtn ˈwɜːdz ðət aɪ ˈjuːz ðət prɒbəbli maɪ ˈhʌzbənd ðət kʌmz frəm ①ˈɔːfə dʌznt juːz | ənd ˈðæts bɪk(ɒ/ə)z aɪ wəz brɔːt ʌp ɪn ˈsændi | ənd ð(ɛ)ərə sɜːtn ˈwɜːdz ðət kʌm frəm ˈɛvri ˈpærɪʃ hɪə ‖ ɪf aɪ hɪə maɪsɛlf ɒn ði ˈɑːnsərɪŋ məʃiːn | aɪ ˈdəʊnt ˈlaɪk ɪt ‖
Inter:	ɔːl ˈraɪt ‖
Inf:	aɪ θɪŋk aɪm prɪti ˈbrɔːd ɪf aɪm rɪˈlækst | aɪm prɪti ˈbrɔːd ˈspəʊkən ‖

GA

Inter:	də jə ˈθɪŋk ðɛrz ɛni p(ə)rˈtɪkjəl(ə)r ˈdaɪəlɛkt ðət rɛprɪˈzɛnts ˈskɑːtlənd ˈbɛst | wɛr jə wəd ˈsɛɪ | oʊˈkɛɪ | ˈðɪs ɪz haʊ ˈskɑːt̬ɪʃ ˈpiːpl ˈspiːk | (ɔː/ə)r ˈðɪs ɪz ðə ˈmoʊst ˈtɪpɪkl ˈskɑːt̬ɪʃ ˈdaɪəlɛkt (ɔː/ə)r ˈæksənt ||
Inf:	ˈpɑːsəbli | aɪ miːn ˈglæ(s/z)goʊ | ɪts ðə ˈwɛl ˈnoʊn ˈwʌn əkr(ɔː/ɑː)s ðə ˈwɜːrld | aɪ səpoʊz | b(ʌ/ə)t ˈaɪ wəd prɪˈfɜːr sʌmwɛr laɪk ðə ˈmɪdl | laɪk ɪnv(ə)rˈnɛs | ˈpɜːrθ | bɪk(ʌ/ɔː/ɑː/ə)z ɪts ə sɔːrt əv ˈnɔːrm(ə)l ˈtoʊnˈdaʊn ˈvɜːr(ʒ/ʃ)n | b(ʌ/ə)t̬ ɪtˈstɪl gɑːt ðə ˈskɑːt̬ɪʃ ˈæksənt
Inter:	jɛə | ɪgˈzæktli | jɛə||
Inf:	ɪn ɪt | jɛə||
Inter:	ðæts ˈɪn(t̬)ərɛstɪŋ | ðæts ən ˈɪn(t̬)ərɛstɪŋ ˈstɛɪtmənt hir || də jə hæv ɛni ˈfɛɪv(ə)rət ˈdaɪəlɛkts (ɔː/ə)r ˈæksənts hir ɪn ˈskɑːtlənd || aɪ miːn | jəv ˈmɛnʃnt | w(ʌ/ɑː)t w(ʌ/ɑː)z ɪt | ɪnv(ə)rˈnɛs ənd ˈpɜːrθ||
Inf:	wɛl
Inter:	aɪ miːn piːpl ðət j(u/ə) ɪnˈdʒɔɪ ˈlɪsənɪŋ tu ˈmoʊst ˈdʒʌst bɪk(ʌ/ɔː/ɑː/ə)z əv ð(ɛ/ə)r ˈæksənts (ɔː/ə)r ˈdaɪəlɛkts ||
Inf:	prɑːbəbli ðə wɛstərn ˈaɪlz ə bɪt | aɪ miːn aɪ (ˈ)k(æ/ə)n ˈlæf ət ðə ˈdʒoʊks ðət kʌm frəm ðə ˈglæ(s/z)goʊ ˈwʌnz | b(ʌ/ə)t̬ aɪ ˈθɪŋk ɪt kən bi vɛri ˈhɑːrd tə ˈmɛɪk ˈaʊt | jə noʊ | fər ˈmi ənd ðɛn ˈpɑːsəbli iːvn ˈwɜːrs fər ˈf(ɔː/ɑː)rənərz (ɔː/ə)r iːvn ði ˈɪŋglɪʃ ||
Inter:	soʊ jə wəd sɛɪ jər ˈfɛɪvərət ˈæksənt wəd bi wɛst(ə)rn ˈaɪlz ɪn ˈskɑːtlənd ||
Inf:	wɛl | ɪts gɑːt̬ ə ˈlɪlt | ənd aɪ ˈlaɪk tə | jɛə | prɑːbəbli laɪk hirɪŋ ˈðæt ||
Inter:	ɪz ðɛr ɛni ˈdaɪəlɛkt (ɔː/ə)r ˈlæŋgwɪdʒ jə ˈdoʊnt p(ə)rtɪkjəl(ə)rli ˈlaɪk | hir ɪn ˈskɑːtlənd | wɛr jəd sɛɪ | ˈm | ɪts ˈnɑːt vɛri ˈplɛznt tə ˈlɪsn tu ||
Inf:	ˈnoʊ | nɑːt ˈriːli || aɪ ˈθɪŋk mɛɪbi ði æbərˈdoʊniənz | ɪts ˈkwaɪt ˈdɪfɪkəlt tə ˈmɛɪk ˈaʊt ||

26	Inter:	jɛə || ɪz ɪt dʒʌst ˈdɪfɪkəlt (ɔ:/ə)r ɪz ɪt ʌnˈplɛzəntə ju ||
27	Inf:	wɛl | aɪ ˈdoʊnt ˈnoʊ | aɪ ˈnɛvər ri:li ˈθ(ɔ:/ɑ:)t̬ əbaʊt skɑ:t̬ɪʃ ˈæksənts |
28		b(ʌ/ə)t̬ aɪ ˈdoʊnt p(ə)rtɪkjəl(ə)rli laɪk ðə ˈbɜ:rmɪŋhəm ˈæksənt ɪn
29		ˈɪŋglənd | bɪk(ʌ/ɔ:/ɑ:/ə)z ɪts ˈtu: ɪts ə ˈdroʊn | ɪts ə
30	Inter:	ðə ˈbrʌm ||
31	Inf:	ɪt saʊndz vɛri | jɛə || aɪ ˈdoʊnt p(ə)rtɪkjəl(ə)rli laɪk ˈðæt | b(ʌ/ə)t̬ aɪ
32		hævnt ri:li ˈθ(ɔ:/ɑ:)t̬ əbaʊt ðə ˈskɑ:t̬ɪʃ ˈæksənts əz biɪŋ ˈgrɛɪt̬ɪŋ ||
33	Inter:	ˈs(ɑ:/ɔ:)ri ||
34	Inf:	aɪ ˈdoʊnt faɪnd ɛni əv ðə ˈskɑ:t̬ɪʃ ˈæksənts ˈgrɛɪt̬ɪŋ ||
35	Inter:	ˈgrɛɪt̬ɪŋ | w(ʌ/ɑ:)t dəz ðæt ˈmi:n ||
36	Inf:	gɛt̬ɪŋ (ɔ:/ɑ:)n jər ˈnɜ:rvz | jə noʊ | ˈgrɛɪt̬ɪŋ | jə noʊ ||
37	Inter:	oʊˈkɛɪ oʊˈkɛɪ | ɑ: ˈjɛə || ɪz ðæt̬ ə ˈskɑ:t̬ɪʃ ˈtɜ:rm || nɛv(ə)r ˈhɜ:rd əv ɪt ||
38	Inf:	prɑ:bəbli dʒʌst ˈmaɪn ||
39	Inter:	haʊ w(ə/ʊ)d jə dɪskraɪb jər ˈoʊn ˈdaɪəlɛkt (ɔ:/ə)r ˈæksənt ||
40	Inf:	wɛ:l |
41	Inter:	aɪ mi:n nɑ:t dʒʌst ˈnaʊ | b(ʌ/ə)t wɛn jə t(ɑ:/ɔ:)k tə ˈfrɛndz (ɔ:/ə)r tə jər ˈfæm(ə)li ||
42	Inf:	wɛl ðɛrər sɜ:rtn ˈwɜ:rdz ðət aɪ ˈju:z ðət prɑ:bəbli maɪ ˈhʌzbənd
43		ðət kʌmz frəm ①ˈɔ:rf(ə)r dʌznt ju:z | ənd ˈðæts bɪk(ʌ/ɔ:/ɑ:/ə)z aɪ wəz
44		br(ɔ:/ɑ:)t ʌp ɪn ˈsændi | ənd ðɛrər sɜ:rtn ˈwɜ:rdz ðət kʌm frəm
45		ˈɛvri ˈpɛrɪʃ hir || ɪf aɪ hir maɪsɛlf (ɔ:/ɑ:)n ði ˈænsərɪŋ məʃi:n | aɪ
46		ˈdoʊnt ˈlaɪk ɪt ||
47	Inter:	(ɑ:/ɔ:)l ˈraɪt ||
48	Inf:	aɪ θɪŋk aɪm prɪt̬i ˈbr(ɔ:/ɑ:)d ɪf aɪm rɪˈlækst | aɪm prɪt̬i ˈbr(ɔ:/ɑ:)d ˈspoʊk(ə)n ||

① Words like *Orfir* (a small town in Orkney) and perhaps also *Sanday* (one of the islands) reveal the limitations of this approach: there may simply not be any RP or GA pronunciations since these words do not exist outside their dialect context. In cases like this, we use the spelling as a guideline for the (hypothetical) RP and GA pronunciations.

B31. Proper nouns 1

1. Aristotle [ˈærɪstɒtl]/[ˈɛrɪstɑːt̬l]
2. Michigan [ˈmɪʃɪgən], not [ˈmɪtʃɪgən]
3. Leicestershire [ˈlɛstəʃə]/[ˈlɛstəʃ(ə)r]. Note that *-shire*, when used after a place name (as in *Aberdeenshire, Lincolnshire* etc.) is usually pronounced [ʃə]/[ʃ(ə)r]. In isolation, it is [ʃaɪə].
4. Portuguese [pɔːt(j/ʃ)(ə/ʊ)ˈgiːz]/[pɔːrtʃəˈgiː(z/s)]
5. Spurgeon [ˈspɜːdʒ(ə)n]/[ˈspɜːrdʒ(ə)n]
6. McDonald [məkˈdɒn(ə)ld]/[məkˈdɑːn(ə)ld]. The interesting question here, of course, is the pronunciation of 'Mc'. The EPD normally uses [mək], but also allows for [mæk] in this case. The LPD states that the choice is "perhaps depending on degree of formality". However, if 'Mc' is followed by an unstressed syllable (as in *McAleese* or *McNamara*), only [mæk] is possible.
7. Greenwich (district of London) [ˈgr(ɛ/ɪ)nɪ(tʃ/dʒ)]
8. February: [ˈfɛb(r/j)u(ə/ɛ)ri], [ˈfɛb(r/j)(ʊ/ə)ri]/[ˈfɛb(j/r)uɛri]. This word allows for a large number of different pronunciations, even more than those listed here.
9. Sioux singular: [suː], plural (same spelling): [suː(z)]
10. Thames (river in London) [tɛmz]
11. Levis [ˈliːvaɪz]
12. Rolls-Royce [ˌrəʊlz ˈrɔɪs]/[ˌroʊlz ˈrɔɪs]
13. Edinburgh [ˈɛdɪnb(ə)rə]
14. Calais [ˈkæleɪ]/[kæˈleɪ] (notice the unexpected stress pattern)

B32. Text: Pygmalion (RP)

ˈhɪgɪnz | əz hi ʃʌts ðə lɑːst drɔː || wɛl | aɪ θɪŋk ˈðæts ðə həʊl ˈʃəʊ ||

ˈpɪkərɪŋ || ɪts rɪəli əˈmɛɪzɪŋ || aɪ ˈhævnt tɛɪkən ˈhɑːf əv ɪt ˈɪn | jə nəʊ ||

ˈhɪgɪnz || wəd jə laɪk tə gəʊ əʊvər ˈɛni əv ɪt əˈgɛ(ɪ)n ||

ˈpɪkərɪŋ | ˈraɪzɪŋ ənd ˈkʌmɪŋ tə ðə ˈfaɪəplɛɪs | wɛə hi ˈplɑːnts hɪmsɛlf wɪð hɪz ˈbæk tə ðə ˈfaɪə || ˈnəʊ | ˈθæŋk j(u/ə) | nɒt ˈnaʊ || aɪm (ˈ)kwaɪt dʌn ˈʌp fə ðɪs ˈmɔːnɪŋ ||

ˈhɪgɪnz | ˈfɒləʊɪŋ hɪm | ənd ˈstændɪŋ b(ɪ/ə)ˈsaɪd hɪm ɒn hɪz ˈlɛft || ˈtaɪəd əv ˈlɪs(ə)nɪŋ tə ˈsaʊndz ||

ˈpɪkərɪŋ || ˈjɛs || ɪts ə ˈfɪəf(ə/ʊ/-)l ˈstrɛɪn || aɪ ˈrɑːðə ˈfænsid maɪsɛlf b(ɪ/ə)k(ɒ/ə)z aɪ kən prəˈnaʊns twɛnti ˈfɔː dɪsˈtɪŋkt ˈvaʊ(ə)l saʊndz || b(ʌ/ə)t j(ʊ)ə hʌndr(ə/ɪ)d ənd ˈθɜːti ˈbiːt mi || aɪ ˈkɑːnt hɪər ə ˈbɪt əv ə ˈdɪfr(ə)ns b(ə/ɪ)twiːn ˈməʊst əv ðəm ||

ˈhɪgɪnz | ˈtʃʌklɪŋ | ənd gəʊɪŋ ˈəʊvə tə ðə piˈ(æ/ɑː)nəʊ tu iːt ˈswiːts || ˈəʊ | ðæt kʌmz wɪð ˈpræktɪs || jə ˈhɪə nəʊ ˈdɪfr(ə)ns ət ˈfɜːst || b(ʌ/ə)t jə kiːp ɒn ˈlɪs(ə)nɪŋ | ənd ˈprɛz(ə)ntli jə ˈfaɪnd ð(ɛ)ər ˈɔːl əz ˈdɪfr(ə)nt əz ˈɛɪ frəm ˈbiː ||

ðə mʌðə || haʊ də jə ˈnəʊ ðət maɪ ˈsʌnz ˈnɛɪm iz ˈfrɛdi | prɛɪ ||

ðə ˈflaʊə gɜːl || ˈaʊ | ˈiːz jəʊə ˈsan ɪz i || wal | fjuːd dan j ˈdjəʉti bɔːmz ə ˈmaðə ˈʃʊd | iːd naʊ ˈbɛtɐn tə ˈspɔːl ə ˈpɔː ˈgɛlz ˈflaːzn ðɛn ran əˈwaɪ əθaːt ˈpaɪɪŋ || wɪl ˈjəʉ ˈpaɪ mi f ðəm ||

This transcription is an attempt to reconstruct what Shaw might have had in mind, informed both by the spelling he used and by what we know about Cockney. Shaw uses the spelling <san> for ‘son’; so obviously, he had a pronunciation other than [sʌn] in mind.The STRUT vowel is quite flexible in London Cockney (as it is on a world scale), and the pronunciation [a] given here is only one possibility. Shaw’s representation is not always true to real Cockney. MOUTH, for example, is usually around [æː] or [æə] in Cockney. Shaw’s representation of MOUTH as <aw>, on the other hand, suggests that he had [ɔː] in mind.

B34. Proper Nouns 2

1. Chicago: [ʃɪˈkɑːgəʊ]/[ʃɪˈkɑːgoʊ]
2. Geoff [dʒɛf]
3. Gloucester [ˈglɒstə]/[ˈgl(ɑː/ɔː)st(ə)r]
4. Gaelic: The pronunciation of this word depends on whether it is used in a Scottish or an Irish context. Approximately 50,000 Scots speak [ˈgælɪk], whereas the Irish talk about their [ˈgɛɪlɪk] speakers (or [ˈgeːlɪk] in their own accent). Note, however, that the Irish usually refer to their national language as Irish, not Gaelic.
5. Niagara Falls: [naɪˌæg(ə)rə ˈfɔːlz]/[naɪˌæg(ə)rə ˈfɑːlz]
6. Boheme [bəʊˈɛ(ɪ)m]/[boʊˈɛ(ɪ)m]. Notice, though, that the pronunciation of *Bohemia* is [bə(ʊ)ˈhiːmiə]/[boʊˈhiːmiə].
7. Sean [ʃɔːn]/[ʃ(ɑː/ɔː)n]
8. Arkansas [ˈɑːk(ə)nsɔː]/ [ˈɑːrk(ə)ns(ɔː/ɑː)]
9. Celtic: The question here is, of course, does this word start with [s] or [k]? The answer is, the sea and the language are usually [ˈkɛltɪk]; the sports teams (most prominently *Celtic Glasgow*) are pronounced [ˈsɛltɪk].
10. Connecticut [kəˈnɛtɪkət]/ [kəˈnɛt̬ɪkət]
11. Cajun [ˈkɛɪdʒən]
12. Louisiana [luː(ˌiː)ziˈænə]
13. Hebrew [ˈhiːbruː]
14. Heligoland [ˈhɛlɪgə(ʊ)lænd]/ [ˈhɛlɪgoʊlænd]

B35. Medley 7

1. hypocrite [ˈhɪpəkrɪt] – 2. heuristic [hj(ʊ(ə)/uː)ˈrɪstɪk] – 3. illocution [ɪləˈkjuːʃ(ə)n] – 4. haphazard [hæpˈhæzəd]/[hæpˈhæzərd] – 5. occurrence [əˈkʌr(ə)ns]/ [əˈkɜːr(ə)ns] – 6. hierarchy [ˈhaɪ(ə)rɑːki]/[ˈhaɪrɑːrki] – 7. xerox [ˈzɪərɒks]/ [ˈzi(ː)rɑːks] – 8. pedagogy [ˈpɛdəg(ɒ/əʊ)(dʒ/g)i]/[ˈpɛdəg(ɑː/oʊ)dʒi] – 9. archipelago [ɑːkɪˈpɛləgəʊ]/[ɑːrkəˈpɛləgoʊ] – 10. lieutenant [lɛfˈtɛnənt]/[luːˈtɛnənt] – 11. affricate [ˈæfr(ɪ/ə)k(ɛɪ/ə)t] – 12. posthumously [ˈpɒstj(ʊ/ə)məsli]/ [ˈpɑːstʃ(ə/ʊ)məsli] – 13. antitheses [ænˈtɪθ(ə/ɪ)siːz] – 14. enthusiasm [(ɪ/ɛ)nˈθ(j)uːziæz(ə)m]/ [(ɪ/ɛ)nˈθuːziæz(ə)m] – 15. miscellaneous [mɪs(ə)ˈlɛɪniəs] – 16. suffice [səˈfaɪs] – 17. subsequent [ˈsʌbs(ə/ɪ)kwənt] – 18. accumulate [əˈkjuːmj(ə/ʊ)lɛɪt] – 19. aesthetic [(iː/ɪ)sˈθɛtɪk]/[(ɛ/ɪ)sˈθɛt̬ɪk] – 20. journalist [ˈdʒɜːn(ə)lɪst]/[ˈdʒɜːrn(ə)lɪst] – 21. simultaneous [sɪm(ə)lˈtɛɪniəs]/[saɪm(ə)lˈtɛɪniəs]

Section C

C1. Casual speech

Since casual speech is not in any way 'standardised', the following transcriptions can be taken as suggestions – and as an encouragement to think about the processes that are at work.

1. [w(ə)dʒə ˈhəʊl ðɪs]/[w(ə)dʒə ˈhoʊl ðɪs]
2. [jə kŋ ˈkiːp ɪt]
3. [fɪʃ n tʃɪps]
4. [ði (i/ɪ)ˈfɛks ə(v) ðæ(t)]
5. [ʃi ˈðʒʌmt (ˈ)ʌp (n/m) ˈdaʊn]
6. [ˈtɛlɪm]
7. [ðə ˈnɛks dɛɪ]
8. [lʊk ət ˈðæp ˈmæn]
9. [ˈðæts ˈkrɛkt]
10. [g(ʊ/ə)(n/ʔ/-) ˈnaɪt]
11. [ˈgɛ(t/t̬)m]/[ˈgɛt̬m]
12. [ˈɪndiərə(n/m) pɑːkɪsˈtɑːn]/[ˈɪndiərə(n/m) ˈpækɪstæn]
13. [præps aɪ ʃd ˈliːv]
14. [km ˈɒn | ˈduː (w) ɪt]/[km ˈɑːn | ˈduː (w) ɪt]

C2. Words with non-canonical speech sounds

1. This is an exclamation of relief or one that is used to indicate that you are hot. It is usually written 'phew'. If you just blow out air through your lips, you produce a voiceless bilabial fricative, and the transcription would be [ɸː]. If you precede the fricative by a homorganic plosive, you create the affricate [pɸː].

2. This exclamation of disgust appears to have two major variants, both of which are transcribed in ordinary (Roman) script as 'ugh'. The first is purely vocalic. It starts with an unrounded high back vowel and ends in a mid-central position, thus [ɯə]. The second has onset and coda and finishes with a voiceless velar fricative: [jʌx].

3. The Welsh have many names that start with <Ll>; Llanfairpwllgwyngyll is the abbreviation for the longest of them, which, in its full length, reads Llanfairpwllgwyngyllgogerychwyrndrobwll-llantysiliogogogoch. (If you want to hear a native pronunciation of the place, go to 'Llanfairpwllgwyngyll' at Wikipedia, and click on 'listen'.) The <Ll> (or <ll>) spelling indicates a voiceless alveolar lateral fricative, which is symbolised as [ɬ]. If speakers of English try to imitate it, they (and others) usually shorten it further to 'Llanfair P.G.', which they tend to pronounce as [ˌhlænfɛə ˌpiː ˈdʒiː] or [ˌθlæn-]. This result is a combination of spelling pronunciation (e.g. 'fair' is pronounced as [fɛə]) and the imitation of the foreign [ɬ], using only phonetic material from English.

4. The velar fricative [x] lies in between the German [ç] (*ich-laut*) and the German [χ] (*ach-laut*). We find it in Scottish words like *loch* or *dreich* ('miserable', 'dreary', 'dull', especially when referring to the weather), and it acts as something like a shibboleth for many Scots (cf. Schmitt 2009: 150f.; 258f.). If someone pronounces it as [k], they know that person must be a foreigner, usually someone from England. A typical Scottish pronunciation of the famous loch would therefore be [lɒx nɛs]. The easiest way to find the position of [x] is to form an affricate (a combination of a plosive and a homorganic fricative as, for example, in [ts]) with the plosive [k] as a starting point (since both [k] and [x] are velar), thus arriving at [kx].

5. This is a sequence of usually two (or more) alveolar clicks, which means that the air is sucked in rather than blown out. The symbol used for this sound is a vertical line: [|], thus 'tut-tut' is [||].

6. French has three or four nasal vowel phonemes: [ɛ̃, ɑ̃, ɔ̃] and possibly [œ̃]. These vowels are illustrated in the French pronunciation of these words: [ʃɔpɛ̃], [ʃɑ̃sɔ̃] and [mɔ̃ blɑ̃]. When speakers of English try to incorporate nasalized vowels, they may arrive at something like [ʃ(ɒ/əʊ)pæ̃]/[ʃoʊpæ̃n], [ˈʃ(ɒ̃/ɑ̃ː)sɒ̃]/[ʃɑ̃ː(n)ˈs(oʊ/ɑː/ɔː)n] (note the different stress patterns between British and American English) and [m(ɒ̃/ɔ̃ː) blɒ̃]/[m(ɑ̃ː/õʊ)(nt) blɑ̃ː(ŋ)], unless, of course, they are very good speakers of French, in which case their pronunciation is closer to the original.

C3. Locating the German 'vocalic r'

The 'vocalic r' is commonly transcribed as a 'turned a', i.e. [ɐ], and this is where you find it:

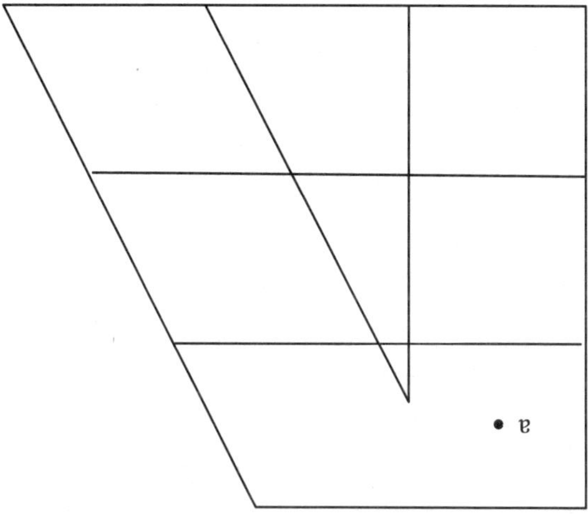

For many Germans, it is a somewhat centralised low to mid-low back vowel, located between the German /a/ and the German /ɔ/. As with all vowels, and especially non-peripheral vowels, however, there is some variation among German speakers. There are some minimal and quasi minimal pairs with /a/ e.g. *Opa* vs. *Oper*, *Kreta* vs. *Kreter, Thea* vs. *Teer* and *Olga* vs. *Holger*. There cannot be any minimal pairs with /ɔ/ since this vowel neither occurs after long vowels (like the 'vocalic r') nor at the end of words. However, if you pronounce the word *Otter* carefully, you will realise that the second vowel is slightly more open and also more unrounded than the first. If you want to locate this vowel, pronounce the German /a/ sound and then move your tongue in the direction of /ɔ/. You should at some stage pass [ɐ]. As an alternative, you may also use minimal pairs that involve a contrast between schwa and vocalic 'r' such as *bitte/bitter* or *Fliege/Flieger*. If you start with the first word and hold your tongue in the schwa position, you have to lower and retract it a little to arrive at [ɐ].

C6. Analysing authentic data 1: Vowels

Here are some of the most important features of the speaker's accent (most of which are fairly typical of Orcadians).

- The KIT vowel is very open. It does not actually extend as far as cardinal vowel 3, so the most appropriate symbol would probably be [ɛ̝], but since we wanted to do (as far as possible) without diacritics, [ɛ] seems to be the most appropriate symbol. It is interesting to listen to the speaker's pronunciation of the word *Inverness* (l. 6), in which she uses three almost identical vowels (rather than three different vowels as in RP).
- As in Scottish Standard English (SSE), FACE and GOAT are monophthongs ([eː] and [oː], respectively). Examples would be *grating* (l. 33, 35, 37), *Glasgow* (l. 4), *drone* (l. 30) and *spoken* (l. 49).
- There is some variation in the TRAP vowel. The speaker pronounces *accent* (l. 7, 28, 29, 35) and *that* (l. 31) with an open [a], whereas in other instances she uses the slightly higher variety of [æ], even in other instances of the words *accent* (l. 33) and *that* (l. 43, 44). In some cases she reaches a quality that resembles CV 3 [ɛ] (*can* in lines 16, 18). What looks like free variation, however, turns out to be fairly regular when more data are included. Most typical Orkney speakers have two distinct allophones of TRAP. They use [æ] (or even [ɛ]) before nasals (e.g. in *language* or *family*) and [a] elsewhere. There are, however, exceptions to this rule, as we see in the excerpt.
- An interesting fact about most accents in Scotland is that the historical NURSE merger has not taken place here, i.e. words that are pronounced with one vowel in RP (the mid-central [ɜː]) are pronounced with various other vowels in Scotland. Usually the spelling is a good indicator for the distribution. Our informant, however, pronounces *world* (l. 5), *Perth* (l. 6), *version* (l. 7), *Birmingham* (l. 29) and *word* (l. 43, 45) uniformly with a mid-low front vowel, here transcribed as [ɛ]. Only in *worse* (l. 19) does she use a back vowel. The question of which r-sound follows this vowel under which conditions (alveolar tap, alveolar trill, schwa, or the next non-/r/ sound) is often difficult to determine auditorily.
- In many Scottish Lowland accents (including those on the Northern Isles), speakers use [uː] for some high-frequency lexical items that are part of the MOUTH set elsewhere. These words typically include items like *out* (l. 18, 26), *about* (l. 28, 33), *town* and *house*. (For a brief introduction, see Millar 2007 ch. 2.2.) In many dialect writings, these words are spelled with <oo>. Usually, *down* is part of this set, too, which here is pronounced with [oː] (l. 7), probably influenced by *toned*. Notice, however, that the informant uses the more common [aʊ] pronunciation elsewhere (*sounds*, l. 32).

C7. Analysing authentic data 2: Consonants

- The distribution and realisation of the 'r-sound' is somewhat variable and appears, at first sight, chaotic or random. However, a closer look may reveal some regularities. Unlike SSE, the informant's accent tends to be non-rhotic (cf. *Perth* in line 6, *version* in line 7, *Western* in line 16, *nerves* in line 37), but there are some exceptions (*normal* in line 6, *Birmingham* in line 29). Most of the time, she uses the alveolar tap [ɾ]. This, however, is not the only realisation. In *normal* (l. 6), she uses a fricative; on other occasions, she employs the RP-like post-alveolar approximant [ɹ] (in *across*, l. 4; *really*, l. 25, *drone*, l. 30). In line 18, the informant uses the word *for* twice. The first *for* is realised with repeated contact between the tongue and the alveolar ridge ('trill'), the second *for* is not realised with an r-sound at all. In the word *Birmingham* (l. 29), she uses the trill again. Since in both cases the words with the trill receive considerable stress, the choice between the tapped [ɾ] and the trilled [r] seems to be determined by the emphasis the speaker puts on a word. If this analysis proves to be robust (the excerpt is too small for a definitive statement), [r] could be considered an allophone of /ɾ/ in the speaker's accent. Variability of the realisation of /ɾ/ is quite common in Scotland, even though it seems to be particularly strong with this speaker. Many Orcadians prefer [ɹ] if it is the only consonant before a high front vowel (as in *really*) or sometimes before any front vowel (as in *relative*, *radio*) and use [ɾ] elsewhere.
- A typical Orkney feature is the merger of /r/ + /s/ or /r/ + /z/ to [ʂ̥], i.e. a voiceless retroflex fricative. In our excerpt, we find it in the words *worse* and *foreigners* (l. 19), and in the construction *there's certain* (l. 43, 45).
- Another typical Orcadian feature is the realisation of initial /dʒ/ as [tʃ]. An example would be the informant's pronunciation of the word *jokes* in line 17.
- In some cases (e.g. *pretty*, l. 48), the speaker realises the phoneme /t/ as a glottal plosive (more commonly known as 'glottal stop'). This 't-glottalling' tends to occur after stressed vowels and is usually associated with London, Glasgow or other varieties of urban speech, but it is quite common in Orkney as well.
- Occasionally, the speaker realises initial /ð/ as [d] (*that* in lines 6 and 22 and *then* in line 18). This feature is referred to as 'th-stopping'. Notice that [d] here refers to a dental plosive rather than to the alveolar plosive and should therefore (if we allow for diacritics) be transcribed as [d̪]. Th-stopping *can* be found in Orkney speech, but it is probably not an overly common feature.

One lesson we have to learn here is that, unlike in the transcription of abstract, pre-defined varieties, real-life speech always involves variation. Often this variation may not fit our ideas or theories. Take, for example, the realisation of /r/ that we have just discussed. Yes, we do find the approximant [ɹ] before a high front vowel (*really*, l. 25), as with most Orcadians, but we also find it before a back vowel (cf. *across* in line 4). Another interesting observation is that the speaker even uses two different hesitation particles ([ɛm] in line 16 and [em] in line 17), both of which are rather exceptional on a world scale but quite normal in Orkney. We should not forget that speakers are not there to confirm our ideas about language, but that the starting point for our theories and descriptions is actual speech as it is used by real people. In the case of dialect description, this may also mean that we need to include more data in our analysis. Our excerpt, for example, does not contain all the phonological features of Orkney English. Like many other Scots, Orcadians distinguish a voiced [w] and a voiceless [ʍ], the latter being used when there is a <wh> in the spelling. There is, however, no wh-word in the speaker's contributions in our passage; but if you listen to the interview at 10:47–49, where the informant struggles with the right choice of *when* and *what*, you can hear her clearly using the voiceless fricative several times. For a more detailed description of the Orkney accent, read McColl Millar 2007 or Melchers 2008.

C8. Analysing authentic data 3: Intonation

When you talk to Orcadians about their accent, most of them will tell you before long that whenever they go to the mainland, people think they are Welsh (cf. Schmitt 2009: 147). The reason in both cases lies in the rather unusual intonation pattern of these accents. There is not much research on Welsh and Orkney intonation, but if you listen to the underlined words in the data provided, you will hear that the speaker employs a distinct rising intonation where other speakers would probably use a fall. From the little data we have, the informant seems to use this pattern if there is a stressed proper noun, especially at the end of an intonation unit. If you listen to the rest of the interview, this observation is partly confirmed. Another example would be "They've kept the dialect pretty strong ... in Westray" (13:12), but in "I was born on the island of Sanday", the informant uses a normal (i.e. falling) intonation. This peculiar pattern of fall-rise can also be found in other contexts, e.g. in "Just for a sort of project or something" (13:40), "I just find a bit of a joke" (15:17), "If the choice is there" (18:33). It is too early to make generalisations based on these few examples, though. For more technical information on the intonation of Orkney English, see van Leyden 2004.

C9. Analysing authentic data 4: Lexis and grammar

- There are two constructions that (a) seem to be so far removed from Standard English and that (b) do not fit the regular sound correspondences found elsewhere in the text that they cannot be considered a feature of the accent: the word *from* is realised as [fə] by the speaker (l. 17, 45), and the *not* as [nə] (l. 33). Both forms have a long tradition and wide distribution throughout the Scottish Lowlands, and they can also be found in various written texts both past and present. The spelling often varies between *fae* and *fra(e)* for the former and *-na(e)* for the latter, which is then directly attached to the preceding auxiliary. *-na(e)* even has something like the status of a shibboleth for Scotland outside the country. This picture of a poster was taken in Belfast, Northern Ireland:

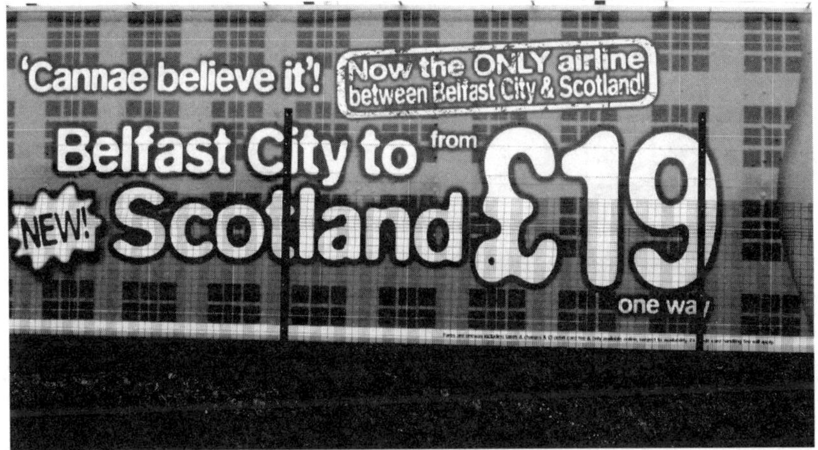

Fig. 4: Poster at Belfast City Airport

- By and large, the speaker's grammar is very similar to Standard English grammar. However, she sometimes uses the third-person singular suffix with plural nouns, as in "the jokes that comes" (l. 16–17) and in "there's certain words comes from every parish here" (l. 45). In the latter case she also drops the relative pronoun, which would normally be required in Standard English. Finally, she uses *me* instead of the possessive *my* ("me husband", l. 43), which is a common feature in various non-standard varieties of English.

C10. Analysing authentic data 5: Idiosyncrasies

Number ① is a clear case of speech accommodation. The informant had just mentioned the city of Perth, and I felt that using the RP pronunciation [pɜːθ] would have created too much of a social distance. However, as often happens in such cases, my accommodation was imperfect. I did use a vowel similar to her vowel in *Perth*, and I also realised the phoneme /r/ in the way my interlocutor did most often, but I failed to notice that she did not use /r/ in the word *Perth*.

Like most prefixed words in English, the word *unpleasant* retains the main stress on the base: [ˌʌnˈplɛzənt]. In German, however, the prefix [ʊn-] often receives primary stress, as it would have in the case of 'unangenehm', the German word for *unpleasant*. Thus in number ②, my German substratum was responsible for the un-English stress on the first syllable. What we have here is therefore a case of interference.

Bibliography

Almeida, Antonio / Braun, Angelika (eds.) (1987): Probleme der phonetischen Transkription. Stuttgart.

Ashby, Patricia (2006): Phonetic Pedagogy. In: Brown, Keith (ed.): Encyclopedia of Language & Linguistics. Amsterdam, 372–378.

Ashby, Patricia (2007): Phonetic ear-training – design and duration. In: Trouvain, Jürgen / Barry, William (ed.): Proceedings of the XVIth International Conference of Phonetic Sciences. Saarbrücken, 1657–1660.

Ball, Martin J. (2006): Transcribing at the segmental level. In: Müller, Nicole (ed.): Multilayered Transcription. San Diego, 41–67.

Bradlow, Ann R. (2008): Training non-native language sound patterns: Lessons from training Japanese adults on the English /ɹ/-/l/ contrast. In: Hansen Edwards, Jette G. / Zampini, Mary L. (eds.), 287–308.

Carroll, Lewis (1993): Alice in Wonderland & Through the Looking Glass. Ware.

Chomsky, Noam / Halle, Morris (1968): The Sound Pattern of English. New York.

Collins, Beverley / Mees, Inger M. (^{2}2008): Practical Phonetics and Phonology. Abingdon.

Cucchiarini, Catia (1993): Phonetic transcription: a methodological and empirical study. Nijmegen.

Davis, John F. (2002): Phonetics and Phonology. Stuttgart.

Deterding, David (1997): The formants of monophthong vowels in Standard Southern British English pronunciation. In: Journal of the International Phonetic Association 27, 47–55.

Dretzke, Burkhard (2008): Modern British and American English Pronunciation. Paderborn.

Duranti, Alessandro (1997): Linguistic Anthropology. Cambridge.

Dziubalska-Kołaczyk, Katarzyna / Przedlacka, Joanna (eds.) (^{2}2008): English Pronunciation Models: A Changing Scene. Bern.

Edwards, Harold T. / Gregg, Alvin L. (^{2}1997): Applied Phonetics Workbook: A Systematic Approach to Phonetic Transcription. San Diego.

Eimas, Peter D. / Siqueland, Einar R. / Jusczyk, Peter / Vigorito, James (1971): Speech perception in infants. In: Science 171, 303–306.

Fabricius, Anne H. (2007): Variation and change in the trap and strut vowels of RP. In: Journal of the International Phonetic Association 37/3, 293–320.

Giegerich, Heinz J. (1992): English Phonology: An Introduction. Cambridge.

Gimson, Alfred Charles (1962): An Introduction to the Pronunciation of English. London.

Gut, Ulrike (2009): Introduction to English Phonetics and Phonology. Frankfurt.

Hansen Edwards, Jette G. / Zampini, Mary L. (eds.) (2008): Phonology and Second Language Acquisition. Amsterdam.

Harrington, Jonathan / Palethorpe, Sallyanne / Watson, Catherine I. (2000): Does the Queen speak the Queen's English? In: Nature 408, 927f.

Hawkins, Sarah / Midgley, Jonathan (2005): Formant frequencies of RP monophthongs in four age groups of speakers. In: Journal of the International Phonetic Association 35/2, 183–199.

Hughes, Arthur / Trudgill, Peter (³1996): English Accents and Dialects: an Introduction to Social and Regional Varieties of English in the British Isles. London.

IPA – The International Phonetic Association (1999): Handbook of the International Phonetic Association: A Guide to the Use of the International Phonetic Alphabet. Cambridge.

Jones, Daniel (various editions): English Pronouncing Dictionary.

Kemp, J. Alan (2006): Phonetic Transcription: History. In: Brown, Keith (ed.): Encyclopedia of Language & Linguistics. Amsterdam, 396–410.

Kennedy, Graeme (1998): An Introduction to Corpus Linguistics. London.

Kohler, Klaus (1999): German. In: IPA – The International Phonetic Association, 86–89.

König, Werner (1988): Zum Problem der engen phonetischen Transkription. In: Zeitschrift für Dialektologie und Linguistik 55, 155–178.

Kortmann, Bernd (2005): English Linguistics: Essentials. Berlin.

Kretzschmar, William A. (2008): Standard American English pronunciation. In: Schneider, Edgar W. (ed.): Varieties of English 2: The Americas and the Caribbean. Berlin, 37–52.

Künzel, Hermann J. (1987): Transkription in der forensischen Phonetik. In: Almeida, Antonio / Braun, Angelika (eds.), 141–164.

Ladefoged, Peter (1960): The value of phonetic statements. In: Language 36, 387–396.

Laver, John (1994): Principles of phonetics. Cambridge.

Leisi, Ernst / Mair, Christian ([8]1999): Das heutige Englisch: Wesenszüge und Probleme. Heidelberg.

Leyden, Klaske van (2004): Prosodic Characteristics of Orkney and Shetland Dialects: An Experimental Approach. Utrecht.

Liberman, Alvin M. / Safford Harris, Katherine / Hoffman, Howard S. / Griffith, Belver C. (1957): The discrimination of speech sounds within and across phoneme boundaries. In: Journal of Experimental Psychology 54, 358–368.

Macaulay, Ronald (1988): RP R.I.P. In: Applied Linguistics 9:2, 115–124.

Mair, Christian (2008): English Linguistics. Tübingen.

Major, Roy C. (2008): Transfer in second language phonology: A review. In: Hansen Edwards, Jette G. / Zampini, Mary L. (eds.), 63-94.

McColl Millar, Robert (2007): Northern and Insular Scots. Edinburgh.

Melchers, Gunnel (2008): English spoken in Orkney and Shetland: phonology. In: Kortmann, Bernd / Upton, Clive (eds.): Varieties of English 1: The British Isles. Berlin, 35–47.

Ohala, Diane K. (2008): Phonological acquisition in the first language. In: Hansen Edwards, Jette G. / Zampini, Mary L. (eds.), 19–39.

Przedlacka, Joanna (2008): Models and Myth: Updating the (Non)standard Accents. In: Dziubalska-Kołaczyk, Katarzyna / Przedlacka, Joanna (eds.), 17–35.

Reetz, Henning / Jongman, Allard (2009): Phonetics: Transcription, Production, Acoustics, and Perception. Malden.

Riper, William R. van (1973): General American: An Ambiuity [sic]. In: Scholler, Harald / Reily, John (eds.). Lexicography and Dialect Geography. Wiesbaden, 232–242.

Roach, Peter ([3]2000): English Phonetics and Phonology: A practical course. Cambridge.

Roach, Peter (2004): British English: Received Pronunciation. In: Journal of the International Phonetic Association 34:2, 239–245.

Roach, Peter (2008): Representing the English Model. In: Dziubalska-Kołaczyk, Katarzyna / Przedlacka, Joanna (eds.), 393–399.

Roach, Peter / Hartman, James / Setter, Jane / Jones, Daniel ([17]2006): Cambridge English pronouncing dictionary. Cambridge.

Romaine, Suzanne (1980): Stylistic variation and evaluative reactions to speech: problems in the investigation of linguistic attitudes in Scotland. In: Language and Speech 23:3, 213–232.

Sampson, Geoffrey (1980): Schools of Linguistics. Stanford.

Sapir, Edward (1949): The Psychological Reality of the Phoneme. In: Mandelbaum, D. G. (ed.): Selected Writings of Edward Sapir in Language, Culture and Personality. Berkeley, 46–60.

Sauer, Walter ([3]2006): A Drillbook of English Phonetics. Heidelberg.

Schmitt, Holger (2007): The case for the epsilon symbol (ɛ) in RP DRESS. In: Journal of the International Phonetic Association 37:3, 321–328.

Schmitt, Holger (2009): Sprache und Identität in Schottland. Eine qualitative Makrostudie zur Rolle des Tiefland-Schottischen (Scots). Heidelberg.

Shaw, Bernard (1957): Pygmalion. A Romance in Five Acts. London.

Strange, Winifried / Shafer, Valerie L. (2008): Speech perception in second language learners: The re-education of selective perception. In: Hansen Edwards, Jette G. / Zampini, Mary L. (eds.), 153–191.

Strange, Winifried / Weber, Andrea / Levy, Erika S. / Shafiro, Valeriy / Hisagi, Miwako / Nishi, Kanae (2007): Acoustic variability within and across German, French, and American English vowels: Phonetic context effects. In: Journal of the Acoustical Society of America 122, 1111–1129.

Skandera, Paul / Burleigh, Peter (2005): A Manual of English Phonetics and Phonology. Tübingen.

Trudgill, Peter (2001): Received Pronunciation: Sociolinguistic Aspects. In: Studia Anglica Posnaniensia 36, 3–13.

Trudgill, Peter / Hannah, Jean ([4]2002): International English: A Guide to Varieties of Standard English. London.

Upton, Clive (2004): Received Pronunciation. In: Schneider, Edgar / Burridge, Kate / Kortmann, Bernd / Mesthrie, Rajend / Upton, Clive (eds.): A Handbook of Varieties of English, Vol. 1: Phonology. Berlin, 217–230.

Upton, Clive / Kretzschmar, William A. / Konopka, Rafael (2003): The Oxford Dictionary of Pronunciation for Current English. Oxford.

Vieregge, Wilhelm H. (1986): Reliabilität und Validität phonetisch-segmenteller Transkriptionen. In: Zeitschrift für Dialektologie und Linguistik 53, 182–186.

Vieregge, Wilhelm H. (1987): Basic Aspects of Phonetic Segmental Transcription. In: Almeida, Antonio / Braun, Angelika (eds.), 5–55.

Wells, John (1982): Accents of English. Cambridge.

Wells, John (2006): English Intonation: An introduction. Cambridge.

Wells, John (2006a): Phonetic Transcription and Analysis. In: Brown, Keith (ed.): Encyclopedia of Language & Linguistics. Amsterdam, 386–396.

Wells, John ([3]2008): Longman Pronunciation Dictionary. Harlow.

Wells, John (2008a): Abbreviatory Conventions in Pronunciation Dictionaries. In: Dziubalska-Kołaczyk, Katarzyna / Przedlacka Joanna (eds.), 401–408.

Windsor Lewis, Jack (2003): IPA vowel symbols for British English in dictionaries. In: Journal of the International Phonetic Association 33/2, 143–152.

Internet sources:

Port, Robert F. (2002): Is There a Universal Phonetic Space? Why Apriori Phonetic Transcription is Not Possible. http://www.cs.indiana.edu/~port/teach/641/against.transcription.html (accessed August 2010)

Wells, John (1999): Transcribing Estuary English: a discussion document. http://www.phon.ucl.ac.uk/home/estuary/transcree-uni.htm (accessed January 2011)

Wells, John (2001): IPA transcription systems for English. http://www.phon.ucl.ac.uk/home/wells/ipa-english.htm (accessed August 2010)